D0895095

Vol. 5

UNIFORMS, ORGANIZATION AND HISTORY OF THE

WAFFEN-SS

HUGH PAGE TAYLOR
Assisted by
ROGER JAMES BENDER

1st EDITION

ISBN No. 0-912138-25-4

COPYRIGHT 1982
by
HUGH PAGE TAYLOR
and
ROGER JAMES BENDER

Printed in the United States of America

Designed and Illustrated
by
Roger James Bender

All rights reserved. This book, or parts thereof, may not be reproduced in any form without permission of the authors.

R. JAMES BENDER PUBLISHING
P.O. Box 23456, San Jose, Calif. 95153

Table of Contents

Introduction

The four volumes published so far in this series have generated a degree of readership feedback which is one of the great joys of 'going into print' and also one of the declared aims of this series. The subject is vast, particularly since we switched to a more in-depth approach to the divisional histories in Volume 3 and the amount of errors corrected and new material received can easily be appreciated by the lengthy appendices appearing at the back of Volumes 2, 3, 4 and now 5.

The Waffen-SS is a difficult subject with huge gaps in its historical and pictorial documentation - had we waited until we "knew it all" (an impossibility we are the first to admit), then not even Volume 1 would have appeared by now. Even the most studious coverages of single units have been found to be imperfect, so we were well aware of the pitfalls in a series covering the Waffen-SS as a whole and so have taken the maximum possible care throughout.

Never before, since the series began, have we received so much help than over the 15th SS Division (1st Latvian) as a result of our coverage of that formation in Volume 4. This was not just the usual response we so welcome and encourage from our readership as a whole, but the result of a genuine and untiring effort on the part of Latvian exiles living in England, Germany, Canada and elsewhere. We were able to contact a large number of these kind and helpful people, and by giving them copies of our work, were in a position to put into motion a program of study perhaps unrivaled in the research of this subject. It would be a betrayal of their trust and efforts for us not to make available the facts they have now given, and this explains the heavy 'Latvian influence' to this present book - a whole separate volume was considered for a time, but abandoned when we felt it more in line with the aims of this series to act in this manner. We feel certain our readers will welcome this new material and have decided to present it in the following way.

Specific corrections and additions are given page-by-page in the appendix to this book as usual. More general and lengthy observations that also apply to the 19th SS Division (2nd Latvian) are incorporated in our coverage of that formation in the body of this book. The others, of which the question of Latvian "collaboration or cooperation?" is so important, have been grouped into a special section that follows the Foreword.

In thanking those Latvians who have made this considerable advance in our knowledge possible, we would like to give special recognition to Artūrs

Silgailis and Indulis Kažociņš, who, denied of their homeland, now live in Canada and England, respectively. Both have given generously of their time and considerable knowledge of this subject, and Mr. Silgailis, former Chief of Staff of the 15th Latvian Division and author of the standard work in Latvian on the history of the whole Latvian Legion, has kindly consented to provide the Foreword to this book.

Latvians are not the only Balts to have answered our call for help and to have allowed us to benefit from their first-hand experience and knowledge. Although too young to have served in the Second World War, USAF Major Henno Uus is well-versed in Estonian history and is one of the four members of the Historical Commission of the Estonian war veterans' organization (Legion of Estonian Liberation, Inc., of New York City). Thanks to Major Uus, the Historical Commission has agreed to help us present an accurate and comprehensive coverage of the Estonian Waffen-SS in this and future volumes. Consequently, the initial draft of our chapter on the 20th (1st Estonian) Division has been proofread by this Commission and benefits in advance from their corrections, additions and suggestions. Mr. Henry Rüütel, who became a Luftwaffe auxiliary (Luftwaffenhelfer or LwH) at the age of 16 and saw active service with an antiaircraft unit (Lsp. Flak-Ers.-Abt. 208) guarding the Estonian town of Kiviõli near the Narva front, now lives near London in England and studies his country's military insignia. He has been kind enough to make his considerable knowledge and photographic collection available to us.

In the six years since publication of Volume 4, two military historians we relied upon for inspiration have sadly died. Friedhelm ("Olly") Ollenschläger shared his friendship and considerable knowledge of military uniforms with RJB and HPT for many years and was one of our hard-working proof-readers from the very beginning of this series - all those who had the privilege of knowing this kind and gentle man will miss Olly very much.

We never actually established contact with François Duprat and certainly do not share his political views, but his prolific writings in French on the Waffen-SS have been listed in our bibliographies and raised a number of questionable points that led to considerable research. His car was overturned during riots at the time of the French parliamentary elections in March 1978, and he died in the ensuing explosion.

Our sincere and renewed thanks to Philip Henry Buss who has again given so much of his time to proof-reading this book, making countless useful suggestions and generally guiding us through from first draft to publication. Phil's own book on the Germanic Legions of the Waffen-SS with Andrew Mollo was published in 1978 and is highly recommended. His 1974 thesis on the non-Germans in the German Armed Forces is also an invaluable source of accurate information (see bibliography for details of both). Special thanks also go to Jost Schneider, whose monumental coverage of the Knight's Cross Holders of the Waffen-SS and Police appeared in 1978.

Acknowledgements

A. Bērziņš
Bill Brooks
P. H. Buss
Stan Cook
Jānis Jēkabsoņš
Indulis Kažociņš
Tim Knight
Richard Landwehr
Rudolf Lehmann
David Littlejohn
Gustav Lombard
Hans-Joachim Nietsch
Philip A. Nix
George Petersen
Jan Poul Petersen
Henry Rüütel
C. Peyton Williams
Jost Schneider
Artūrs Silgailis
Hans Stöber
Daugavas Vanagi (Latvian Relief Society, Inc.)
Wolfgang Vopersal
James van Fleet
Pierre C. T. Verheye
Lennart Westberg

Foreword

The authors of this historical work did not have an easy task to leave to posterity a true reflection of the German Waffen-SS.

As outsiders, not being personally involved, they encountered great difficulties in learning the true facts and sequence of events due to the chaotic state of Germany in the last stage of the war. Many factors contributed to this, such as documents became lost or were destroyed, orders from higher authorities frequently failed to reach subordinates or could not be implemented because of the timing, and evidence given by eye witnesses was sometimes contradictory. The difficulty in gathering the data especially refers to units of foreign ethnic origin. These units, particularly from Eastern Europe, which had nothing in common with National Socialist ideology, participated in the Second World War only by the desire to defend their people and homelands from communist domination. In order to do this they had to accept German support and were forcibly attached to the Waffen-SS.

In my former capacity as colonel of the General Staff of the Latvian National Army and later Chief of Staff of the Inspection-General of the Latvian Legion, I was closely connected with the events which led to the participation of Latvians in the Second World War, and the formation of the Latvian Legion as well as its heroic battles. I acknowledge with admiration the efforts and meticulous research of the authors of this work to present an accurate and objective portrayal of the Baltic Waffen-SS. By their objective approach to the subject of the German Waffen-SS, the authors, Hugh Taylor and Roger Bender, have created a document of great historical value. Moreover, their work will be appreciated for its trustworthiness as many previous publications in this regard, published outside of Germany, were often misleading because of prejudice.

ARTŪRS SILGAILIS
Chief of Staff of the Inspector
General of the Latvian Legion

ARTŪRS SILGAILIS
(A Biographical Sketch)

Born on 13 November 1895, Artūrs Michael Silgailis graduated from the Military College at Vilna in September 1915 as Second Lieutenant in the Czarist Russian Army. He was promoted to Lieutenant in 1916 and with the proclamation of Latvian independence in 1918 became an officer of the Latvian Army. He graduated from the Latvian Staff College in December 1928 and returned to serve as a lecturer there from 1934 to 1939. During 1934 and 1935 he was attached to the 6th Rīga Infantry Regiment to acquire experience as a battalion commander.

When Russia occupied Latvia in 1940, Silgailis was a colonel and Chief of Staff of the 4th Infantry Division. This was to be his last rank in the Latvian Army; he managed to escape to Germany disguised as a German.

After Germany's attack on the Soviet Union on 22 June 1941, Silgailis was attached to the German 18th Army as an interpreter with the appointment of "Sonderführer Z." At the demand of the Latvian Self Administration, Silgailis was released from the Wehrmacht in March 1942 and appointed Director of the Department of Personnel Affairs of the Self Administration.

Chosen by the Self Administration as Chief of Staff of the Latvian Legion and appointed Legions-Standartenführer and Chief of Staff of the "1st Division of the Latvian SS Volunteer Legion" with effect from 1 March 1943,* in fact, he became second-in-command (Infanterieführer) of the 15th SS Division in March 1943, a post he held permanently until 6 July 1944. Promoted to Oberführer on 9 November 1943, he became Chief of Staff to the Inspector General of the Latvian Legion** in July 1944, standing in for General Bangerskis when he was away for long periods.

Silgailis was imprisoned by the British in Belgium after Germany's capitulation. He was released in March 1946 and in 1948 became Chief Liaison Officer of Baltic Units of the Mixed Service Organization of the British Army of the Rhine. He held this post until his emigration to Canada in September 1953, where he lives today.

Artūrs Silgailis' history of the Latvian Legion, "Latviešu Leģions," was published in Copenhagen in 1964 and ran to two editions. He is now working on an enlarged English edition.

**See footnote 35 on page 71 of Volume 4.*
***Chef des Stabes der Generalinspekteur der lettischen SS-Freiwilligen-Legion.*

Pulkvedis (1940)

Legions-Standartenführer (1943)

Our thanks go to Artūrs Silgailis for supplying the two original studio protraits from his private files that we reproduce above. At left he wears the uniform of a Pulkvedis (colonel) of the Latvian National Army. This photograph was taken on 9 September 1940 - just two days before the Latvian National Army was taken over as the XXIVth Territorial Infantry Corps of the Red Army. The silver aiguilette worn from his right shoulder strap to the top tunic button was from the Military Staff College of Latvia. His medals (from left to right as you look at the photograph) are:

- Triju Zvaigžņu Ordenis (the 3 Stars Order - 4th Class)
- Aizsargu Nopelnu Krusts (Aizsargi Cross of Merit)
- Latvijas Atbrivošanas Kara Pieminas Zīme (Medal for Participation in the Independence War of Latvia)
- Latvijas Republikas Atbrivošanas Cīņu 10 Gadu Jubilējas Piemiņas Medaļa (10 Years' Jubilee Medal of the Independence War of the Republic of Latvia)

The metal badge worn below the row of medals was the badge of the 6th Riga Infantry Regiment (6 Rīgas Inf.Rgt.), to which AS was attached in 1934/1935.

In the photograph at right Artūrs Silgailis wears the uniform of a Legions-Standartenführer. This photograph was taken between 1 March 1943 (the date of his appointment) and 9 November 1943 (when he was promoted to Legions-Oberführer).

General Bangerskis and the Latvian Self Administration

It is hardly surprising that former officers of the Latvian Legion such as Artūrs Silgailis have reacted strongly against our branding Rudolfs Bangerskis and the Latvian Self Administration as "a group of collaborators under puppet leaders"[1] and in all fairness to them and the history of the Latvian people, we feel obliged to examine the question in more detail and place before our readers the Latvians' point of view. We present this impartially and without bias and, as always, invite other points of view which will be expounded in just the same detail in future books in this series.

It is thanks to the likes of Pétain and Quisling that the word "collaborator" has taken on such a sinister and ugly meaning, and by defining it as someone "cooperating traitorously," Silgailis refuses to accept it as applicable to Bangerskis and the Latvian Self Administration. He explains the cooperation they gave as being forced upon them in order to avert a second Russian occupation of Latvia, adding how his people chose Germany as the lesser of two evils. "The one year of Bolshevik occupation and terror was sufficient to change the Latvian feelings in favor of Germany. All activities of the Latvian leaders were directed to achieve the maximum possible benefits for their people and country."

Silgailis feels the description of his former senior officer, General Bangerskis, as a "collaborator" particularly unjustified, since he did not offer his services to lead the Latvian Legion, but was invited to come out of retirement and do so by the Latvian Self Administration.[2]

He extends the same argument to the Latvian Self Administration itself, stressing how they cooperated but never "collaborated" with the Germans - on the contrary, defending the interests of the Latvian people against encroachments of the German authorities as much as was then possible, repeatedly demanding the recognition of Latvia as a sovereign state, and a better lot for the Latvians generally. "They were not a government appointed by Germans or self-imposed rulers, but a local Latvian administration, selected by Latvians, which had to act under the direction and supervision of the German civil administration - the Generalkommissar in Riga."

To give even greater perspective to this interesting and important aspect of the Latvian story, we quote below in full Silgailis' recapitulation of the events that led to the formation of the Self Administration.

---

[1]First two lines of page 67 of Volume 4. See Stein: "Latvian puppet regime" (pg. 176) - "indigenous collaborators" (pg. 178).

[2]Silgailis refers to the petition of 23 February 1943 signed by the Director General of the Interior on behalf of the Latvian Self Administration and submitted to the Reichskommissar für das Ostland (see appendix in German on page 341 of Silgailis' book Latviešu Legions). For bibliographical details of Rudolfs Bangerskis, see page 12 of this book.

"After the Red Army had abandoned the capital of Latvia and the commander of the advancing German forces had greeted the Latvian people with their liberation from Bolshevik terror over the radio station in Rīga, finishing his address with the Latvian anthem, the Latvians were convinced they had regained their independence. In the afternoon of the same day (1 July 1941) officers of the former Latvian army, leading Latvian personalities who succeeded in escaping Bolshevik persecution and deportation as well as representatives of previous Latvian organizations assembled at the former Latvian club, called "Latviešu biedriba," in Rīga under the chairmanship of Colonel E. Kreismanis to form a provisional government under the leadership of B. Einsbergs - minister of the former Latvian government - as well as to organize the administration of the country. The assembly was called "Latvian Organization Center." To the disappointment of the Latvians, this idea was strictly rejected by the Höherer SS und Polizeiführer beim Befehlshaber im Rückwärtigen Gebiet der Heeresgruppe "Nord," SS-Brigadeführer und Generalmajor der Polizei Walter Stahlecker.

"In order to administer the country and run its economy, the same body, abbreviated "L.O.C.," appointed "director generals" to take charge of former ministries of Latvia with the task of reinstating the functions of these ministries (of course, not all former ministries were reinstated, those of Foreign Affairs, Defense and others were not for example). After several changes in the structure of these "general directorates," they were officially approved by the German civil administration at the end of 1941, and the beginning of 1942 as the local administration (Landeseigene Verwaltung - Zemes Pasparvalde in Latvian - or what I translate as Self Administration).

"It was specially pointed out by the Germans that the Self Administration was not a Latvian government, not even a collective Latvian body, but separate general directorates (nebengeordnete Generaldirektore) which had to cooperate directly with the corresponding departments of the Generalkommissar in Riga.

"Nevertheless, the director generals acted as a collective body under the chairmanship of the Director General of the Interior, General Oskars Dankers, held regular meetings and made joint decisions of common concern, complying with the laws and regulations which were in force before the occupation of Latvia by the Soviet Union on 17 June 1940 - as far as these laws and regulations did not conflict with German orders.

"Defending the interests of the Latvian people caused relations between the Self Administration and German authorities to become so strained that the Germans even considered arresting the Director General of the Interior, General Dankers.

"Events forced the Germans in time to increase the authority of the Self Administration and to recognize it as a representative body of the Latvian people."

The biographical sketch of Rudolfs Bangerskis that follows is drawn mainly from information supplied to the authors by Artūrs Silgailis:

RUDOLFS BANGERSKIS
(A Biographical Sketch)

Born 21 July 1878. Graduated from the Vladimir Military College at Petrograd (now Leningrad) in 1901.

Fought in the Russo-Japanese War 1904-1905.

Graduated from the Russian Staff College in 1914.

Last rank in the Czarist Russian Army: Colonel and C.O. 17th Siberian Rifle Regiment.

After the Bolshevist Revolution of 1917, he joined the White Russian Army of Admiral Koltchak and was given command of a division - he later commanded a corps and at the end an army group.

Following the collapse of Admiral Koltchak's Army, Bangerskis returned to Latvia, where he commanded various divisions and was twice Minister of Defense (1924-25 and 1928-29) before his retirement in 1937.

In March 1943 he was chosen to head the Latvian Legion by the Self Administration. With effect from 1 March 1943, he was given the rank of Legions-Brigadeführer und Generalmajor der lettischen SS-Freiwilligen-Legion.

Although Bangerskis was originally intended to command the 15th SS Divison, he was denied doing so by not being a German citizen.[3] Instead, he became Inspector General of the Latvian SS Volunteer Legion with the rank of SS-Gruppenführer und Generalleutnant der Waffen-SS.[4]

On 20 February 1945 Bangerskis was elected President of the Latvian National Committee, a provisional Latvian government proclaimed with German approval in Potsdam to take over the administration of that part of Latvia still unoccupied by the Russians (the province of Kurzeme - Courland in English and Kurland in German) from the German Civil Administration. Bangerskis continued as President of this Committee even after German capitulation, concentrating his efforts on trying to organize Latvian refugees in Germany and secure a better lot for the men of the Latvian Legion. To this end he wrote to Field Marshal Alexander, then C-in-C Middle East, from Lübeck on 23 May

---

[3]Hansen's order of 19 March 1943 (see footnote 125 on page 96 of Volume 4) confirmed that Himmler had appointed Bangerskis with effect from 1 March 1943 "Legions-Brigadeführer und Generalmajor der Lett. SS-Freiw.-Legion mit der Führung der 1. Division der Lett. SS-Freiw.-Legion Beauftragt."

[4]Generalinspekteur der lettischen SS-Freiwilligen-Legion.

1945.[5] As a colonel, Alexander had commanded the 13th Infantry Regiment of the former Latvian National Army during the Latvian War for Independence 1919-1920, and Bangerskis asked him to intervene to have the Allies regard the Latvians as political refugees and not "war prisoners, belonging to the German SS (political) formations."[6]

Not long after writing this letter, Bangerskis was denounced as a "Nazi" by one of his fellow countrymen (whose identity was never made public), arrested by the British Intelligence Service on 21 June 1945, and confined to his room at the Hotel-Restaurant Bleiche in Goslar. He was moved from the hotel to a jail in Goslar on 2 July, and the following day to a prison in Brunswick. Transfer followed to a POW camp at Westertimke on 19 July, and to another POW camp at Sandbostel on 23 July. He was discharged from Sandbostel on 20 November 1945 and sent to the Latvian POW camp at Westerbuhr, Aurich county in Friesland. He was finally released on Christmas Day 1945 and settled down at the Displaced Persons Camp at Oldenburg.

Rudolfs Bangerskis died in a traffic accident at Oldenburg in the night of 24/25 February 1958, 15 years to the day from the raising of the 15th SS Division.

Petition for a 100,000 strong Latvian Army

Mr. Silgailis has kindly provided further details of the petition "for the reestablishment of a 100,000 strong Latvian army":[7]

"A proposal for the establishment of a 100,000 strong Latvian army was submitted privately and on his own initiative by the Director General of Justice, Alfred Valdmanis on 30 November 1942. In this petition Valdmanis outlined that the Latvians could raise an army of 100,000 men if Germany would legally

---

[5]*Text reproduced on pp. 109-110 of Bangerskis' Mana Mūža Atmiņas, vol. 4.*

[6]*The Nuremberg Military Tribunal made no distinction between the various branches of the SS, and so the Waffen-SS was condemned as part of a criminal organization along with the Allgemeine-SS, SD, etc. A different view was taken by the U.S. authorities when considering Latvian immigrants as the following extract from a Memorandum of the U.S. Department of State dated Washington, D.C., 16 March 1951 shows:*

"In connection with the immigration of Latvian refugees to the United States, also here the true nature of the Latvian Legion was studied under scrutiny and in its decision of 1 September 1951 the Displaced Persons commission made the following statement:

Baltic Waffen SS units (Baltic Legion) are to be considered as separate and distinct in purpose, ideology, activities and qualifications for membership from the German SS, and therefore:

The Displaced Persons Commission holds them not to be a movement hostile to the Government of the United States under Section 13 of the Displaced Persons Act of 1948, as amended."

[7]*Page 67 of Volume 4 - see Stein, The Waffen-SS, pg. 176.*

and effectively recognize Latvia as an independent state. The petition was returned to Valdmanis by the Generalkommissar in Rīga in the presence of the other Director Generals on 2 December 1942 with the remark that he was unable to submit it to higher German authorities because it contained inappropriate political demands and, besides, had been signed only by Valdmanis and therefore could not be regarded as a petition of the Latvian people. The same day the Self Administration submitted a new petition with the same content and demands, signed by all the Directors General and using a more diplomatic style of language."

Recruiting Difficulties

There can be no doubt that recruiting for the Latvian Legion and therefore for the 15th SS Divison in 1943 got off to a bad start and was far from a success, but Latvians claim this failure was not due to any slowness or inefficiency on their part, but rather was the fault of the Germans. Since this is a very different situation to that described in Volume 4 (pp. 71-76), it is worthy of further investigation.[8]

The Germans took care to camouflage their unlawful conscription of Latvians for military service. They based it on Alfred Rosenberg's[9] compulsory labor decree of 19 December 1941 and had the Department of Labor of the Latvian Self Administration carry it out, commencing in early 1943 with the compulsory recruitment of Latvian citizens born between 1919 and 1924.

In March 1943 the Inspector General of the Legion, General Bangerskis, did not have his own recruting office,[10] nor was any such office ever opened. The Germans had, however, opened an SS-Ergänzungskommando in Rīga in the second half of February 1943. This was soon renamed SS-Ersatzkommando Ostland and was under the command of SS-Standartenführer Hierthes. Originally, call-up notices from this office carried the rubber stamp of the Inspector General, but were signed on Bangerskis' behalf with neither his knowledge nor consent by an unknown German NCO. Since this led to some

---

[8]Stein gained the impression from the OKW war diary that the difficulty encountered by the Germans over conscription in Latvia was due to the inefficiency of Bangerskis and the "indigenous collaborators" (op.cit., pg. 178).

[9]Rosenberg was Minister of the Occupied Eastern Territories - Reichsminister für die besetzten Ostgebiete.

[10]Pg. 71 of Vol. 4.

[11]Other reasons stemmed from the harsh treatment the Latvians felt they were receiving from the German authorities: lack of national recognition and independence; persecution and arrest of Latvian nationalists; failure to return property nationalized by the Russians to their former owners; poorer rights of Latvians compared with Germans (food, wages, supplies, etc.); assignment of inappropriate duties to the Latvian "Schuma" or police battalions. Silgailis, Latviešu Leģions, pg. 23.

Latvian officers refusing to obey, the stamp was changed to read "Ersatzkommando der Lettischen Legion," although effectively there never was such an office.

The reasons why the recruiting agencies of the Department of Labor of the Self Administration and Hierthes' "SS-Ersatzkommando Ostland" met with so little initial success was to a large extent that the Latvian Self Administration had not yet agreed to the formation of the Latvian Legion and so the majority of Latvians were reluctant to step forward.[11] The resultant failure led Berger to draw Himmler's attention to the problem by his letter of 15 April 1943, in which he stated that a bare 16½ percent of the men registered had in fact been called up.[12]

Konstantin Hierrl, leader of the German Labor Service (Reichsarbeitsdienst or R.A.D.) and other R.A.D. leaders visit the 15. SS-Artillerie-Regiment in Jelgava, Latvia, in the summer of 1943. Hierrl had come to Latvia to investigate recruitment of Latvian youths for the R.A.D. and wanted to see Latvians who had recently completed their one year's labor service in Germany and were enrolled in the Latvian Legion.
Behind Legions-Gruppenführer und Generalleutnant der lettischen SS-Freiwilligen-Legion Rudolfs Bangerskis and to the extreme left of the photograph is Legions-Standartenführer Voldemārs Skaitslauks, commander of 15. SS-Artillerie-Regiment. An unidentified SA-Untersturmführer involved in pre-military training stands in the background behind Skaitslauks and Bangerskis. To Bangerskis' left is SS-Hauptsturmführer Mäder, in charge of Abteilung VI (Propaganda und Fürsorge - propaganda and welfare) of the 15th SS Division. The (German?) officer (SS-Hauptsturmführer?) giving explanations to Hierrl remains unidentified but almost hidden behind him can just be seen Artūrs Silgailis. The two officers behind Silgailis were aides to General Bangerskis: the taller Legions-Untersturmführer Zēgners and the shorter Legions-Hauptsturmführer (later Legions-Sturmbannführer) Mednis.

---

[12] *Pg. 72 and footnote 39 of Vol. 4.*

Recruiting became more effective once it was known that the Self Administration had agreed to the formation of the Legion and General Bangerskis had addressed the Latvian people on 23 March, appealing to them to join the Legion. In spite of other setbacks[13] a degree of success was thenceforth achieved, the Germans organizing the recruiting campaign as a whole, while the General Inspector of the Legion called up individual officers.

The real turning point, however, came on 15 November 1943 when the Self Administration, worried by the worsening front situation on the Latvian border and wary of German intentions to conscript more Latvians for military service on other fronts, took over the mobilization from the Germans. The Inspector General was made responsible for recruitment and the General Inspection was accordingly enlarged by an additional department and the required recruiting offices were set up over the country.[14] Recruiting was conducted in accordance with the laws and regulations in force in Latvia before the Russian occupation of 17 June 1940, the only difference being that it was General Bangerskis as Inspector General of the Latvian Legion who was vested with the corresponding rights and authority, rather than the then non-existent Minister of Defense and C-in-C of the Army.[15]

It was thus the Latvian Self Administration that took over mobilization from the Germans on 15 November 1943 and not the SS.[16] Of course, since the Legion was a component of the Waffen-SS, it was natural that the SS should look after recruitment, and in this connection the SS-Ersatzkommando was upgraded to Ersatzinspektion Ostland and attached to the office of the HSSPF Ostland, SS-Obergruppenführer und General der Polizei Friedrich Jeckeln.[17]

Difficulties that continued even after the Latvians had taken over the recruitment program can be blamed in large part upon German interference. The German civil administration in Rīga, in order to keep the economy running and to meet the requirements of the war industry, classified too many Latvians for reserved occupations (i.e., indispensable and therefore exempt from military service - the German term "unabkoemmlich," abbreviated as "uk.," became a term of derision among Latvians). This cut down the number of

---

[13]*On 29 March 1943 a thousand raw recruits were sent as reinforcements for the 2nd Latvian Brigade on the Leningrad front without training, Latvian officers or NCOs. This was in spite of German promises that the Legion would be trained in Latvia for at least six months before combat engagement. At the same time, it became known that the appointment of General Bangerskis to command the "1st Latvian Division of the Latvian Legion" was a misunderstanding and that the post had to be given to a German.*

[14]*This is a possible explanation for Stein's curious statement that the German Army set up some 50 recruiting offices in Latvia in late 1943 (op.cit., pg. 178).*

[15]*Bangerskis was well-qualified for the post, having twice been Latvian Minister of Defense (1924/1925 and 1928/1929).*

[16]*Vol. 4, pg. 76.*

[17]*See footnote 58 on pg. 76 of Vol. 4.*

men drafted and created dissatisfaction, especially among those men who had been drafted and led Bangerskis to complain on several occasions.

In addition to this, confusion and waste resulted from the uncoordinated efforts of different German agencies all doing their best to recruit Latvians for their own purposes.[18] Latvians quite willing to join the Legion were being approached by the R.A.D.[19] for labor service, the Military C-in-C "Ostland"[20] to serve as Army auxiliaries,[21] the German police and so on. The result was utter confusion[22] and there were cases of men receiving call-up papers from several different organizations at the same time and not knowing which to obey.

Finally, a note on minimum height requirements. Such had been laid down for the Latvian Legion by the Germans, but apart from SS-Erstazkommando Ostland applying them for a time in the very beginning, they were generally ignored.[23]

The officer with his hands clasped behind his back is SS-Hauptsturmführer Mäder, in charge of Abteilung VI (Propaganda und Fürsorge - propaganda and welfare) of the 15th SS Division. Mäder talks with a Latvian Waffen-Standartenoberjunker (recognizable by his wearing silver piping to his NCO collar patches and an officer's forage cap) who may have been a photographer from SS-Kriegsberichter-Kompanie 15 (or -Trupp or -Zug, depending upon the date on which the photograph was taken - which we do not yet know). The three German NCOs to Mäder's right wearing "Feldgendarmerie" gorgets are from SS-Waffen-FeldgendarmerieTrupp 15.

---

[18]*Latviešu Karavīrs Otra Pasaules Kara Laikā, Vol. 3, pg. 256.*
[19]*Reichsarbeitsdienst - the German labor service which also recruited outside the Reich.*
[20]*Wehrmachtsbefehlshaber Ostland.*
[21]*Hilfswillige or "Hiwis."*
[22]*Latviešu Karavīrs Otra Pasaules Kara Laikā, Vol. 3, pg. 79.*
[23]*Vol. 4, pg. 74.*

Combat History of the 15th SS Division

(November 1943 - August 1944)[1]

As a component of the Waffen-SS, the 15th SS Division was administratively subordinated to the VIth SS Volunteer Corps in late 1943, but operationally it was in reserve at the disposal of the XXXXIIIrd Army Corps, 16th Army, Army Group "North."[2]

At the beginning of 1944, the Division's 34th and part of its 33rd infantry regiments were gradually attached to German formations and suffered heavy losses in the fighting in the area of Novosokolniki that lasted until almost the end of the month. The rest of the Division was, meanwhile, still in reserve at the disposal of the XXXXIIIrd Army Corps. At the end of January, the Division was ordered to move to Belebelka, and on 15 February took up positions on the west bank of the river Radja. It was on the west bank of the Radja that the 15th SS Division was engaged in battle for the first time as a formation, not at Novosokolniki.

The Russian offensive around Leningrad in the beginning of January 1944 coupled with the retreat of the German 18th Army forced the high command to pull back its positions also in the Welikije-Luki area.[3] In the course of this withdrawal, the 15th Division fought rearguard actions, sustaining very few casualties in spite of most unfavorable conditions, until it regrouped at the so-called "Panther Position" on the Velikaya River. There it was reunited with its 34th and that part of its 33rd infantry regiments that had stayed behind with German elements and had been so mauled at Novosokolniki and linked up with its sister division and fellow component of the VIth SS Volunteer Corps, the 19th SS.

The VIth SS Volunteer Corps, under command of the 18th Army of Army Group "North," took up positions that stretched some 30 kms. along the west bank of the Velikaya, south of Ostrov; the 15th SS Division being responsible for the defense of a front some 15 kms. in length. Only a matter of days later, the Latvian SS divisions became involved in continuous fighting with the advancing Russians, who in spite of all attempts failed to cross the river.

Particularly fierce fighting broke out on 16 March when the Russians captured Hill 93,4 on the boundary between the two Latvian SS Divisions. Elements of both the 15th and 19th SS were engaged in heavy fighting for three days until the hill was finally retaken.

---

[1]*See pp. 78-83 of Vol. 4.*

[2]*It was the HQ of the 16th Army and not the 15th SS Division itself that was in the Pskov area in January 1944 (Vol. 4, pg. 79).*

[3]*This was not a personal decision of SS-Oberführer Heilmann (vol. 4, pg. 80).*

On 26 March 1944, under heavy artillery and air cover, the Russians launched an attack on the front section of the 15th SS Division. While they managed to establish a bridgehead on the western bank of the Velikaya, about 5 kms. wide and 3 kms. deep, all further efforts by the Red Army to enlarge the bridgehead were repulsed in heavy fighting by the Latvians with assistance from some German elements. Continuous fighting on the whole front of the VIth SS Corps lasted until the middle of April 1944 when the Latvian divisions, due to sustained losses, were withdrawn to a quieter sector of the eastern front in the Bardovo/Kudever area, some 50 kms. east of Opochka.[4] Here the VIth SS Volunteer Corps with its two Latvian divisions came back under the command of the 16th Army.

Static fighting began on 24 April and carried through May to end on 21 June 1944. General Bangerskis visited the Division in its positions in the Bardovo/Kudever area on 8 June 1944, accompanied by Waffen-Oberführer Silgailis, second in command (Infanteriеführer) of the 15th SS Division. Silgailis, dressed in shirtsleeve order, accompanied Bangerskis on his tour of the Latvian positions, and the three photographs, kindly provided by Silgailis himself, show the two most senior Latvian officers of the Waffen-SS visiting the 33rd and 34th infantry regiments (see next page).

On 22 June 1944, exactly three years after Germany's surprise attack on Russia in Operation "Barbarossa," the Red Army started an offensive that was to inflict terrible losses on the 15th Division and the whole German Army Group "North," forcing them westwards to the Latvian border. The Russians' attack on 10 July forced the 15th Division to retreat from its positions at Bardovo/Kudever and terrible losses were suffered in the process, especially by the 32nd Infantry Regiment. While the 19th Division held the front in Latvia, south of Lake Lubāna, the survivors of the 15th were sent to the relative safety of West Prussia[5] for reforming. There at Sophienwalde on 28 October 1944, Bangerskis and Silgailis visited the reforming 15th SS Division. Artūrs Silgailis has also provided photographs of this occasion, from one of which it can be seen that the widow of Karlis Aperāts, killed on 16 July 1944 while commanding the 32nd Infantry Regiment, was with them.

---

[4] *Opotschka in German and Opočka in Latvian.*

[5] *See Vol. 4, pg. 83 and footnote 85.*

This group of three photographs was taken on 8 June 1944 when General Bangerskis and Waffen-Oberführer Silgailis (in shirtsleeve order) toured the 15th SS Division in its Bardovo-Kudever positions.

Waffen-Standartenführer Vilis Janums, commander of the 33rd infantry regiment, wears the badge of the Military Staff College of Czechoslovakia on his right breast pocket. This group photograph was taken at the village of Borchavitsi at the HQ of the 33rd regiment.[6]

Here Bangerskis, Silgailis and others are at a field gun position behind the front line at Bardovo, listening to Waffen-Untersturmführer Bergtāls, commander of the 13th (infantry gun) company of the 34th infantry regiment. From left to right of the photograph: unidentified Waffen-Obersturmführer in peaked cap, Waffen-Hauptsturmführer Vilis Ziemelis (aide-de-camp of Bangerskis - he wears a forage cap and what appears to be shield pattern "B" on his upper right sleeve), private soldier in forage cap with his back to camera, Bergtāls, Bangerskis, Waffen-Obersturmbannführer Alberts Vīksna (acting commander of the 34th infantry regiment), Waffen-Obersturmführer Pēteris Vītols, Silgailis.

Bangerskis and Silgailis with other Latvian officers at the HQ of the 33rd infantry regiment. From left to right of the photograph: Waffen-Oberführer Artūrs Silgailis, Waffen-Hauptsturmführer Vilis Ziemelis, Bangerskis, Waffen-Untersturmführer Jānis Zēgners, Waffen-Obersturmführer Pēteris Vītols, Janums, Waffen-Untersturmführer Verners Gusevs, Waffen-Hauptsturmführer Akermanis.[7]

---

[6]Borchavitsi is given by Silgailis (letter dated 18.9.80) and Waffen-Hauptsturmführer Jānis Rulliņš, former adjutant of the 33rd regiment. Latviešu Kaŗavīrs otra pasaules Kaŗa Laikā, Vol. 4, pg. 207 places the photograph at the artillery positions in the nearby village of Detkovo - this would appear to be wrong since Janums did not accompany Bangerskis to Detkovo (Silgailis).

[7]According to Silgailis (letter dated 18.9.80) Zēgners and Gusevs did not accompany Bangerskis on this visit to the front lines, and so these identifications are subject to confirmation.

Silgailis, shaking hands at left, wears the pattern "D" Latvian sleeve shield. The woman in traditional Latvian costume is the widow of Karlis Aperāts, who fell at the head of the Division's 32nd Infantry Regiment on 16 July 1944. She was in charge of the Latvian "Soldiers' home" (Soldatenheim).

Sophienwalde railway station in West Prussia, 28 October 1944. General Bangerskis, Waffen-Oberführer Silgailis and others have just arrived by a train of the German Railways to visit the 15th SS Division while reforming. A bespectacled military railway station commandant (Silgailis remembers him as being the Bahnhofskommandant at Sophienwalde) with silver infantry assault badge looks on as Bangerskis and Silgailis (both facing the camera) talk with SS-Standartenführer Hierthes (back to the camera - he was previously in charge of SS-Ersatzkommando Ostland but when this photograph was taken was temporarily in command of the Division's 33rd Infantry Regiment) and SS-Obersturmbannführer Erich Wulff (Chief of Staff of the 15th SS Division).

The Surrender of the 15th SS Division

The survivors of the 15th SS Division surrendered in a number of groups at different places and times and did all possible to fall into American rather than Russian hands.[8] The following detailed analysis is drawn from all available published Latvian sources.[9]

TO THE WESTERN ALLIES (U.S., British & Canadian armies):

1. SCHWERIN AREA:

Most survivors of the Division surrendered to the Americans around the town of Schwerin in Mecklenberg, about 90 kms. east of Hamburg.

1.1 MECKLENBERG - 0600 Hours, 2 May 1945:

The main body of the Division surrendered at 0600 hours on a road at the southeastern corner of the Schwerin Forest.

The senior officers present were three Latvian majors (Waffen-Sturmbannführer): Jūlijs Ķīlītis (who had taken command of the 33rd Regiment on 20 April 1945), Valdemārs Baumanis (commander of SS-Versorgungs-Regiment 15) and Leonards Trēziņš (leading what remained of his SS-Panzerjäger-Abteilung 15).

Regimental commanders Ķīlītis and Baumanis decided that while Baumanis should go and report to the Americans, Ķīlītis would assume temporary command of the whole contingent. He ordered his men to remove the death's head emblems from their caps and replace them with the sun and stars badges from their collar patches and then, on horseback, led the long column into captivity. Reluctantly the Latvians agreed to comply with an American demand and carried a white flag at the head of the column.[10]

A United States Air Force officer accepted the surrender of what Ķīlītis reported to be 3,500 men.[11] This large group was made up of:

- most of Ķīlītis' 33rd Regiment (IInd battalion and 13th, 14th and HQ companies - the Ist battalion had been detached to form SS-

[8] *As will be seen here, it was an over-simplification (Vol. 4, pg. 87) to say that SS-Kampfgruppe "Janums" surrendered to the Americans at Güterglück on 27 April 1945 and all the rest to the Red Army at Neuruppin in early May. In fact, although some Latvians may have surrendered at Neuruppin individually or in small groups, there is no evidence of any closed units surrendering there. The Archive of the Latvian Legion has estimated that about 30,000 Latvian soldiers managed to slip through Russian hands in one way or another and surrender to the Western Allies. The misleading impression that most of the 15th SS Division surrendered to the British is due to the fact that soon after surrendering to the U.S. Army, they were turned over to the British (Indulis Kazocins, letter of 22.5.81 & Artūrs Silgailis, letter of 23.6.81).*

[9] *Particular thanks to Indulis Kažociņš for his systematic analysis upon which this coverage is largely based, and to Artūrs Silgailis for general clarification.*

[10] *Ķīlītis: Es kaŗā aiziedams, 1956.*

[11] *Four thousand, according to Latviešu Kaŗavīrs Otra Pasaules Kaŗa Laikā.*

Kampfgruppe "Janums" - see below)
- SS-Versorgungs-Regiment 15 (under Waffen-Sturmbannführer Valdemārs Baumanis)
- SS-Panzerjäger-Abteilung 15 (under Waffen-Sturmbannführer Leonards Trēziņš)
- SS-Ausbildungs- und Ersatz-Btl. 15[12]
- antiaircraft auxiliaries from the Luftwaffe (Flakhelfen)
- civilians.

Waffen-Sturmbannführer Jūlijs Ķīlitis

Survivors of Waffen-Grenadier-Regiment der SS 33 (lettische Nr. 4) under the temporary command of Waffen-Sturmbannführer Julijs Ķīlitis prepare to surrender to the Americans on a road near Schwerin/Mecklenberg on 2 May 1945.

1.2 MECKLENBERG - 1400 hours, 2 May 1945:

A second group of over 2,300 Latvians surrendered under a white flag at the same location.[13] Waffen-Sturmbannführer Mežgrāvis was in command of 53 officers, 247 NCOs and 1,333 other ranks of the Ist and IInd battalions plus HQ company of the 34th Regiment as well as the 3rd

[12]*Having been destroyed by the Red Army at Šiauliai, the Latvian training and replacement unit was reformed as a depot and organized into three construction regiments which surrendered with the main part of the Division near Schwerin.*

company of SS-Pionier-Bataillon 15. Waffen-Hauptsturmführer Tute commanded the 700 survivors of the Ist and IIIrd detachments of SS-Artillerie-Regiment 15.

Note:
The total number of Latvians surrendering on 2 May 1945 at Schwerin Forest has been estimated at 5,000.[14]

1.3 SCHWERIN LAKE - 2 May 1945:

IIIrd battalion, HQ company and individual survivors of the 32nd Regiment surrendered to the Canadians under regimental C.O. Waffen-Obersturmbannführer Osvalds Meija, north of Schwerin Lake (Schweriner See), some 20 kms. north of Schwerin.[15] The Canadians disarmed them but rather than taking them prisoner on the spot, allowed them to move freely to the west.[16] After a march of about 20 kms. the men were met by Americans at the village of Damlock and sent to a POW camp at Rehna.[17]

1.4 12 KMS. SOUTH OF SCHWERIN - 2 May 1945:

SS-Nachrichten-Bataillon 15 under Waffen-Hauptsturmführer Jānis Vēveris.

1.5 NEAR HAGENOW - 25 KMS. SOUTHWEST OF SCHWERIN - 2 May 1945:

Divisional staff and elements of the 34th Regiment under Waffen-Sturmbannführer Pēteris Balodis.

1.6 WISMAR - 30 KMS. NORTH OF SCHWERIN:

The three SS Construction regiments managed to escape the advancing Russians and surrendered to the U.S. Army at Wismar. The 1st Regiment had been forced-marched for several days and the 3rd had suffered heavy losses during the continued Russian attacks en route. The bulk of the 2nd surrendered at Wismar, but a small group (including the regimental HQ) surrendered nearer to Schwerin.

1.7 SÜLSDORF NEAR LUDWIGSLUST - 35 KMS. SOUTH-SOUTHEAST OF SCHWERIN - 3 May 1945:

---

[13] *Schwerin Forest - though possibly at the northeastern rather than southeastern corner.*

[14] *Archive of the Latvian Legion, via Indulis Kažociņš.*

[15] *The Ist battalion had been detached to form SS-Kampfgruppe "Janums" - see 2. below. A report that 11th company of the 32nd Regiment was taken prisoner by the British at Lübeck (50 kms. northeast of Schwerin) in May 1945 must be in error since no armed Latvian elements were able to reach so far west. 11./III./32. was completely destroyed in January 1945 in the fighting near Kleschin in Pomerania, but may have been reformed in that it was reported (with a strength of only 17 men!) on 24 March 1945. These men are thought to have surrendered with their battalion (III./32.) at Schwerin Lake on 2 May 1945.*

[16] *Regimental C.O. Meija took the opportunity to search for his family and handed command over to Waffen-Hauptsturmführer Kronis.*

[17] *Artūrs Silgailis, letter of 23.6.1981.*

SS-Waffen-Pionier-Bataillon 15 (lacking its 3rd company) surrendered to the U.S. Army under Waffen-Untersturmführer Raitums.

2. GÜTERGLÜCK - 26/27 April 1945:

The Ist battalions of the 32nd and 33rd regiments (40 officers, 126 NCOs and 658 men - temporarily grouped as SS-Kampfgruppe "Janums") under Waffen-Standartenführer Vilis Janums surrendered during the night of 26/27 April 1945 at Güterglück near Zerbst, 190 kms. south-southeast of Schwerin and 40 kms. southeast of Magdeburg.

TO THE RED ARMY:

1. BERLIN - 3 May 1945:

SS-Füsilier-Bataillon 15 had been placed under Waffen-Standartenführer Vilis Janums with the Ist battalions of the 32nd and 33rd infantry regiments to form SS-Kampfgruppe "Janums" but transferring to the combat zone near Berlin became separated from the battle group and its commander, the German SS-Hauptsturmführer Wally. The battalion suffered heavy losses in the defense of Berlin under the Latvian Waffen-Obersturmführer Neilands (Wally's aide). At the end, Neilands and some 80 survivors surrendered to the Red Army.[18]

2. DANZIG, GOTENHAFEN, HELA AREA - May 1945:

What remained of the 15th Division at Sophienwalde after its principal combat elements left in January 1945 were placed under Waffen-Obersturmführer Rēbergs, commander of the divisional artillery regiment. He marched his force of 114 officers, 564 NCOs and 3,170 men, comprising the IIIrd battalion of the 33rd regiment, SS-Feldersatz-Bataillon 15 and 1,486 men from his own SS-Artillerie-Regiment 15, to Danzig where they arrived on 7 March 1945. The following day they were forced to hand over their weapons and on 13 March were disbanded and scattered among the German forces defending Danzig and Gotenhafen. Those who survived but were not able to get away by sea were captured by the Russians. In all, about 3,000 men were taken prisoner by the Red Army in the Danzig, Gotenhafen, Hela area.

3. COURLAND - May 1945:

The 2,500 men of Kampfgruppe Rusmanis, formed from the original five SS Construction Regiments, had been shipped to Courland on 12 April 1945. Unarmed and not attached to any front elements, they were taken prisoner after the capitulation of Courland.

---

[18]Neilands was able to escape the fate of his fellow Latvians by pretending to be a German and following a term in captivity was released and allowed to return to West Germany.

ESCAPE BY SEA - April/May 1945:

Some Latvian elements that took part in the defense of Danzig managed, thanks to the initiative of their Latvian officers, to find transport to Swinemünde, Kiel and even to Denmark and Sweden.

The IIIrd detachment of the 15th Artillery Regiment (6 officers, 30 NCOs and 180 men) and the IInd battalion of the 32nd regiment were transported by sea from Gotenhafen to Swinemünde on the 5 and 14 April respectively and rejoined their regiments (for their subsequent fate, see above).

Sixty-eight officers and 604 other ranks of SS-Sanitäts Bataillon 15 (including its two medical companies) under Waffen-Hauptsturmführer Jansons were shipped from Danzig to Denmark, and 99 men of the divisional artillery regiment reached Kiel from Danzig on 9 May 1945.

One hundred seventy-six men pursuaded the masters of two Latvian tug boats to take them from Weichselmünde to Gotland, but having been transferred to Sweden and interned, they were repatriated to the Soviet Union.

Divisional Commanders

1. Peter Hansen:

   When the SS-FHA appointed Peter Hansen commander of the "Formation Staff of the Latvian Legion" on 26 February 1943, it was generally understood, at least by Hansen himself, that he was to look after the raising and training of the 15th Division, while General Bangerskis would be its actual commander. When it became known that this was not to be (see below), Hansen took over command of the Division.[19]

2. Rudolfs Bangerskis:

   On 9 March 1943, General Oskars Dankers (Director General of the Interior of the Latvian Self Administration), General Bangerskis and Colonel Silgailis were in SS-Brigadeführer Hansen's Riga office when a telephone call came through from the SS-FHA in Berlin. Hansen was given instructions about the Latvian Legion which, or so the Germans were to declare later, left him convinced that General Bangerskis was to be given command of the "1st Division of the Latvian SS Legion" (i.e. what later became the 15th (1st Latvian) SS Division). Ten days later, at a meeting of the Self Administration's Directors General on 19 March 1943, General Dankers was able to give the welcome news that Berlin had agreed to allow the command of the Division to go to a Latvian. At this news the Directors General agreed unanimously to sup-

---

[19] *Artūrs Silgailis, letter of 13.9.1977.*

port the formation of the Legion and authorized Dankers to address the Latvian people on behalf of the Self Administration. That same 3 March, Hansen signed the official appointment order making Bangerskis "Legions-Brigadeführer und Generalmajor der Lett. SS-Freiw.Legion mit der Führung der 1. Division der Lett. SS-Freiw.Legion Beauftrage," which Bangerskis was to receive the following day, 20 March 1943.

The Latvians were understandably disappointed when, before the end of March 1943, they heard that it was all a mistake. They were told that Hansen had misunderstood the SS-FHA's instructions over the telephone on 9 March, and that under German law only a German citizen could command a division.[20]

The Germans realized the damaging effect this "mistake" could have on Latvian support for the Legion, and so acted to avert a crisis. They appointed Bangerskis as Inspector General of the Latvian Legion, pointing out that this gave him authority over not just a single division, but also a brigade and the police battalions. He thus had authority to supervise and inspect both formations and the police battalions and the right to report his observations and suggestions directly to the High Command of the Army and to Reichsführer-SS Heinrich Himmler.

For other details of the life and career of General Bangerskis, see page 12 of this volume.

3. Carl Graf von Pückler-Burghauss:

Artūrs Silgailis provides the accompaning letterhead which shows the unquestionably correct spelling of this officer's name. Silgailis comments: "Graf von Pückler-Burghauss was not a Baltic German name.[21]

GRAF v. PÜCKLER-BURGHAUSS
SS-BRIGADEFÜHRER UND
GENERALMAJOR DER WAFFEN-SS

It was a very old German noble surname related to the Hohenzollern family of the late German Kaiser. Count Pückler told me that he had privately visited the Kaiser while in exile in the Netherlands before the Second World War."

Duprat was wrong in saying von Pückler-Burghauss "fell heroically at the head of his Division."[22] In fact, he handed over his command to Heilmann on 17 February 1944[23] and on 20 March 1944 became Waffen-

---

[20] *Since a divisional commander was vested with the same authority as a judge, he had to be a German citizen.*

[21] *Vol. 4, pg, 75, footnote 55.*

[22] *Vol. 4, pg. 80, footnote 73 - quoting from Duprat, op.cit., pg. 358.*

[23] *Vol. 4, pg. 79, last paragraph.*

SS C-in-C Bohemia and Moravia in Prague (Befehlshaber der Waffen-SS Böhmen und Mähren). He was killed in May 1945 when Prague was captured by the Red Army.[24]

4. Herbert von Obwurzer:

Doubt surrounds von Obwurzer's fate and Hans Stöber was not aware of his capture by the Russians at Nakel in West Prussia on 26 January 1945.[25] Thanks to Artūrs Silgailis,[26] we are able to provide this following eyewitness testimony of Waffen-Untersturmführer Putniņš, von Obwurzer's "Ordonanzoffizier" (staff officer) and interpreter:

> "On 26 January 1945, after a visit to the 34. Gren.Rgt., von Obwurzer, accompanied by a German "Kriegsberichter" (war correspondent), a driver and myself, was on the way to the HQ of the 32. Gren.Rgt. Approaching the Gut Gregau estate, von Obwurzer suddenly caught sight of a well camouflaged tank by a barn. At the same time, ten or twelve Russian soldiers came running down a hill and opened fire. We left the car and started running back. The Kriegsberichter was hit and fell. After a while von Obwurzer cried in a loud voice "ich erschiesse mich" (I'm going to shoot myself!). I was about to commit suicide, too, but in my excitement, I couldn't release the safety catch of my pistol. While I was struggling with my pistol, I was grabbed by a Russian. During my interrogation I was told that the three other occupants of the car were dead."

However, Putniņš may have been misinformed. Years later, Silgailis heard a rumor that von Obwurzer had not committed suicide or been killed, but after release from Russian imprisonment had returned to live in West Germany.[27] German sources say he died after the war.[28]

5. Eduard Deisenhofer:

Deisenhofer was suggested to replace von Obwurzer as commander of the 15th SS Division but died in action in the East on 31 January 1945 (less than a week after von Obwurzer is believed to have been taken prisoner).[29] It is not known whether Deisenhofer was considered as divisional commander from 26 January to 31 January 1945 - in any event, he never reached the Division and the Ia probably took over temporary command.

---

[24]Silgailis received a letter from him dated Prague 20 July 1944, and his last contact was in January 1945 when his wife met von Pückler-Burghauss in Prague. Silgailis questions whether it is really von Pückler-Burghauss in Prague in the photograph on pg. 95 of Vol. 4 - "it doesn't look like Pückler."

[25]Letter from Hans Stöber dated 16.9.1977.

[26]Letter from Artūrs Silgailis dated 1.12.1978.

[27]ibid.

[28]Walter Harzer via P. A. Nix.

[29]Hans Stöber, letter dated 16.9.1977.

6. Adolf Ax:

Julijs Ķīlītis (commander of the IInd battalion of the 33rd regiment) was told in the evening of 26 January 1945 that von Obwurzer had been taken prisoner and that the new divisional commander was to be Adolf Ax, who had just arrived from the Corps staff.[30] According to Vilis Janums (commander of the 33rd regiment), Ax took over command of the Division on 29 January 1945.[31]

Jost Schneider

Adolf Ax

---

[30]*Ķīlītis, op.cit., pg. 152.*
[31]*Janums, op.cit., pg. 165.*

Divisional and Unit Insignia

COLLAR PATCHES OF THE 15th SS DIVISION:[32]

Our knowledge of the regulations governing the collar patches of the 15th SS Division is incomplete in that we do not yet know the date of introduction of the special collar patch with sun and stars. As will be seen below, this was probably soon after 9 September 1944, but research has still not brought to light the relevant SS-FHA or divisional order. Even though this key date has eluded us, we feel it worthwhile setting out what continuing research has brought to light - hopefully the complete story can be told in a future volume in this series.

A) OFFICIAL USAGE:

1) PLAIN BLACK:

The SS-FHA order of 26 February 1943 establishing the Division forbade under "Ziffer 10" the wearing of the SS runes and prescribed a plain black right hand collar patch.[33]

Indulis Kažociņš

Official use of the plain black right hand collar patch. In the photograph at left a young Latvian recruit poses for his first photograph in uniform, 1943. In the photograph below a group of Latvian privates on an NCO training course in Germany, 1943.

Indulis Kažociņš

2) SS RUNES:

Although specifically forbidden for the Division from the very beginning by SS-FHA order of 26 February 1943,[33] the Siegrunen were authorized for SS-Wach-Kompanie 15.[34] Von Obwurzer's order of 9 September 1944 sanctioned the wearing by those men of the Division who already wore the runes until issue of the sun and stars patches (see below).

The differing colors (reflections?) of the "S" runes worn by the Waffen-Rottenführer at right suggest they are hand made. He wears Pattern "D" sleeve shield on his upper right sleeve.

3) FIRE CROSS:

The brief follow-up SS-FHA order of 11 March 1943 qualified that of 26 February 1943 in two respects:[35]

- the "Lettische SS-Freiwilligen Legion" had been raised, and
- contrary to "Ziffer 10" of the previous order, a "Hakenkreuz" (swastika) was to be worn on the right collar.[36]

---

[32]*See pg. 97, Vol. 4.*

[33]*SS-FHA, Amt II Org.Abt. Ia/II, Tgb. Nr. II/1501/43 g.Kdos., v. 26.2.1943, Aufstellung der Lett. SS-Freiw.Div.*

[34]*Artūrs Silgailis.*

[35]*SS-FHA, Kdo.Amt der Waffen-SS, Org.Tgb.Nr. 340/43 g.Kdos., v. 11.3.1943, Aufstellung der Lettischen SS-Freiw.Legion (T-175/111/2635266).*

[36]*German orders referred to the emblem as a "Hakenkreuz" or swastika, but the Latvians looked on it as their Thunder or Fire Cross (Pērkona krusts or Uguns krusts, the first form being the older), which had been used in Latvia for centuries and*

This order suggests a degree of contemporary German confusion over the newly formed Latvian Waffen-SS because it leads one to believe that what had been raised as a Division had been renamed a Legion. But as we know, the Legion was a generic term to describe all Latvian elements serving with the German armed forces, and so the 15th SS Division was a part of the Legion - it was not the Legion itself and vice versa.[37]

If there was confusion over terminology, it certainly spread to the allocation of the Fire Cross collar patch, but assuming the SS-FHA in Berlin knew what they were about, we must conclude that the Fire Cross became the official insignia of the 15th SS Division on basis of the 11 March 1943 order. It was certainly worn and General Bangerskis recorded in his note on an inspection he made to the front from 6 to 9 June 1944 that it had been introduced by an order dated 1 June 1944.[38] Later that year the decision was taken to allocate the Fire Cross to the 19th Division and introduce a new patch with sun and stars for the 15th. The commander of the 15th anticipated this change in his "Divisional Order No. 10 (Dress Regulations)" of 9 September 1944, which were to become effective on 1 October 1944.[39] Section "3.) Kragenspiegel"

---

was adopted by the former Latvian army as a distinctive mark for its aircraft and was painted on the wings of Latvian warplanes. So although it was identical to the swastika and most Germans took it to be one and the same, its origins were purely Latvian, and it had nothing to do with the emblem of Nazi Germany - in fact, it has even been suggested that a member of a Freikorps, while in Latvia, saw the symbol in a Latvian farmstead, liked it so much that he copied it and took it back to Germany with him, and it was in this way that the swastika became the badge of the National Socialists! The symbol will thus be referred to as "Fire Cross" when dealing with the Latvian Waffen-SS.

[37]Order from SS-Obergruppenführer und Polizeigeneral Jeckeln, Rīga, to the Inspector General of the Latvian Legion Gruppenführer und Generalmajor Bangerskis dated 22 June 1943: "1) The Reichsführer has stipulated in his order of 24 February 1943 that the term "Latvian Legion" has to be used as a generic term for all elements conscripted by the SS and Police. . . "

[38]Bangerskis, Mana mūža atmiņas, Vol. 3, pg. 197. To be noted, however, that not all of Bangerskis' observations were accurate, as the following extract demonstrates:

"All formations are now grouped into three main groups: the original German SS divisions with the SS runes; the volunteer SS divisions ("Wiking" and "Nordland") with the Wolfsangel (sic!) on the collar patches, and lastly the Waffen-Grenadier SS Divisions (two of them Volksdeutsche from Hungary, the Latvians and the Estonians), with the Fire Cross on the collar patches."

Wherever he got his information, Bangerskis was confused over Waffen-SS insignia. The Wolfsangel was never worn by "Wiking" and "Nordland" (it was only worn by the Dutch). Perhaps the Fire Cross or swastika was at some stage intended for the Waffen-Grenadier Divisions (if so, then it would have been as a German swastika and not the purely Latvian Fire Cross), but in fact it was only worn by the Latvians.

[39]15. Waffen-Gren.Division der SS, Ia, Divisionsbefehl Nr. 10 (Anzugsordnung), Div.St.Qu. Bütow, den 9.9.1944 - reproduced in full in Der Freiwillige, Heft 6, Juni 1978, pp. 15-17 & 22. This order did not refer specifically to that of the SS-FHA of 11.3.43 (see footnote 35 above).

referred to special collar patches for the two Latvian SS divisions, but because they had not as yet been distributed to the troops, did not describe them. The Order went on to provide that until issue of the new divisional collar patch, members of the Division were to continue wearing the collar patches already on their uniforms, but:

- new recruits joining the Division were to wear the plain black collar patch without SS runes or the Fire Cross
- home-made SS runes and Fire Crosses of aluminum or tin that had been added to the plain black regulation patches were to be removed.[40]

Consequently, the use of SS runes and the Fire Cross was officially sanctioned by von Obwurzer's Order of 9 September 1944 until issue of the new patches with sun and stars. A firm date for such substitution can probably never be determined in that with divisional elements being recommitted prematurely to battle, not all received the new insignia at the same time - if at all. The 15th Division should have stopped wearing the Fire Cross in the autumn of 1944, but as will be seen below, some elements did not receive the sun and stars until mid-January 1945.

4) SUN & STARS:

No order introducing this collar patch for the 15th Division has been found and so no exact date of adoption can be given. In practice, divisional elements will either have received supplies at different dates - or not at all. Distribution certainly began after von Obwurzer's Order of 9 September 1944 and is said to have taken place during the autumn of 1944,[41] but elements were still receiving them as late as mid-January 1945.[42]

---

[40]Indulis Kažociņš provides an interesting insight into this practice, which he heard from a fellow Latvian living in England, L. Ceriņš. Ceriņš was with a group of Latvians attending an NCO training course for Waffen-Artillerie-Regiment der SS 15 at Josefstadt/Jaromer in Czechoslovakia which lasted from 20 September to 20 December 1944. The recruits were very badly dressed without proper footwear, they were issued with Italian boots that were generally too small and second hand uniforms, more often than not German Army issue rather than Waffen-SS, even Afrikakorps breeches. When it came to being photographed for their paybooks, they borrowed the better looking tunics and added to their right hand collar patches SS runes they cut by hand from the tin of empty ration cans. To be noted that at the time (late 1944) they were still not aware of the sun and stars emblem authorized for the collar patches of the 15th Division.

[41]Artūrs Silgailis.

[42]L. Ceriņš, a former NCO of Waffen-Artillerie-Regiment der SS 15, was put in charge of distribution of the new insignia and recalls how exactly the correct number of patches was received for the strength of the regiment at that time - one per man and who did not get the sun and stars patch on that date were never to get them later. According to Ceriņš, an order was issued between 8 and 12 January 1945 whereby all SS runes patches had to be removed immediately. and the sun and stars patch sewn on at once. Some men were punished for not having sewn on the new insignia by the evening of the day they got them (Indulis Kažociņš, letter dated 17.2.1979).

Daugavas Vanagi

The "sun and stars" collar patch being worn by Waffen-Untersturmführer Voldemārs Akmens (commander of the 1st company of SS-Pi.-Btl. 15, who disappeared with his whole company at Nakel in February, 1945).

B) UNOFFICIALLY:

1) SS RUNES:

Photographs show a widespread use of the SS runes from the very beginning when they were expressly forbidden (SS-FHA order of 26 February 1943)[43] until they were tolerated by von Obwurzer's Order of 9 September 1944. Latvian sources have been checked over this practice, for apart from a few Latvians who still believed in a German victory as late as the end of 1944 and aspired to full membership of the SS,[44] the men of the Latvian Legion did not see any kind of 'honor' or 'privilege' in wearing the SS runes on the collar as did their counterparts in the German SS. Some are reported to have added the SS runes because they thought it was the correct thing to do, others did not want to be mistaken for SD personnel by wearing plain black collar patches. It is also reported, although as yet unconfirmed, that in spite of regulations, uniform jackets were issued to the Latvians with German-made SS runes collar patches already stitched to the collar.[45] Some legionnaires wore SS rune collar patches supplied by the Germans when they were unable to obtain the authorized pattern.[46]

---

[43] *See footnote 33 on pg 33.*

[44] *Letter from Ķīlītis to Indulis Kažociņš, dated 23.1.79.*

[45] *Silgailis and Kažociņš.*

[46] *Silgailis.*

OFFICIALLY:
Authorized 26.2.43 until replaced by Fire Cross on 11.3.43 and eventually (end 1944/early 1945) by sun & stars. Only patch for new recruits from 1.10.1944 until issue of sun & stars.

UNOFFICIALLY:
If worn after other patterns introduced.

OFFICIALLY:
Forbidden for the Division on 26.2.43, but those who wore it permitted on 9.9.43 to continue until issue of the sun & stars. Specifically authorized for SS-Wach-Kompanie 15.

UNOFFICIALLY:
Widespread use throughout.

OFFICIALLY:
Authorized for the Latvian Legion (and therefore for the 15th Division) 11.3.43 - confirmed for the Division 1.6.44. Later authorized for the 19th Division, but 15th permitted on 9.9.43 to retain it until issue of the sun & stars.

UNOFFICIALLY:
If worn after sun & stars issued (no record).

OFFICIALLY:
Authorized for 15th Division in autumn 1944, but still being issued as late as January 1945.

UNOFFICIALLY:
If worn outside the 15th Division (no record).

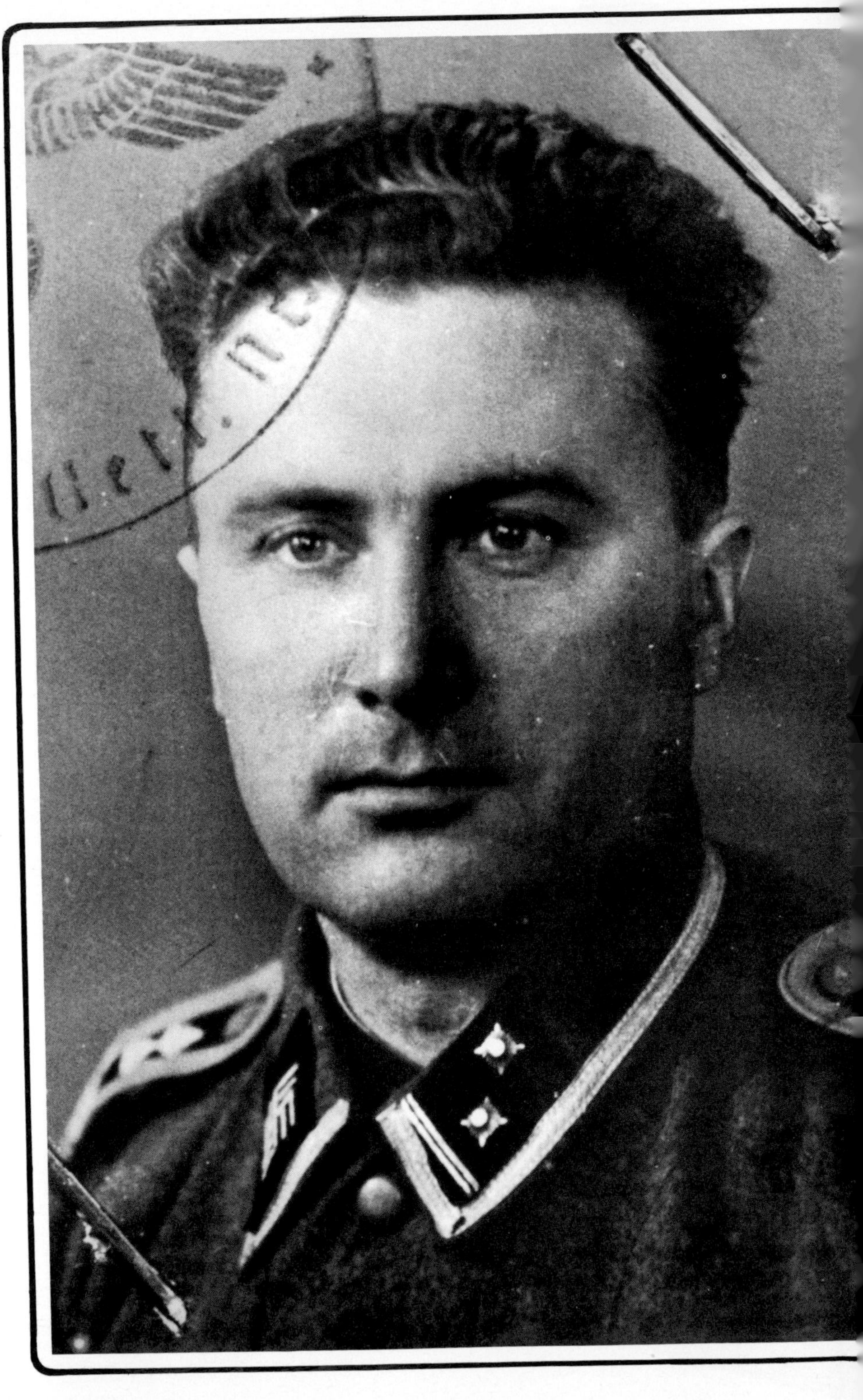

Two different embroidery patterns of the "double-armed swastika" collar patch.

'he photograph at left proves that at least in one case the so-called "double-armed wastika" was worn by a member of the 15th SS Division. This photograph is an nlarged reproduction from that appearing in a bilingual German/Latvian Soldbuch f a Waffen-Hauptscharführer issued in November 1944. He was recruited by SS-rsatz-Inspektion (Ersatz-Kommando Ostland der Waffen-SS) on 29.8.1944 (Rekruten Depot Libau), trained in SS-Grenadier-Ausbildungs- und Ersatz-Bataillon 15 (lett. Nr.) at Berent in West Prussia, took the oath on 8.11.1944 and joined Waffen-Grenadier-Regiment der SS 34 (lett. Nr. 5) on 12.11.1944. Since this patch does not appear to have een authorized for the Latvian Legion or the 15th SS Division, it is possible that it emonstrated that this particular soldier had previously seen service as a concentra-on camp guard (the "double-armed swastika" was authorized for non-German con-entration guards by order SS-WVHA Amtsgruppenchef D, AV/4 Az.: Tgb. Nr. 759/44 eh., Uniformenspiegel). See footnote 173 on page 111 for details. Alternatively, it is ossible that this member of the Latvian Legion was issued by error with a "double-rmed swastika" rather than the Fire Cross (which was, after all, a "single-armed wastika").

SLEEVE SHIELDS OF THE 15th SS DIVISION[47]

There were many different types of Latvian sleeve shield as has been seen in Volume 4, and although a number of orders were issued, no particular type was ever authorized - that is unless an order prescribing the final "Waffen-SS pattern" was issued but has so far eluded researchers.

While military historians and insignia collectors may take great interest in these variations, the Latvians themselves did not really care which type they wore - what was important to them was simply to have one. It was extremely important to the Latvians that their uniform clearly showed their nationality. At first they had been able to wear old Latvian Army uniforms, but when these were replaced by German issue, Latvian nationality was shown by a sleeve badge, showing the colors of the national flag (2/5 ths dark red - 1/5th white - 2/5 ths dark red). The soldiers were proud of their country and so everyone wore the badge - even some members of the German commanding staff.

In the absence of regulations there was no uniformity and shields, often homemade, were worn of varying shapes and sizes - some with and others without the word "LATVIJA." Wearing the Latvian colors was all-important to the Latvians - the actual design of the badge itself was of little concern to them.

The first step towards standardization came soon after the establishment of the General Inspection of the Latvian Legion in April 1943.[48] According to Artūrs Silgailis the General Inspection placed an order for type "E" with the Lenta manufacturing company of Riga and distributed only this type to the men of the Legion.[49] The many available photographs, however, fail to show type "E" being worn by any Legion men at the front and it appears to have found its way onto the uniforms of Latvian police units.[50] Type "E" was in any case not the official pattern,[51] even though having been approved by the General Inspection, it may have been the one the Latvians felt should have been official.

Latvians in the Waffen-SS continued to wear various other types of shield right up to the end of the war: in Latvia a number of different types were on the

---

[47]*See Vol. 4, pp. 98-102.*

[48]*Not an easy date to determine exactly. Silgailis gives 30 April, but Kažociņš chooses 1 April because this was the date of Bangerskis' Order No. 1 as General Inspector (letter of 23.1.79 and Latviešu karavīrs otra pasaules kara laikā, Vol. 3, pg. 60).*

[49]*Artūrs Silgailis, letter of 27.5.77.*

[50]*Einzeldienst and closed units. Kažociņš, letter dated 23.1.79.*

[51]*Artūrs Silgailis, letter of 13.9.77. Jochen Nietsch was therefore quite wrong in captioning type "E" as "Einziger offiziell genehmigter Landesschild für die 15. Waffen-Grenadier-Division der SS (lettische Nr. 1)" in Der Freiwillige, Heft 6, June 1978, pg. 15.*

open market and soldiers bought them as their old ones wore out;[52] in Germany the chaotic situation prevailing in the closing months of the war made it impossible for Latvians to lay hands on any particular type of shield - some will have found those made in Latvia (by the Lenta company and others), some will have received the Waffen-SS pattern on black cloth backing, and others will have made their own by hand.[53]

At a date as yet unknown (probably in June 1944), the Germans introduced a "Waffen-SS pattern" sleeve shield on a black cloth backing (type "F"). By German standards this should have been the one and only official pattern, but for the Latvians it had little appeal. Heraldically it was all wrong, having an incorrect shade of red and the white bar too wide. The black backing was also unpopular and earned "F," the ironical nickname of "badge (or colors) of mourning" (Sēru zīme).[54] In any event, appearing as it did so late in the war, it was worn by only a few.[55]

Note:

Examples of "F" are often found today to have been distorted out of shape, taking on a noticeable "list" to the left. This is thought to have been caused by uneven shrinkage of the red and white thread, some sort of artificial yarn.

Those regulations that were laid down over sleeve shields are summarized below in chronological order:

12.7.1943 Shield to be worn on upper right sleeve - the top edge to be positioned 15cm below the base of the shoulder strap.[56]

---

[52] *Indulis Kažociņš, letter dated 26.1.78.*

[53] *Artūrs Silgailis, letter of 27.5.77.*

[54] *Indulis Kažociņš, letters dated 23.1.79 and 12.6.79.*

[55] *Jochen Nietsch, Der Freiwillige, Heft 4, April 1978, pg. 16, was in error in saying that this type was never made - it is clearly shown being worn in the photograph on page 102 of Volume 4 in this series. The illustration in Der Freiwillige by artist Kurt Geiss is also wrong, for in copying it from the "1.2.1945 map" he mistakenly included the German word for Latvia "LETTLAND" at the top of the design, whereas this was merely a label appearing on the "map" and was never a part of the shield's design. These are not the only flaws in this two-part article on the uniforms and insignia of the 15th SS Division, which although appearing in 1978 failed to take into consideration our detailed coverage in Volume 4 (published in 1975). In a photograph appearing on page 16 of Heft 4, a soldier's sleeve rank chevron is described as a Latvian sleeve shield. In this article are illustrated the patterns of shield we labelled "B," "D," "E," and "F" in Volume 4 - as well as another variation we reproduce here and call "AA."*

[56] *Nr. 20, Divisionsbefehl Nr. 2, vom 12.7.1943.*

13.9.1943	Reichsführer-SS Heinrich Himmler ordered that the Latvian Legion should wear a shield in Latvian national colors with the word "LATVIJA" on the upper right sleeve.[57]
15.4.1944	Sleeve shield henceforth to be worn on the upper left sleeve of the uniform -- one finger's width below the SS sleeve eagle.[58]
1.6.1944	Bangerskis referred to an order whereby from this date sleeve shields had to be transferred from the right arm to the left sleeve under the sleeve eagle.[59] Type "F" - what the Germans considered the official Waffen-SS pattern - probably introduced during June 1944.
1.8.1944	Type "F" already introduced (for it was illustrated in the 25th edition of Der Soldatenfreund - Taschenjahrbuch für die Wehrmacht mit Kalendarium für 1945. Ausgabe D: Waffen-SS, updated to 1.8.1944).
9.9.1944	The previous order of 15.4.1944 was repeated and to be complied with no later than 1.10.1944.[60]
1.2.1945	Type "F" appeared on the "1.2.1945 map" of Amtsgruppe D of the SS-Hauptamt.[61]

To Sum up:

a) the shield should have had the word "LATVIJA" from 13.9.1943

b) it should have been worn on the upper right sleeve until April 1944

c) it should have been transferred to the upper left sleeve in April 1944 - although a reminder was necessary, ordering compliance by the end of September 1944[62]

d) the Germans introduced a final "Waffen-SS pattern" ("F") prior to the end of July 1944, probably in June

---

57 *Der HSSPF für das Ostland, H./Gy., Riga den 13.9.1943, Lettische SS-Freiwilligen-Legion.*

58 *Verordnungsblatt der Waffen-SS, 5. Jahrgang, Berlin, 15.4.1944, Nr. 8, Z. 165. The sleeve eagle had to be moved three finger widths up the sleeve and lower ranks' sleeve rank insignia had to be added ½ a finger's width below the bottom of the shield.*

59 *Service note from inspection at the front, 6 to 9 June 1944, quoted by Bangerskis in Mana, mūža atmiņas, Vol. 3, pg. 197 (see also footnote 38 on page 34 of this volume).*

60 *4.) Landesschilde, 15. Waffen-Gren.-Division der SS, Ia, Div.St.Qu. Bütow, den 9.9.1944, Divisionsbefehl Nr. 10 (Anzugsordnung).*

61 *Captioned "Offizielle Musterzeichnung des SS-Hauptamtes, Amtsgruppe D.Stand: Februar 1945" in Der Freiwillige, Heft 5, April 1978, pg. 15 (see footnote 42 on pp. 90/91 of Volume 3).*

62 *According to Ķīlītis, his men never complied with the orders to transfer the sleeve shield from right to left sleeves. The explanation has been given that Latvian pride did not permit their national colors being placed below the German eagle (which the Latvians called the "Hunger Crow" - "Spassvogel" in German or "Bada vārna" in Latvian) which of course was worn on the upper left sleeve of the Waffen-SS uniform. Just before the surrender at Schwerin, Ķīlītis advised his men to remove the SS sleeve eagle and transfer the Latvian sleeve shield from the right sleeve to its correct place on the left sleeve, but not all did so.*

Latvian Sleeve Shield Variations

"AA"

One of the five types illustrated in Jochen Nietsch's not always accurate article for Der Freiwillige.[63] It could have been a different type or, as appears to be the case from photographs, the result of distortion to the frame through stitching to uniform sleeves.

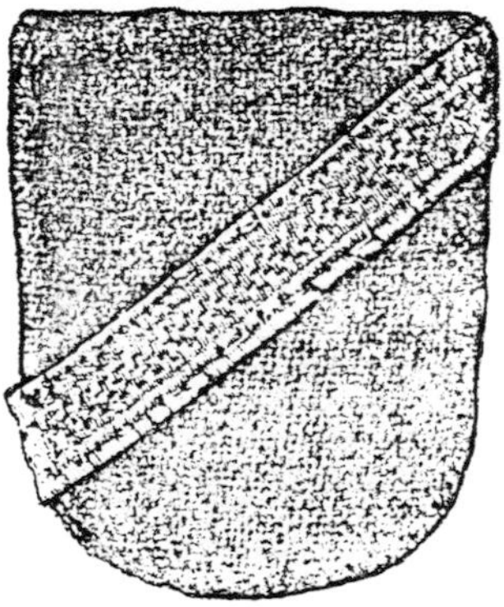

"BB"

A home-made example using a field postcard as backing (J van Fleet collection).

The Latvian sleeve shield should have been worn on the upper right sleeve until April 1944.

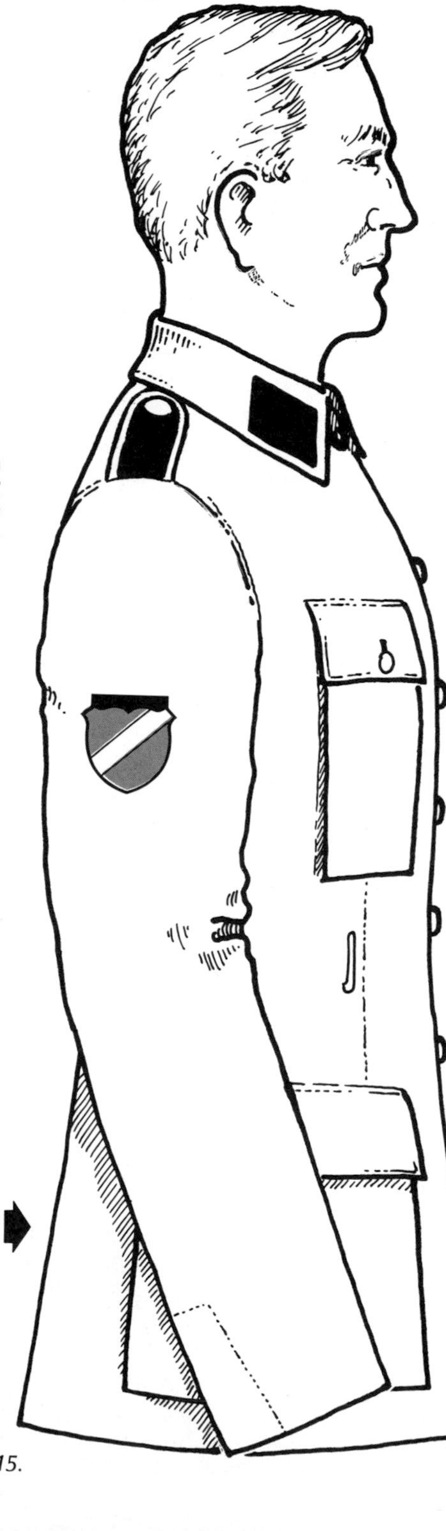

[63] *Der Freiwillige, Heft 4, April 1978, pg. 15.*

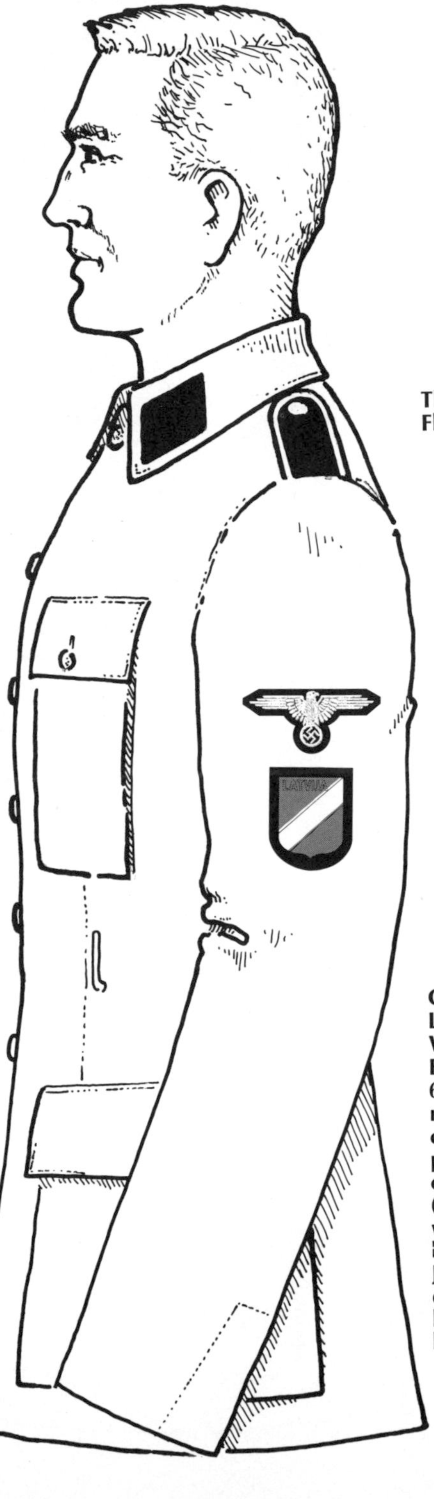

"CC"

The same as "C" but with a black border (J van Fleet collection).

"DD"

One of the many variations of type "D," that is Latvian-made badges with the word "LATVIJA." This example was made by the Johanna Egle handicrafts workshop of Ad. Hitlera ieta 62/64 in Rīga for "members of the Latvian military units under German command." The original from which this illustration is taken was purchased in early 1943 and worn on the sleeve of an officer of the Latvian Youth Organization (LJO) - but this pattern was almost certainly also worn on Waffen-SS uniform. Note the different lettering to that of "D" (especially the A's and J), the different top-right positioning of the diagonal bar and the fact that the horizontal backing to the lettering was black rather than blue.

From April 1944 the sleeve shield should have been worn on the upper left sleeve.

"E"

Another "D" variation. Here, the top-right positioning of the diagonal white bar is as "DD," but the lettering is different and the shield has no outer border. Note the (metal?) SS runes worn on this private's collar patch.

Col. C. M. Dodkins

Similar to "DD" but with different lettering and an outer border. This Waffen-Unterscharführer is from the Guard Company ("Wach-Kompanie") of the 15th SS Division, and the photograph was taken in Rīga in the summer of 1943. The Wach-Kompanie was a temporary element made up for guard duties by the Division while its HQ was in Rīga in 1943.

Note: This photograph has been incorrectly identified as showing men of "Lettisches Grenadier-Ersatz- und Ausbildungs-Regiment 15 at Rīga-Bolderāja.[64]

In this rare photograph of a Latvian Waffen-Untersturmführer wearing the black Waffen-SS "Panzer" uniform in Rīga on 30 May 1944 can be seen:

- "D" sleeve shield
- SS runes collar patch.

---

[64]*ibid.*

Col. C. M. Dodkins

This officer wears the Latvian-made pattern "E" sleeve shield on the left sleeve of his camouflage jacket. Contrary to regulations, he wears shoulder straps.

Indulis Kažociņš

CUFFBANDS[65]

A) DIVISIONAL:

No cuffbands were ever authorized for this Division. One bearing the word "LATVIJA" (in fact, the Germans misspelled the Latvian word for "Latvia" by writing it "LATTVIJA") appeared in SS-FHA order of 22 October 1943[66] but was cancelled in the follow-up order of 12 November 1943.[67] Either a mistake had been made in giving the cuffband in the first place, or more likely, the Germans changed their minds and considered the appearance of the word "LATVIJA" on the sleeve shield (ordered 13 September 1943)[68] adequate indication of the wearer's nationality.

Unofficially at least two patterns of cuffband are reported:
- "Lett. SS-Freiw.Legion"
- "Lett. SS-Frw.Div."

which were forbidden to be worn after 1 October 1944.[69] Former members of the Division do not remember ever having seen these cuffbands and their use - if they were worn at all - must have been very limited.

B) REGIMENTAL:

Divisional commander von Obwurzer submitted an application to the SS-FHA for a cuffband "Karlis Aperāts" for the 32nd Grenadier Regiment to commemorate its late commander, killed in action on 16 July 1944. This proposal was rejected.[70]

C) MISCELLANEOUS:

A cuffband with golden letters on red cloth was worn on the sleeve under the Latvian sleeve shield by members of the Latvian Front Theatre when they entertained the troops on the Leningrad front in 1942.[71] The wording of this cuffband is not known.

SHOULDER STRAPS[72]

At first it was thought that the order quoted in Volume 4 did not reach the divisional elements and so was never complied with,[73] but confirmation has

---

[65]*Vol. 4, pg. 102.*
[66]*Ibid., footnote 133.*
[67]*Ibid., footnote 134.*
[68]*Vol. 4, footnote 131, pg. 99.*
[69]*8.) Schulterstücke, Dienststellenabzeichen, Ärmelstreifen, 15. Waffen-Gren.-Division der SS, Ia, Div.St.Qu.Bütow, den 9.9.44, Divisionsbefehl Nr. 10 (Anzugsordnung).*
[70]*Artūrs Silgailis, letter dated 13.9.1977. The wording on the cuffband was to have been "Regiment Aperats" (sic - "Aperāts" should be written with an accent thus) according to Stöber: Die lettischen Divisionen im VI. SS-Armeekorps, pg. 96.*

now been received that colored cords were being worn on the shoulder straps by a number of men of the 15th SS Division at Sophienwalde. A former NCO of Waffen-Artillerie-Regiment der SS 15 remembers what he thought were two colored cords loosely twisted together that indicated the wearer's regiment.[74] These cords were positioned between the base of the shoulder strap and the Anwärter or Bewerber bars,[75] and although such positioning appears to have been left to the individual, the cords were not placed too close to the base. The accompanying photograph clearly shows a Waffen-Untersturmführer wearing the divisional "sun and stars" collar patch and a colored bar close to the base of his right shoulder strap.

These colored cords had vanished from shoulder straps by the time the Division was fighting in Pomerania; they had either been removed or had been torn off during the fighting.

Indulis Kažociņš

[71]*Latviešu karavīrs otra pasaules kara laikā*, vol. 7.
[72]*Uniform Notes 2*, Vol. 4, pg. 103.
[73]Silgailis, letter dated 13.9.77.
[74]L. Ceriņš, via Indulis Kažociņš, letter dated 12.6.79.
[75]See Vol. 1, pg. 133.

CAP BADGES

Before surrendering to the U.S. Army at Schwerin on 2 May 1945, Waffen-Sturmbannführer Ķīlītis ordered his men[76] to remove the death's head emblem from their caps and replace them with the sun and stars badges from their collar patches.[77] This was presumably an attempt to "Latvianise" their uniforms just before capitulation and strip them of German - especially SS - insignia and appearance, and was not the only instance of this being done. Photographs show the death's head replaced by a sun and stars badge on the cap of Anna Bormane, a doctor traveling from Swinemünde to Denmark with SS-Ausbildungs- und Ersatz-Bataillon 15 in March 1945.[78] Similar reasoning would explain the absence of the eagle and swastika badge from the service cap of the Waffen-Untersturmführer in the photograph on page 97 of Volume 4.[79]

COLORS[80]

Colors were sometimes presented to a unit by the local organizations or government offices of the locality in which it was formed and in some cases the unit was even adopted by the locality.

Three colors are reported for the 15th SS Division:

32nd Infantry Regiment - given by the local government and civil organizations of Liepāja (Libau in German)

34th Infantry Regiment - given by the Cēsis (Wenden in German) urban council (destroyed in an air attack at the front in the night of 25/26 March 1944)

SS-Waffen-Panzerjäger-Abteilung 15 - given by the urban district and rural district organizations of Liepāja (Libau).

---

[76] *He had taken command of the 33rd Regiment from Janums on 20 April 1945 but assumed temporary command of the whole 3,500 - 4,000 strong contingent for the surrender (see page 24 of this book).*

[77] *Indulis Kažociņš, letter dated 15.2.78. Imperial War Museum photograph BU 7146 shows a Russian boy (possibly a mascot) wearing such a badge on his cap instead of the "Totenkopf" while being deloused by two British soldiers.*

[78] *Latviešu karavīrs otra pasaules kara laikā, Vol. 6, pg. 276. She also wore type "F" sleeve shield under her Waffen-SS sleeve eagle.*

[79] *Silgailis doubts this: "I don't believe that the absence of the eagle was an attempt to "Latvianise" the cap. Why would he have taken off the eagle and swastika, the insignia worn by all members of the German armed forces, the Navy included, and not the death's head of the Waffen-SS?" He also suggests that the photograph may even be a montage, basing this on the "strange shape" of the cap ("the front top is too steep") and "imitation look of the sun and stars collar patch." This photograph was originally published on page 59 (incorrectly attributed to the 19th SS Division!) of Beadle & Hartmann's Divisionsabzeichen der Waffen-SS its Divisional Insignia, and was the only one available when Volume 4 in this series went to press. See pages 36 and 49 of this book for unquestionably original photographs of the sun and stars collar patch being worn.*

[80] *Vol. 4, pg. 103.*

The 33rd Infantry Regiment, which had been raised near Priekule, was not given a color.

The colors of all three units were identical, being a plain Latvian flag with the sun and stars device as a pole top.

THE VEHICLE SYMBOLS OF THE 15th SS DIVISION[81]

The capital "L" with Roman ordinal "I" was assigned to the 15th Division, but no copy of the corresponding order ever reached the General Inspection of the Latvian Legion or the divisional elements and so the symbol never appeared on vehicles.[82] Photographic evidence confirms at least one case of the outline of a Latvian sleeve shield being roughly painted or stencilled onto a Waffen-SS vehicle.[83]

Waffen-Oberführer Artūrs Silgailis' Volkswagen (Kübelwagen Kfz. 1 (type 82)) stuck in the spring mud on its way from the 15th to the 19th SS Divisions at Svinuchovo in the Bardovo-Kudever area on 9 May 1944. At this time Silgailis was second-in-command (Infanterieführer) of the 15th SS Division, as well as temporary commander of the 19th. The vehicle carries registration number "SS 223 277" but no divisional symbol.

---

[81] *Ibid.*

[82] *Artūrs Silgailis, letter of 3.2.78.*

[83] *J. P. Petersen, 1.5.81.*

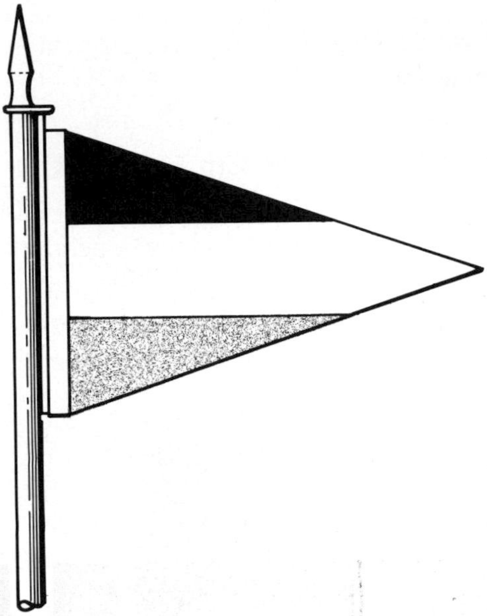

15.(lett.) SS-Freiw.Division

Div.St.Qu., den 25.11.1943

Ausweis.

Leg.Standartenführer S i l g a i l i s , geb.13.11.1895, ist Inf.Führer der 15.(lett.) SS-Freiw.Division und daher zum Führen der verkleinerten Kommandoflagge am Kfz. berechtigt. Es steht ihm freie Durchfahrt nach OKH.GenStH/Ausb.Abt.(Ia) Nr. 2600 zu.

Für das Divisionskommando:
Der 1.Generalstabsoffizier

SS-Sturmbannführer.

As "Infanterieführer" of the 15. (lett.) SS-Freiw.Division, Legions-Standartenführer Artūrs Silgailis was entitled to fly a divisional pennant on his car - illustrated above is the permit to do so issued to him by the divisional HQ on 25 November 1943.

A German NCO instructs Latvian recruits in the use of the Panzerschreck, late 1944.

19. Waffen-Grenadier-Division der SS (lettische Nr. 2)

EVOLUTION AND TITLES OF 19. WAFFEN-GRENADIER-DIVISION DER SS (lettische Nr. 2)

18 May 1943[1] - 22 October 1943	Lettische SS-Freiwilligen-Brigade
22 October 1943[2] - 7 January 1944 ..	2. Lettische SS-Freiwilligen-Brigade
7 January 1944[3] - May 1944	19. Lettische SS-Freiwilligen-Division
May 1944[4] - July 1944	19. Waffen-Grenadier-Division der SS (lettische Nr. 2)
July 1944[5] - late August 1944	Kampfgruppe Streckenbach
Late August 1944[6] - 8 May 1945[7] ...	19. Waffen-Grenadier-Division der SS (lettische Nr. 2)

Note:
At no time was this Division officially named either "Latvija" or "Lettland."

---

[1]*SS-FHA, Kdo, Amt d. W.-SS, Org.Tgb.Nr. 660/43 g.Kdos., v. 18.5.43, Umgliederung der 2. SS-Inf.Brig. (mot.) in Lett. SS-Freiw.Brig. (T-175, Roll 111, frames 2635286-90).*

[2]*SS-FHA, Amt II Org.Abt. Ia/II, Tgb.Nr. 1574/43 g.Kdos., v. 22.10.43, Bezeichnung der Feldtruppenteile der Waffen-SS - Anlage 3: III. Brigaden und Sturmbrigaden.*

[3]*Date the SS-FHA ordered immediate conversion of the brigade into a division (SS-FHA, Amt II Org.Abt. Ia/II, Tgb.Nr. 40/44 g.Kdos., v. 7.1.44, Umgliederung bzw. Neuaufstellung der 2. Lett. SS-Freiw.-Brig. zur 19. Lett. SS-Freiw.Div. - T-175/141/2669370).*

In practice the Brigade was too heavily involved in retreating battles with the Red Army during January and February 1944 to have been able to comply with the order and work on conversion could only begin at the end of February 1944 when the Brigade took up defensive positions on the banks of the Velikaya river. It is probably impossible to give a definite date for the achievement of true divisional status. Silgailis (letter of 31.3.81) assumes 22 March 1944 as this was the date he gives for the renumbering of the original two infantry regiments from 39 and 40 to 42 and 43, and the forming of the new third regiment and its numbering as the 44th. He adds that it may even have been a few days earlier, since the newly raised 44th regiment had already participated in the battle for the retaking of Hill 93,4 (16-19 March 1944) at which time the Brigade was called "19th Division." The German Red Cross and Finke were wrong in dating achievement of divisional status later (April 1944 and 16 May 1944, respectively).

[4]*Introduction of the word "Waffen-" in the title was indicated by V.O.SS 1495 of 16.5.44, although it seems to have been used by both the 15th and 19th SS divisions as early as March 1944 (Silgailis and DRK), that is from when the formation effectively became a division.*

[5]*Kažociņš, letter of 26.1.78.*

[6]*Latviešu karavīrs otra pasaules kaŗa laikā, Vol. 5, pp. 24 and 42. According to Stīpnieks (ibid, Vol. 5, pg. 49) Kampfgruppe "Streckenbach" was renamed as the 19th SS Division once the 43rd infantry regiment had been reinforced in early September 1944.*

[7]*Date the Division surrendered to the Russians in Courland.*

History

The histories of the two Latvian Waffen-SS divisions differ dramatically, especially their beginnings and their fates. The 15th was raised with some difficulty but at least peacefully in Latvia during 1943, whereas the 19th was formed by reorganizing and expanding a Waffen-SS brigade while it was fighting the Russians on the eastern front. In 1944 Latvians of the badly mauled 15th were transferred to Germany and so had no chance of defending their country. Their compatriots of the 19th fought desperately and with great bravery for every foot of Latvian soil, trapped in Courland they held out against impossible odds until the very end of the war. Two completely different stories, that which follows will exclude as far as possible repetition of what has already been written about Latvia, the Latvian Legion and the 15th SS Division in this series. As will be seen, what the two Latvian divisions did have in common was heroism and sacrifice in the face of certain defeat and a total commitment to the defence of Latvia against a return to Russian domination.

OCTOBER 1941 - MAY 1943: ON THE LENINGRAD FRONT: FROM POLICE BATTALIONS TO SS BRIGADE:

Latvians remember the Russian occupation of their country from June 1940 to July 1941 as "the year of horror."[8] They welcomed as a lesser evil the Germans when they drove the Red Army out of Latvia as a part of the seemingly inexorable "Operation Barbarossa," but all the heroism and sacrifice that was to follow was to give Latvia only three years of freedom from Russian oppression in exchange for German occupation.

Soon after establishing themselves in Latvia in July 1941, the Germans raised a number of police battalions of Latvian volunteers.[9] The original intention was to use them for maintaining law and order within the country, but when the Russian winter-offensive of 1941/1942 inflicted severe losses on the German Army, it was decided to use these Schuma battalions at the front as reinforcements.

The first Latvian Schuma battalion to be sent to the eastern front was the 16th. It left home on 22 October 1941 and fought in the Dno area until the end of

---

[8]Kažociņš, letter of 26.1.78.

[9]The police battalions were raised under the auspices of the Higher SS and Police Leader for the Ostland, Friedrich Jeckeln (hanged in Riga on 3.2.1946). They soon became known as Schutzmannschafts-Bataillone, referred to henceforth as "Schuma" battalions (although this abbreviation appears to have been coined by the Germans after the war - A. J. Bērziņš of the Archive of the Latvian Legion has found no trace of any Latvian or German document in which this abbreviation was used). They were renamed "Latvian Police Battalions" (Lettische Polizei-Bataillone) with effect from 24.5.1943 (see Vol. 4, pg. 66, fn. 17).

1942. On 30 March 1942 the 21st Schuma battalion was sent to the Leningrad front, followed on 12 May 1942 by the 19th. It was not until 5 November 1942 that the 24th Schuma battalion left Latvia for Leningrad and was attached to the German 380th Infantry Regiment near Peterhof. While the 16th and 24th served under command of the German Army, the 19th and 21st were attached to a formation of the Waffen-SS, the 2nd (motorized) SS Infantry Brigade, an international formation in that during its time on the eastern front, it included not only the Latvian Schuma battalions but also the Dutch, Flemish and Norwegian volunteer Legions.[10]

A private (Kareivis) of an unidentified Latvian Schutzmannschafts battalion on the Leningrad front in 1942. He wears a Czech steel helmet with a German police transfer (decal) on its left side. The rifle is a Russian Vintovka obr.1891/30g.

---

[10]The Brigade had been formed on 1.5.1941 (SS-FHA, I. Org.Tgb.Nr. 1445/41, v. 24.4.41 - T-175/109/2633308-9) on basis of SS-Totenkopf-Standarte 4 and 14, which were renamed SS-Inf.Rgt. 4 and 14. The Brigade went into action on the northern sector of the eastern front at the end of 1941 (for photocopies of its original war diaries, see Unsere Ehre Heisst Treue, Europa Verlag, 1965).

Men of the 16th Schuma battalion (16. Schutzmannschafts-bataillon) receive the Iron Cross 2nd Class from their battalion commander, pltn. Rudolf Kociņš while serving under German Army command in the Dno area of the Leningrad front in 1942. Kociņš was later promoted to Legions-Sturmbannführer and on 1 November 1942 to Legions-Obersturmbannführer and was to lead the 19th SS Division's third infantry regiment (the 44th). The 16. Schuma-Btl. became III./Lettische Legion at Krasnoje Selo on 8 February 1943.

The desire to join the Germans in crushing the Red Army for once and for all and so postpone indefinitely a return of their country to Russian control drove the Latvian Schuma battalions to fight bravely and with considerable sacrifice. This was certainly better than being tied to the internal police duties the Germans had originally planned for them at home, but it was far from the Latvian ideal of a reborn national army. There had been misunderstandings between certain Schuma battalion commanders and the German authorities - the battalions were engaged separately, and those attached to elements of the German armed forces were thus scattered along the eastern front - used by German commanders to fill gaps torn in their lines by the Red Army, it is hardly surprising that Latvians felt they were being used as mere cannon-fodder.

Dissatisfaction spread amongst the Latvians at home as well as at the front and reached a head when it became known that the Germans had agreed to allow the small neighboring country of Estonia to raise an Estonian Waffen-SS legion on 28 August 1942, the first anniversary of the ousting of the Russians from the Estonian capital of Tallinn.[11] The Latvians saw no good reason for the Estonians to be privileged in this way, they had both aided the German war effort by volunteering for the German-controlled Schuma and both had had their share of losses. With the collapse of the German offensive in the east at Stalingrad and with Allied troops in North Africa, Latvia could no longer count on what had at first seemed a certain Axis victory and fear of a return of the Russians became a reality. What hope could there possibly be for Latvia with the few meager battalions the Germans allowed her to raise spread among and subordinated to German elements, especially should the stiuation continue to worsen and the Wehrmacht and Waffen-SS be driven back to and then out of Latvia? Unless the volunteers serving in the Schuma battalions could be grouped into an independent Latvian force, open to all those able and

[11]*See the following chapter in this book.*

willing to fight for the common cause, there could be no chance of Latvia making a last stand against another Russian invasion.

Leaders of the Latvian Self Administration presented a petition to the German civil authorities in December 1942 for the establishment of a 100,000 strong Latvian national army. At a time when a militarily strong Latvia could only have been of great assistance to the German war effort, they chose to pay greater heed to their real or imagined fears of nationalism in the countries they occupied and the petition was turned down.

If the German civil authorities were wary of letting an increased number of Latvians fight the Red Army in closed units, there was one man at least who was not. As Reichsführer-SS and Chief of the German Police, Himmler knew the Schuma battalions and was interested in channeling the hardy Latvian soldiers into his Waffen-SS. Less than a month after the Latvian petition for a national army had been presented and rejected, Himmler paid a visit to the Leningrad front in the second half of January 1943. Of the four Latvian Schuma battalions then fighting in the east, he certainly saw men of the two (19th and 21st) serving with the 2nd SS Brigade and may well have visited the others under Wehrmacht command. Himmler was impressed and upon his return to Germany suggested to Hitler that a Latvian volunteer SS legion should be raised.[12] Hitler agreed on 23 January 1943[13] and the following day Himmler sent a radio message to the commander of the 2nd SS Brigade at the front that his formation should be rebuilt as a Latvian brigade and that all Latvian battalions should henceforth be known collectively as the "Latvian Legion."[14] Two days later, on 26 January 1943, SS-Brigadeführer und Generalmajor der Waffen-SS Gottfried Klingemann handed over command of the brigade he had led since 28 June 1942 to SS-Brigadeführer und Generalmajor der Waffen-SS Fritz von Scholz.[15]

---

[12]*The Latvians were told by the Germans that they were to be formed into a Legion because of the valor they had shown on the battlefield (Silgailis, letter of 27.5.77).*

[13]*Aktennotiz (memorandum) v. 30.1.43 des RF-SS.*

[14]*Funkspruch (radiotelegram) RF-SS, v. 24.1.43. Hitler's official order establishing the Latvian Legion followed on 10.2.43 (the order had no reference and was headed simply "Führer-Hauptquartier, 10.2.43" - Silgailis was given a photocopy by SS-Standartenführer Hierthes in March 1943 (letter of 31.3.81)). Thus the 2. SS-Inf.Brig. (mot.) provided the basis for the 19th Division of the Waffen-SS in much the same way as the 1. SS-Inf.Brig. (mot.) was to be used in January 1944 to form the 18th SS Division "Horst Wessel" - the difference being that the 1st Brigade was predominantly racial German (Volksdeutsche), whereas the 2nd had become heavily Latvian.*

[15]*Klietmann gives the date of this change in command as 26.1.43 when dealing with the 2. SS-Inf.Brig. (mot.) (op.cit., pg. 317) but "beginning March 1943" in his coverage of the Latvian SS Brigade (pg. 375). Stöber and Silgailis confirm 26.1.43. Two days after receiving the message, Klingemann took over command of SS-Junkerschule Bad Tölz. By the end of January 1944 he was Inspector of Infantry within the SS-FHA but later that year seems to have become involved in security matters and by 9.11.44*

Kapt. Rudolf Kociņš awards men of his 16th (Zemgales) Schuma battalion with the Iron Cross 2nd Class. The soldier at left (with officers' collar piping and shoulder straps but other ranks' belt buckle) and two NCOs in the center of this photograph all wear SS uniform with plain black right hand collar patches. Kociņš wears a German Police officer's uniform.

The first Latvian to hear the welcome news that the Germans had agreed to the formation of a Latvian Legion was Legions-Hauptsturmführer Žanis Jansons, temporarily in command of the 21st Schuma battalion serving under the 2nd SS Brigade, for he was told by SS-Sturmbannführer Josef Fitzthum, commander of the Dutch Volunteer Legion.[16] Jansons enthusiastically started to sign orders in the name of 'Volunteer SS Legion "Latvia" ' (Freiwilligen SS

was attached to the RSHA (Reich Security Head Office). Von Scholz, a Brigadeführer since 21.12.42, had previously commanded SS-Regiment "Nordland."

[16]Silgailis. Jansons was commander by proxy of the 21st Schuma battalion and later commanded its 4th (MG & PAK) company (Kažociņš, 19.2.81). SS-Sturmbannführer (later SS-Standartenführer) Josef Fitzthum commanded Freiwilligen-Legion Niederlande from July 1942 until 20.5.43 and was acting commander of the Flemish volunteer legion (Freiwilligen-Legion Flandern) from 20.6.42 until 15.11.42 (Buss/Mollo, op.cit., pg. 137). In fact, Fitzthum had held the higher political SS rank of SS-Oberführer since 12.3.38. He became SS-Brigadeführer und Generalmajor der Waffen-SS on 30.10.43 and was SS and Police Leader in Albania at the end of January 1944. Promoted to SS-Gruppenführer und Generalleutnant der Waffen-SS on 1.8.44, he was Higher SS and Police Leader for Albania by November 1944. See Volume 6.

Souvenir diploma given to the men of 2. SS-Infanterie-Brigade (mot.) who fought on the Leningrad front during the winter of 1942/1943. Signed by the brigade commander, SS-Brigadeführer und Generalmajor der Waffen-SS Gottfried Klingemann, it was given to the men of the 19th and 21st Latvian Schuma battalions as well as to the Germans, Dutchmen, Flemings and Norwegians serving with the Brigade.

Legion "Lettland"), but this was considered premature and in any case an inaccurate designation, and he was forbidden from doing so a few days later.[17]

Back in Latvia the first reports from the Schuma battalions at the front that they had been renamed "Latvian Legion" were met with some scepticism but on 27 January 1943 the SS and Police Leader in Latvia, SS-Brigadeführer und Generalmajor der Waffen-SS und Polizei Walther Schröder, informed the Latvian Self Administration that Hitler had given his permission for the forming of a Latvian Legion.[18]

So it was that in early 1943 the "Latvian Legion" was created, a generic term coined by Himmler to describe all Latvian elements serving with the German armed forces.[19] The plan was to bring all the Schuma battalions back from the

[17]*Silgailis.*

[18]*In fact, Hitler did not sign the order until 10.2.43 - see footnote 14 above. All did not go as smoothly over the announcement as Schröder may have anticipated. First of all, he invited a group of Latvian leaders of his own choosing to his office at Kalpaka bulvaris 1 in Rīga on the morning of 26.1.43. Since this group did not technically represent the Self Administration, a second meeting had to be called that afternoon, and their initial reaction was to refuse to accept the idea of a Latvian Legion - on the grounds that such had not been a request of the Self Administration, and that it was physically impossible to recruit volunteers at the time. They later agreed, not only because of Latvia's need for a military force should the Wehrmacht be driven out of their country and so leave it defenseless, but also to prevent Germany's illegal conscription of Latvians born between 1919 and 1924.*

[19]*Usually reference is limited to Latvians in the Waffen-SS and police, but the same equally applied to those serving in the German Army, Luftwaffe, etc. To be*

front to Latvia and there build them into a division, but German requirements at the front were such that these men could not be spared and so two separate formations had to be built, a division formed at home (the 15th) and a brigade (later to be upgraded to become the 19th SS Division) raised on the battlefield.

The 19th and 21st Schuma battalions, those serving with the 2nd SS Brigade, were withdrawn from the fighting at the end of January 1943 and assembled for training at Krasnoje Selo. On 8 February 1943 they were joined there by the 16th Schuma battalion, the first to have been sent to the front, which was back after a month and a half's rest in Latvia. These three battalions were renamed at Krasnoje Selo on 8 February 1943:

21. Schuma-Btl. - I./Lettische Legion
19. Schuma-Btl. - II./Lettische Legion
16. Schuma-Btl. - III./Lettische Legion

Men of an unidentified Latvian Schutzmannschafts battalion at Rīga-Bolderāja in April 1943. They were already part of the Latvian Legion and from 24 May 1943 would be renamed "Latvian Police." The NCOs have German Police uniforms whereas the privates (Kareivis) wear Latvian Army uniforms with the national shield without name (type "A") on their upper left sleeves.

---

precise, there was, in fact, no Latvian police, and what the Germans called "Polizei" was formally called Schutzmannschaft, which consisted of Einzeldienst, geschlossene Einheiten, Feuerschutzmannschaft and Hilfsschutzmannschaft (Latviešu kaŗavīrs otra pasaules kaŗa laikā, Vol. 2, pg. 366).

Knight's Cross holder, SS-Brigadeführer und Generalmajor der Waffen-SS Fritz von Scholz presents a private (Kareivis) of a Latvian Schuma battalion serving with the 2. SS-Inf.Brig. (mot.) with the Iron Cross IInd Class. The two Legions-Untersturmführer in the background are wearing SS insignia, but the private at right still wears the uniform of the former Latvian Army with national shield (without name and therefore type "A" but without outer piping) on the upper left sleeve. He also wears a German 1st World War steel helmet, whereas his officers appear to have the more modern M1935. Von Scholz later gave up command of the Brigade and was replaced by Hinrich Schuldt.

Just as all did not go entirely smoothly over recruiting and raising the 15th SS Division in Latvia,[20] so there arose difficulties between Germans and Latvians over the new brigade. One particular incident is worth recording as an example of lack of communication between Germans and Latvians which only served to widen this gap. The SS-FHA in Berlin had agreed not to commit Latvians to combat until they had completed a minimum of six weeks' training in Latvia, but on 29 March 1943 sent 1,000 raw recruits as replacements for the 2nd SS Brigade at the front. SS-Brigadeführer Peter Hansen[21] sent a cable to the SS-FHA (which Artūrs Silgailis also signed) in which he stressed the harm such action could do, for it clearly demonstrated how little the Germans cared for the fate of the Latvian legionnaires and the promises they made to their leaders. The whole affair probably resulted from a bureaucratic error in Berlin, for no merit can be found in the decision. It was politically disastrous and could only have harmed future recruitment for the Legion. From a

---

[20]*See Vol. 4, pg. 71, et seq. and Vol. 5, pp 14-17.*

[21]*See Vol. 4, pg. 70 and footnote 33.*

military point of view, the arrival of such untrained replacements can hardly have been of much help to the hard-pressed and depleted Brigade.[22]

Training of the Legion's three new battalions at Krasnoje Selo had only begun when they had to be rushed to the front to make up for serious German losses. They took up positions opposite and to the east of Pulkowo which they held until April 1943. Reassembled at Krasnoje Selo, they were formed into the 1st (Latvian) SS Volunteer Regiment.[23] Soon afterwards the 24th and 26th Schuma battalions also arrived at Krasnoje Selo and were redesignated as the first and second battalions of a new second Latvian infantry regiment.[24] On 12 June 1943 the 18th Schuma battalion arrived to complete the second regiment by becoming its third battalion.[25]

Voldemārs Veiss, commanding a Latvian battalion on the eastern front near Osveya in February 1943, checks for Russian partisans with his binoculars. With his trousers tucked into gaiters, M1935 steel helmet painted white and white fur-lined and collared parka, Veiss wears a pair of the woolen mittens that were hand-knitted by Latvian women in colorful patterns dating back hundreds of years and sent as very welcome gifts to the men at the front.

---

[22]*Brigade commander Fritz von Scholz, in fact, told Bangerskis the untrained replacements had been unwelcome to the brigade when Bangerskis visited him at the front in April 1943.*

[23]*SS-Freiw.Rgt. 1 (lettisch) also, perhaps incorrectly, reported as "1. Lettisches Infanterie-Regiment."*

[24]*SS-Freiw.Rgt. 2 (lettisch) also, perhaps incorrectly, reported as "2. Lettisches Infanterie-Regiment."*

[25]*According to Silgailis (letter of 31.3.81) the renumbering of the 24th, 18th and 26th Schuma battalions as Ist, IInd and IIIrd battalions respectively is a misprint in Klietmann, op.cit., pg. 376. If Klietmann had been correct, there would have been no logical reason for not numbering the battalions chronologically as they arrived.*

Once the two Latvian infantry regiments had been raised from the six former Schuma battalions, it was time to reflect the change in nationality of the Brigade and - the Dutch, Flemish and Norwegian legions having departed - the 2nd (motorized) SS Infantry Brigade was renamed the Latvian SS Volunteer Brigade on 18 May 1943.[26] Controlled by an HQ (Stab der Brigade), the two infantry regiments were redesignated "SS-Freiw.Gren.Rgt. 1 & 2 (Lettische Brigade)." The Brigade's infantry was thus complete, most of its existing German support elements and services would be converted to Latvian during the nine months the Brigade was to be engaged in defending a comparatively quiet section of the front on the west bank of the Volkhov river.

MAY 1943 - JANUARY 1944: ON THE VOLKHOV RIVER: COMPLETION OF THE 2ND LATVIAN SS VOLUNTEER BRIGADE:

Completion of the Latvian Brigade was hampered by the impossibility of withdrawing the Latvians from the front, and so it had to be carried out while the formation continued fighting on the west bank of the Volkhov river. Its two triangular infantry regiments were completed by mid-June 1943, but at that time brigade support elements and services were mixed, some of them left over from the original Brigade and still identified by the number "52," others being new Latvian elements. The following order-of-battle for the summer of 1943 is drawn from various sources and shows this transitional stage:

Stab der Brigade	HQ
SS-Freiw.Gren.Rgt. 1 (Lett. Brigade)[27]	volunteer infantry regiment
Stab und Stabskompanie	HQ & HQ company
I. Btl.	Ist battalion
II. Btl.	IInd battalion
III. Btl.	IIIrd battalion
13. Infanterie-Geschütz-Kp	13th infantry gun company
14. Panzerjäger-Kp.	14th antitank company
SS-Freiw.Gren.Rgt. 2 (Lett.Brigade)[27]	volunteer infantry regiment
Stab und Stabskompanie	HQ & HQ company
I. Btl.	Ist battalion
II. Btl.	IInd battalion
III. Btl.	IIIrd battalion
13. Infanterie-Geschütz-Kp.	13th infantry gun company
14. Panzerjäger-Kp.	14th antitank company
SS-Panzerjäger-Abteilung 52[28]	antitank battalion

[26]*See footnote 1 on pg 56 of this volume for the SS-FHA order. The Brigade was numbered "2nd" on 22.10.43 (see footnote 2 on pg 56). The Dutch Legion was pulled from the front on 27.4.43, sent home and disbanded on 20.5.43. In May 1943 the Flemish Legion was sent to Poland and the Norwegian Legion, reported to have been virtually wiped out, was under the Ist Army Corps of the 18th Army (Buss/Mollo, op.cit.).*

[27]*Reports and documents vary as to the numbering of the two infantry regiments in the summer of 1943, and a precise situation is impossible due to contemporary confusion and changes. The form taken is the official one as given by the SS-FHA in their order of 22.10.43 (see footnote 2 on pg. 56: Anlage 4: IV. Regimenter).*

[28]*According to the SS-FHA order of 7.1.44 (see footnote 3 on pg. 56) the antitank battalion and light artillery detachment were still numbered "52" in June 1943 (PHB).*

le. Art.Abt. 52[28]/I. Lettische SS-Art.Abt.	(light) artillery detachment
SS-Flak-Abt. 52	AA detachment
SS-Fla.-Kompanie[29]	AA company
1. Lettische Pionier-Kompanie	engineer company
(gem.) SS-Nachrichten-Kompanie 52	(mixed) signals company
SS-Feldersatz-Btl. (Lett. SS-Freiw.-Brig.)	field replacement battalion

Note:
For a time the Latvian Brigade's regiments had a 13th infantry gun and a 15th engineer company each and had no 14th antitank company.

By the end of June 1943, the Latvian Brigade also had the following subunits:

Kradmeldezug	motorcycle dispatch rider platoon
Kriegsberichter-Trupp (mot.)	(motorized) war correspondent section
San.Komp. (mot.)	(motorized) medical company
Kr.Kw.Zug	MT ambulance section
Feldgendarmerie-Trupp	military police section
Feldpostamt	field post office
Werkstatt-Kp.	workshop company
Instandsetzungs-Kp.	repair company
2 Kraftfahrkolonne	2 MT columns
2 Fahrkolonne	2 horsed columns
Vet.Kp.	veterinary company

Legions-Obersturmbannführer Voldemārs Veiss presents the Iron Cross Ist Class to a member of the Latvian Volunteer SS Brigade, summer 1943, Volkhov front. The officer with moustache and glasses holding other decorations is Legions-Hauptsturmführer Nikolajs Galdiņš, Veiss' adjutant while he commanded the 1st Latvian Infantry Regiment of the Brigade and later commander of the 19th SS Division's 42nd Infantry Regiment.

[29]*Provided by the 1. SS-Inf.Brig. (mot.) - the German Red Cross erroneously reported this as "SS-Flak-Kp. 52."*

To help build up the brigade, the artillery, antiaircraft and veterinary elements were supplied from Latvia by the formation staff of the 15th SS Division.[30] The original Brigade's signals battalion and field police section were retained and thus remained exclusively German throughout the war.

The need for a higher formation to provide the necessary strategic command for the two Latvian Waffen-SS formations had been realized for some time and Gottlob Berger, Chief of the SS-HA, had mentioned the possibility of forming a Latvian army corps as early at 17 April 1943.[31] The SS-FHA established the HQ of the VIth SS Volunteer Corps on 8 October 1943,[32] and it was formed at Grafenwöhr under SS-Gruppenführer und Generalleutnant der Polizei Karl von Pfeffer-Wildenbruch. Transferred to Pskov north of Ostrov, it was moved again to take over command of the two Latvian formations soon after they took up positions on the Velikaya river in late February 1944. Corps troops were raised which at first were numbered "106," but were renumbered by the addition of a base of 400 to become "506."[33]

On 5 September 1943 von Scholz gave up his command of the Brigade to lead the 11th SS Division "Nordland," and he was succeeded by SS-Standartenführer Hinrich Schuldt.[34]

In the late summer of 1943 a labor unit of Belorussian nationals under German command was attached to the Latvian Brigade for fortification work.[35]

Although in practice the change may have been made earlier, it was only by order of the SS-FHA on 22 October 1943 that the Brigade's two infantry regiments were numbered in the main sequence of Waffen-SS infantry regiments

---

[30]That the Brigade should receive men from the Aufstellungsstab für die 15. (lett.) SS-Freiw.Div. was laid down by SS-FHA, Kdo.Amt der Waffen-SS, Org.Tgb.Nr. 660/43, v. 18.5.43 (T-175/111/2635286-90).

[31]RF-SS, C.d. SS-HA, Be/Rü Az 2, v. 17.4.43 (No. 3379).

[32]SS-FHA, Amt II Org.Abt. Ia/II, Tgb.Nr. 1471/43 g.Kdos., v. 8.10.43, Aufstellung des Gen.Kdo. VI. SS-Freiw.-Korps (T-175/111/2635214-5).

[33]See Vol. 2, pg. 40.

[34]Klietmann provides conflicting dates for this changeover. When writing about "Nordland" and 2. SS-Inf.Brig. (mot.) (op.cit., pp. 179 & 317), he says von Scholz took over "Nordland" on 1.5.1943, the very same day he gave up command of the Brigade. But when dealing with the Latvian Brigade (pg. 376), he says von Scholz commanded it until 5.9.1943! The later date is supported by Silgailis (letter of 31.3.81) and Stöber, who adds that von Scholz had commanded the Brigade from 1.7.43.

Schuldt, who had begun his career as an SS officer with the Leibstandarte in 1933, went on to serve in SS-Regiment "Germania" and by May 1940 was commanding the Ist battalion of the 4. SS-Totenkopf-Standarte. This was one of the two infantry regiments of the 2. SS-Inf.Brig. and having been named "Langemarck" on 20.4.42, Schuldt wore the "Langemarck" cuffband - he was still wearing it in May 1943 when as an SS-Standartenführer he assumed command of the Latvian SS Brigade. Schuldt was awarded the Knight's Cross on 5.4.1942 as an SS-Obersturmbannführer and commander of SS-Totenkopf-Infanterie-Regiment 4. He received the Oakleaves on 2.4.1943 as an SS-Standartenführer and commander of Kampfgruppe "Schuldt" (not to be confused with the battle group of the same name he later led in January/February 1944).

[35]Silgailis (letter of 28.12.78) does not believe this to have been the labor company ("Arbeitskompanie") reported to have been formed by the Brigade in early 1944.

A sniper of the Latvian SS Brigade adjusts his telescopic sight while an NCO wearing SS runes on the collar looks on, Volkhov front, September 1943. (Captioned "Latvian Volunteers on the Eastern Front," this photograph was taken by SS-PK Hoffmann and released by the Atlantic press agency of Berlin on 10 September 1943.)

from "SS-Freiw.Gren.Rgt. 1 & 2 (Lett.Brigade)" to "SS-Freiw.Gren.Rgt. 39 & 40."[36] The formation of additional infantry regiments in the senior formations soon necessitated a further change ordered on 12 November 1943[37] which renumbered the Latvian Brigade's infantry regiments to "SS-Freiw.Gren.Rgt. 42 & 43."[38]

As 1943 drew to its close, the Latvian SS Brigade was still on the Volkhov river, under the XXXVIIIth Army (later Armored) Corps of Army Group "North." Although not made official until 7 January 1944, it became known in late 1943 that the Germans intended to up-grade the Brigade to divisional status. Hauptmann der Schutzpolizei Burkhardt was told of this change and how he was to raise a third infantry regiment[39] even before he was put in charge of the "formation staff of the 2nd Latvian SS Volunteer Brigade" on 1 December 1943.[40] The plan was to build the third regiment from the third battalions of the formation's existing two regiments, and as these battalions in turn had to be replaced, two new battalions were formed behind the front lines from recruits trained at Gatchina, Luga,[41] Batetskaya and Olchovna.

The Brigade was still part of the XXXVIIIth Army Corps on 7 January 1944 when the SS-FHA ordered its conversion and reforming to the "19th Latvian SS Volunteer Division" to begin at once and that the commander of the Brigade, SS-Oberführer Hinrich Schuldt, should take over temporary command of the new Division.[42] The Brigade's formation staff in Rīga issued an order of its own a week later, referring to that of the SS-FHA and instructing 2,000 new recruits to be added to the Brigade to bring it up to divisional status.[43] Building the new Division would have been hampered by conditions at the front just as had happened the previous summer with the Brigade, but the Latvians' days of relative peace on the Volkhov were numbered. In mid-

---

[36]*See footnote 2 on pg. 56: Anlage 4: IV. Regimenter.*

[37]*SS-FHA, Amt II Org.Abt. Ia/II, Tgb.Nr. II/9542/43 geh., v. 12.11.43, Bezeichnung der Feldtruppenteile der Waffen-SS.*

[38]*According to Silgailis, the actual renumbering from 39 and 40 to 42 and 43 took place later in March 1944, when the third regiment (numbered 44) was formed.*

[39]*A Waffen-SS Grenadier-Division was supposed to be tri-regimental, preferably completely triangular. According to Army practice, a third regiment was not absolutely essential, providing the existing two had three battalions each and there was a complete Füsilier-Bataillon (PHB, letter of 14.9.75).*

[40]*Leiter des Aufstellungsstabes der 2. lett. SS-Freiw.Brig. (Kažociņš, letter of 19.2.81).*

[41]*Reports that the Brigade itself was at Luga in December 1943 are incorrect and stem from confusion with the men stationed there at that time who were undergoing training for the new third battalions of the 39th and 40th (later 42nd and 43rd) regiments.*

[42]*See footnote 3 on pg 56. Schuldt, in fact, led the formation until his death on 15.3.44.*

[43]*2. lett. SS-Freiw.Brigade, Aufstellungsstab Riga, Tgb.Nr. 2/44 geh., Riga, den 14.1.44, Auffüllung der 2. lett. SS-Freiw.Brigade zur 19. lett. SS-Freiw.Division.*

January 1944 the Russians launched a new offensive that broke the German encirclement of Leningrad, and the two new battalions forming at Gatchina and Luga had to be transferred back to the safety of Latvia. They were based in Rīga and Vaiņode and on arrival were reinforced with recruits conscripted for border guard duties and enlarged to regimental status as the 1st and 2nd Training Regiments of the 2nd Latvian Brigade.[44]

JANUARY AND FEBRUARY 1944: WITHDRAWAL FROM THE VOLKHOV TO VELIKAYA RIVERS: BATTLE GROUPS "VEISS" AND "SCHULDT"

The Russian offensive along the Volkhov front launched on 14 January 1944 was to force the Latvian Brigade[45] to withdraw from the positions it had held since the previous summer and retreat throughout what remained of January and most of February in the westerly direction Luga/Pskov. In such circumstances and with the additional infantry required to make up a division back in Latvia, it was impossible to proceed with the conversion to divisional status at this time.

To understand developments and apparent contradictions in this period, it is necessary to distinguish between theory to be found in orders and regulations (such as were produced by the SS-FHA in Berlin) and the reality at the front. For example, on paper the formation was already a division with three infantry regiments and one artillery regiment when an SS-FHA order changing the titles of foreign regiments in the Waffen-SS was issued on 22 January 1944 - in fact at that time the formation was still only a brigade, badly under strength as a result of losses and being driven back from the Volkhov by the Red Army. This order[46] laid down that all foreign regiments should have their nationality and their progressive numerations within that nationality added parenthetically to their titles. The theoretical "19th Latvian SS Volunteer Division" thus contained the following four regiments:

SS-Freiw.Gren.Rgt. 42 (lettisch Nr. 4)
SS-Freiw.Gren.Rgt. 43 (lettisch Nr. 5)
SS-Freiw.Gren.Rgt. 44 (lettisch Nr. 6)
SS-Freiw.Art.Rgt. 19 (lettisch Art.Rgt. Nr. 2)

Leaving theory and returning to the front, we find the Latvian Brigade under the Xth Army of Group "Friessner," Army Group "North" in February 1944, and towards the end of the month it was near Pskov. Moving south it took up new battle positions on 27 February some 30 kms. southeast of Ostrov and soon afterwards linked up for the first time with its sister formation, the 15th

---

[44] *Ausb.Rgt. der 2. Lett.Brig. Nr. 1 and 2.*

[45] *Since it was a division in name only, the formation will be referred to as a brigade until the completion of its three infantry regiments in March 1944.*

[46] *SS-FHA, Amt II Org.Abt. Ia/II, Tgb.Nr. 166/44 g.Kdos., v. 22.1.44, Bezeichnung der SS-Freiw.Rgter.*

SS Division, at the so-called "Panther Position" (Panther-Stellung) on the banks of the Velikaya river, north of Novi-Putj.

The Latvian SS Brigade played an important rôle in the tough defensive fighting during its withdrawal from the Volkhov sector in January and February 1944 and sustained severe losses. During the retreat from Leningrad, the German High Command made numerous changes in the subordination of units and various "battle groups" (Kampfgruppen) were formed for specific purposes and to achieve specific goals.[47] When the Red Army's offensive on the Volkhov front launched on 14 January 1944 in the direction of Novgorod/Luga broke through the German front lines 5 kms. south of the Latvian Brigade, Kampfgruppe "Veiss" was formed to protect the formation's right flank. Made up of the first battalion of the 42nd and third battalion of the 43rd infantry regiments plus some German elements, this battle group became involved in the heavy fighting with the advancing Russians at Nekochovo.[48] In the heroic and bitter fighting, Kampfgruppe "Veiss" not only succeeded in fulfilling its allotted task, but also managed to help two German regiments break out from a Russian encirclement. For this action Waffen-Standartenführer Voldemārs Veiss was awarded the Knight's Cross of the Iron Cross.[49] Kampfgruppe "Veiss" was disbanded on 5 February 1944, but Veiss was to lead another battle group bearing his name that was formed soon after on 11 February and is believed to have existed until the retreat from the Volkhov was completed later that month.

Legions-Standartenführer Voldemārs Veiss

[47]Although one would expect those battle groups led by Waffen-SS officers and/or made up principally of Waffen-SS elements to have been named "SS-Kampfgruppen," this does not appear to have been the case with the Latvians (Silgailis, letter of 28.12.78).

[48]No confirmation can be found for the statement that men of the Army's 215th Infantry Regiment fought in either battle groups "Veiss" or "Schuldt" (Silgailis, letter of 28.12.78).

[49]Veiss was awarded the Knight's Cross on 9.2.44 following recommendation by the XXXVIIIth Army Corps, Army Group "North" (Schneider, op.cit., pg. 398).

Voldemārs Veiss, at left as a lieutenant colonel and battalion commander in the 3rd Jelgavas Infantry Regiment of independent Latvia's Army in 1939 (that year he was also on the General Staff and in February 1939 was appointed Latvian Military Attaché in Tallinn, Estonia) and at right as a Legions-Obersturmbannführer and commander of the 1st regiment of the Latvian Volunteer SS Brigade on the Volkhov front on 7 September 1943, after being decorated with the Iron Cross Ist Class (Veiss went on to win the Knight's Cross on 9 February 1944, following recommendation by the XXXVIIIth Army Corps HQ, Army Group "North").

In both photographs Veiss wears on his left breast pocket the Fire Cross badge of the Students' Company (Studentu rota - also referred to as the Separate Students' Company - Atseviška Studentu rota) of Colonel Kalpak's battalion (Kalpaka Bataljons), which he joined at the age of 19 when it was forming in November 1918. The Company was based on young volunteers from a number of Latvian universities and performed special guard duties to the Latvian Provisional Government during the Independence War 1918-1919. After the successful conclusion of the war in 1919, the Company was incorporated into the newly-formed 3rd Infantry Regiment and was thus one of the first-formed units of independent Latvia's Army, of which Veiss held the distinction of being the youngest officer.

The badge of the Students' Company consists of a 45mm-wide Fire Cross made of amber, a yellow translucent fossil resin, attached to a metal backplate and having a silver upright sword superimposed. (From the illustration of this badge appearing in the bottom left quarter of the Kalpaka Battalion's coat of arms, it would appear that Veiss wore his upside-down - at least in the 1943 photograph - for the blade of the sword should have been pointing downwards.) This is probably the rarest of all Latvian badges because the Students' Company only numbered 216, and being cut by a jeweler from a single piece of amber, the badges were expensive and delicate. The example shown by courtesy of Jānis Jēkabsons on the next page (to whom and Indulis Kažociņš thanks are also given for the information contained in this note) is a faithful replica in yellow plastic copied from a damaged original. It is amusing to note that Veiss did nothing to dispel the belief held by some Germans that the 'yellow swastika' badge he wore was a personal and very special award from Hitler himself!

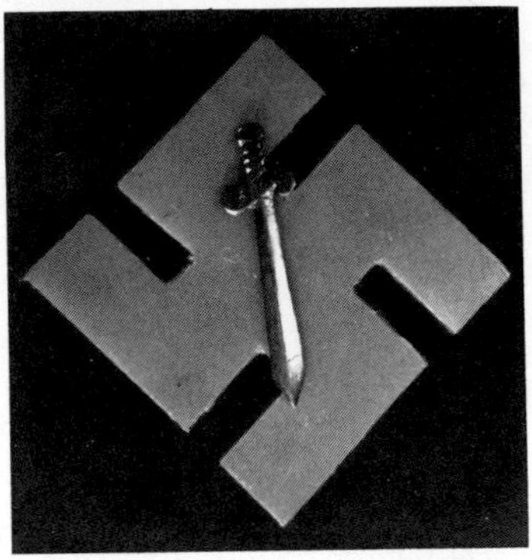

Students' Company Badge

Kalpaka Battalion
coat of arms

On 29 January 1944, Kampfgruppe "Schuldt" was made up of the Latvian Brigade itself, Kampfgruppe "Bock," Kampfgruppe "Aira," Jagdkommando Herrmann, the 405th Infantry Regiment from the 121st Infantry Division and some elements of the 28th Jäger-Division.[50] Led by Brigade commander SS-Standartenführer Hinrich Schuldt, the battle group was subordinated to the 21st Luftwaffe Field Division[51] and was disbanded on 5 February 1944.[52] On 12 February 1944 the Brigade was included in yet another battle group, Kampfgruppe "Speht."[53]

END FEBRUARY - MID-APRIL 1944: ON THE VELIKAYA RIVER: FROM BRIGADE TO DIVISION:

When the two Latvian formations[54] arrived at the "Panther Position" at the end of February 1944, they linked up for the first time and together constituted the VIth (Latvian) SS Volunteer Army Corps, 18th Army, Army Group

---

[50]*See footnote 48 above. During the retreat from the Volkhov, the German element "Jagdkommando Herrmann" was attached to the Latvian Brigade (Silgailis, letter of 28.12.78), and the Brigade is shown to have had a Jagdkommando in a chart of 1.1.1944 (Buss, letter of 11.4.81). KG "AIRA" may have been led by a Latvian and KG "BOCK" came from the 4. SS-Polizei-Division and was led by SS-Standartenführer Friedrich-Wilhelm Bock who commanded the 19th SS Division for a few days between Schuldt and Streckenbach.*

[51]*21. Luftwaffen-Feld-Division, formed December 1942 on the eastern front and served under Army Group "North" at Staraja-Russa from January 1943 until November 1944, when it was transferred to the Army as Felddivision 21(L).*

[52]*This was not the first formation Schuldt was to lead and give his name to. On 21.12.43 the SS-FHA put Hitler's order into effect and raised SS-Brigade Schuldt. On 2.4.43 Schuldt received the Oakleaves to the Knight's Cross of the Iron Cross for his services as commander of this Brigade (which is also reported as "Kampfgruppe Schuldt" - not to be confused with that formed later on 29.1.44).*

[53]*No details have been found for Kampfgruppe "Speht."*

[54]*The 15th Division and the 2nd Brigade, which was in the process of expansion to become the 19th Division.*

"North." To provide strategic command, the Corps HQ, which had been formed the previous October and had been held pending assignment near Pskov north of Ostrov, was transferred to the area held by the Latvian troops on the Velikaya.

The VIth SS Army Corps held positions that stretched 30 kms. along the west bank of the Velikaya south of Ostrov and to the north and south of Novi Putj[55] and it was here that work was continued in the building of the 19th SS Division.

Soon after their arrival at the "Panther Position," the Latvians were involved in continuous fighting with the advancing Russians who, in spite of vastly superior numbers, were unsuccessful in their attempts to cross the river. Particularly fierce fighting broke out on 16 March when the Russians captured the strategically important Hill 93,4 on the boundary between the two Latvian formations. Elements of both, directed by Legions-Oberführer Artūrs Silgailis, were engaged in fierce fighting for three days until the hill was finally retaken.

On 15 March 1944, divisional commander Schuldt was killed near the Velikaya, and his body was later taken to Rīga for burial. He was posthumously promoted from SS-Oberführer to SS-Brigadeführer und Generalmajor der Waffen-SS and awarded the Swords to the Knight's Cross of the Iron Cross.[56] Schuldt, whose name was to be given to the Division's second infantry regiment on 15 January 1945, was succeeded at first by SS-Standartenführer Friedrich-Wilhelm Bock who had been leading a battle group from the 4th SS-Polizei-Division serving with the Latvians as part of Battle Group "Schuldt." Bock is given as commanding his battle group as late as 1 April 1944 and being appointed artillery commander of the IInd SS Armored Corps effectively led the 19th SS Division for only a few days.[57] On April 13 SS-Oberführer Bruno Streckenbach, an experienced security police officer but with questionable military experience, took command of the division he was to lead with distinction until the end of the war.[58]

---

[55]Streckenbach, who took command of the Division on 13.4.44, was wrong when he stated that the 19th Division was at Novorzhev at this time, presumably because he did not join the Division until later (Klietmann, op.cit., pg. 219, gives the Division forming in 'Noworhsew' in the summer of 1944). Streckenbach's own HQ was based at Voronkovo. Other reports that the VIth SS Army Corps was north of Ostrov and around Pskov between 4 and 12 March 1944 are also unfounded - battle reports for this period refer constantly to the same positions being held to the north and south of Novi-Putj (Silgailis, op.cit., pp. 87 and 113 and Latviešu karavīrs otra pasaules kaŗa laikā, Vol. 4, pp. 138-194).

[56]On 25.3.44 - the 56th recipient. Given as 28.3.44 by Schill, op.cit., pg. 30.

[57]Bock was listed as "Arko II. SS-Pz.Korps" in the SS-Dienstaltersliste der Waffen-SS Stand vom. 1. Juli 1944. A month later he was promoted to SS-Oberführer and assumed command of the 9. SS-Pz.Div. "Hohenstaufen," which he led until 10.10.44 when he was reappointed "Arko II. SS-Pz.Korps."

[58]Confusion over Streckenbach's ranks stem from the fact that he rose to such a high level as a police officer in the pre-war SS that he could not be given equivalent

Latvian Waffen-SS troops in a trench on the west bank of the Velikaya river, March/April 1944. Note the camouflage parkas and that the SS runes have been roughly scratched off the transfer shield on the right side of the M1935 steel helmet (in conformity with the order dated 1 November 1943 prohibiting the wearing of the SS runes shield for the duration of the war: Verordnungsblatt der Waffen-SS, 4. Jahrgang, Berlin, 1.11.1943, Nr. 21, Z. 402).

Waffen-Standartenführer Voldemārs Veiss in forage cap and right arm in a sling talks with Dr. med.R. Strautmanis, sometime after receiving his Knight's Cross on 9 February 1944. (Strautmanis was a medical doctor and captain in the 1st Latvian infantry regiment (1. lett. Gren.Rgt.) in April 1943.)

---

military rank when he was transferred to the Waffen-SS in the autumn of 1940. Commissioned as an SS-Untersturmführer on 24.12.32, he rose rapidly within the SD; becoming attached to the SD Main Office, he became Reinhard Heydrich's deputy. During the German invasion of Poland in September 1939, he led Action Group I of the Security Police (Einsatzgruppe der Sicherheitspolizei I) which was attached to the 14th Army and from 1939 until 1941 was commander of the Security Police (Befehlshaber der Sicherheitspolizei - BdS) in Cracow. From 1941 until 1942 he headed the Personnel Office of what had by then become the Reich Security Main Office (Chef Amt I, RSHA) and shortly before, on 9.11.41, had been promoted to SS-Gruppenführer und Generalleutnant der Polizei. The 15.5.43 Dienstaltersliste der SS confirms this rank and the fact that Streckenbach was still attached to the RSHA, but adds that he was at the time serving in the Waffen-SS (z.Zt. W.SS) and it would appear that when he was attached to the Waffen-SS he had to accept the lower rank of SS-Oberführer. This was his rank in April 1944 when he assumed command of the 19th SS Division and a hand-written entry in SS-Obergruppenführer von Herff's personal copy of SS-Dienstaltersliste der Waffen-SS Stand vom 1. Juli 1944 shows his promotion

Knight's Cross holder Legions-Standartenführer Voldemārs Veiss, "Infanterieführer" (divisional infantry commander and second-in-command) of the 19th Division was mortally wounded in the fighting near the Velikaya river on 7 April 1944 and having died in an SS military hospital in Rīga ten days later was buried after an impressive funeral on 21 April 1944.[59] He was temporarily replaced as "Infanterieführer" from 7 April until 1 May by Legions-Oberführer Artūrs Silgailis (Infanterieführer of the 15th SS Division). Veiss's name was given to the 19th Division's senior infantry regiment, Waffen-Gren.Rgt. der SS 42 (lett. Nr. 1) on 15 January 1945.

21 April 1944: the funeral of Legions-Standartenführer Voldemārs Veiss at the Rīga cathedral. All senior German military and political leaders attended, including General Georg Lindemann, G.O.C. Army Group "North." Shortly before, Veiss, second-in-command (Infanterieführer) of the 19th SS Division and commander of its 43rd infantry regiment, had been badly wounded near the Velikaya River and was sent for treatment to the SS hospital (SS-Lazarett) in Rīga. He died there of his wounds on 17 April and was buried four days later after the impressive funeral.

Continuous fighting on the whole of the VIth Army Corps' front lasted until the middle of April 1944 when the two Latvian divisions, due to sustained losses, were withdrawn to a quieter sector of the eastern front in the Bardovo-Kudever area, some 50 kms. east of Opochka.

It was on the Velikaya in March 1944 that the transformation of the Latvian SS Brigade into the 19th SS Division is believed to have been accomplished. The following summary gives the progress made in building up the principal arms of the service:

---

to SS-Brigadeführer und Generalmajor der Waffen-SS dating from 9.11.44. This usually reliable source does not tally with other data: a) photographs of Streckenbach taken on 20.8.44 (see pp 80/85 of this volume) show him clearly wearing the insignia of an SS-Brigadeführer; b) Streckenbach was awarded the Knight's Cross on 27.8.44 as an SS-Brigadeführer und Generalmajor der Polizei und Waffen-SS (Schneider, op.cit., pg. 379); c) according to Stöber, Streckenbach was already an SS-Brigadeführer in August 1944 during the Vidzeme battles north of Lake Lubāns. By the time he was awarded the Oakleaves on 21.1.45, his military rank matched that which he held in the Police, for he was by then an SS-Gruppenführer und Generalleutnant der Polizei und Waffen-SS and according to Stöber already held this rank during the "Christmas battles" in Courland (21.12.44 - 12.1.45).

[59]According to Silgailis (letter of 31.3.81) Schill, Die Geschichte der lettischen Waffen-SS, pg. 29, is wrong in saying Veiss died holding the rank of Waffen-Oberführer (this confirms Schneider, op.cit., pg. 398, who gives Veiss' last rank as Standartenführer).

INFANTRY:

Three divisional infantry regiments had existed on paper since the end of January 1944[60] but as has been seen, circumstances at the front prevented them from being raised until later. At the beginning of March 1944, the whole of the 1st and the Ist battalion of the 2nd Training Regiment[61] were sent from Latvia to join the formation. The 1st Training Regiment was disbanded and its men used to replenish losses sustained by the Brigade's two infantry regiments during the fighting retreat from the Volkhov to the Velikaya rivers and to bring them up to the required three battalions each. The Ist battalion of the 2nd Training Regiment was used as the Ist battalion of the Division's third infantry regiment and thus became I./Gren.Rgt. 44. Between mid-April and mid-May 1944 the remainder of the 2nd Training Regiment was brought to the front from Latvia and put at the disposal of the 19th SS Division, its IInd battalion (II./Ausb.Rgt. 2) becoming the new Division's field replacement battalion (Feldersatzbataillon 19).

When the two original infantry regiments were brought back up to the required strength of three battalions each and a third raised in March 1944, the three triangular infantry regiments were complete and the Brigade can effectively be considered to have grown into the 19th SS Division.[62] But of course there was still much to be done to make the formation completely battleworthy and other divisional units and services were still in the process of forming or had yet to be raised.

ARTILLERY:

The existing artillery detachment was used as the Ist detachment of a new artillery regiment, while the regiment's IInd detachment was raised on the battlefield during May and June 1944 and was combat ready on 23 June 1944. To complete the artillery regiment, IIIrd and IVth detachments plus sub-units were raised in Latvia in the Vaiņode area, but although ready in July 1944 were not to join the Division until it was near Dobele in Courland in October 1944.[63] Officially, the artillery regiment had been designated "SS-Freiw.Art.Rgt. 19 (lettisch Art.Rgt. Nr. 2)" since the end of January 1944.

---

[60] *SS-FHA, Amt II Org.Abt. Ia/II, Tgb.Nr. 166/44 g.Kdos., v. 22.1.44, Bezeichnung der SS-Freiw.Rgter (T-175/141/2669368-9).*

[61] *Ausb.Rgt. 1 + I./Ausb.Rgt. 2.*

[62] *Confirmed by Silgailis who was "Infanterieführer" of the formation at the time, replacing Waffen-Standartenführer Veiss who was on leave.*

[63] *The two detachments were attached to German units at the end of July 1944 when the Russians succeeded in driving towards the Bay of Rīga and cut off the German forces in Estonia and the north of Latvia. They took part in the German counteroffensive to restore contact with the encircled German forces and then joined the 19th Division in October 1944.*

ANTITANK & ANTIAIRCRAFT:

New divisional antitank and antiaircraft detachments were raised in Latvia and transferred to the Division at the front as soon as ready.[64]

ENGINEERS:

The divisional engineer battalion was raised while the Division was at the front from Latvians assembled at the SS Engineer School at Benešov in the Protectorate of Bohemia and Moravia and after training was brought to join the Division in the second half of August 1944, by then retreating towards the Latvian border.[65]

APRIL - JULY 1944: REST AT BARDOVO-KUDEVER & RETREAT TO LATVIA:

The VIth SS Army Corps, made up of the 15th and 19th Latvian Waffen-SS divisions, took up positions in the Bardovo-Kudever area some 50 kms. east of Opochka in mid-April 1944. The Corps HQ was set up at Duchnovo while the 19th Division's HQ was brought forward from Bogdanovo to Aloļ.

May and June 1944 were spent in relative inactivity under the VIth SS Army Corps, 16th Army, Army Group "North" east of Opochka. In early May, Waffen-Oberführer Artūrs Silgailis was temporary commander of the 19th Division as well as second-in-command (Infanterieführer) of the 15th and divided his time between the two formations, traveling through the spring mud separating their positions in his Volkswagen.

In May 1944 the SS-FHA decided to change the numbering of the two Latvian formations' regiments to reflect their seniority. The 19th Division's original two infantry regiments were renumbered from "4th and 5th Latvian" to "1st and 2nd Latvian," while its new third infantry regiment remained as "6th Latvian" since it was the youngest. Similarly the divisional artillery regiment changed over from being the "2nd" and became the "1st Latvian Artillery Regiment." Such niceties may appear out of place with the regiments about to enter the last desperate phase of their lives and undue importance should not be given to them. Latvians at the front, senior officers among them, were either ignorant of such changes in unit designation ordered by the Waffen-SS bureaucrats in far-off Berlin, or paid little attention to them.

---

[64] *Panzerjägerabteilung and Flak-Abteilung.*

[65] *SS-Pionierschule Beneschau had been established by the SS-FHA on 29.6.42 to form with effect from 1.7.42 on the SS military training area at Benešov (SS-Truppen-Übungsplatz Beneschau), some 35 kms. to the southeast of Prague in the Protectorate of Bohemia and Moravia (SS-FHA, Org.Tgb.Nr. 3793/42, v. 29.6.42 - T-175/109/2633460-1). Sometime later the title of the school was changed to SS-Pionierschule Hradischko - named after the Hradisko mountain a further 80 kms. to the southeast in the direction of Vienna. An SS-Pionier-Lager at Hradischko is mentioned on 5.10.42, but this may, of course, have been in use earlier (SS-FHA, Kdo.Amt der Waffen-SS, Org.Tgb.Nr. 6125/42, v. 5.10.42 - T-175/105/2627630-1).*

Gruppenführer Bangerskis and Obergruppenführer Krüger at the HQ of the VIth Latvian SS Army Corps near Tirza, Vidzeme, 20 August 1944. Krüger had taken over command of the Corps less than a month before (on 25 July 1944).

HQ of the VIth Latvian SS Army Corps near Tirza, Vidzeme, 20 August 1944. From left to right: SS-Standartenführer Sommer (German Corps Chief of Staff) - Waffen-Oberführer Artūrs Silgailis - Gruppenführer Bangerskis - Waffen-Untersturmführer Varlejs (Latvian interpreter attached to the Corps HQ) - SS-Obergruppenführer und General der Waffen-SS Walter Krüger (G.O.C. VIth Latvian SS Army Corps).

Gruppenführer Rudolfs Bangerskis visits the HQ of the 19th SS Division at the Davisi Farm (Davisa majas) near Tirza in Vidzeme on 20 August 1944. From left to right: unidentified officer (whom Silgailis believes to have been German) - Waffen-Standartenführer (later Waffen-Oberführer) Voldemārs Skaitslauks, artillery commander of the VIth Latvian SS Army Corps and commander of the 15th Division's artillery regiment - Bangerskis - SS-Brigadeführer und Generalmajor der Polizei und Waffen-SS Bruno Streckenbach, commander of the 19th SS Division (seven days after this photograph was taken, he was awarded the Knight's Cross of the Iron Cross) - Waffen-Oberführer Artūrs Silgailis.

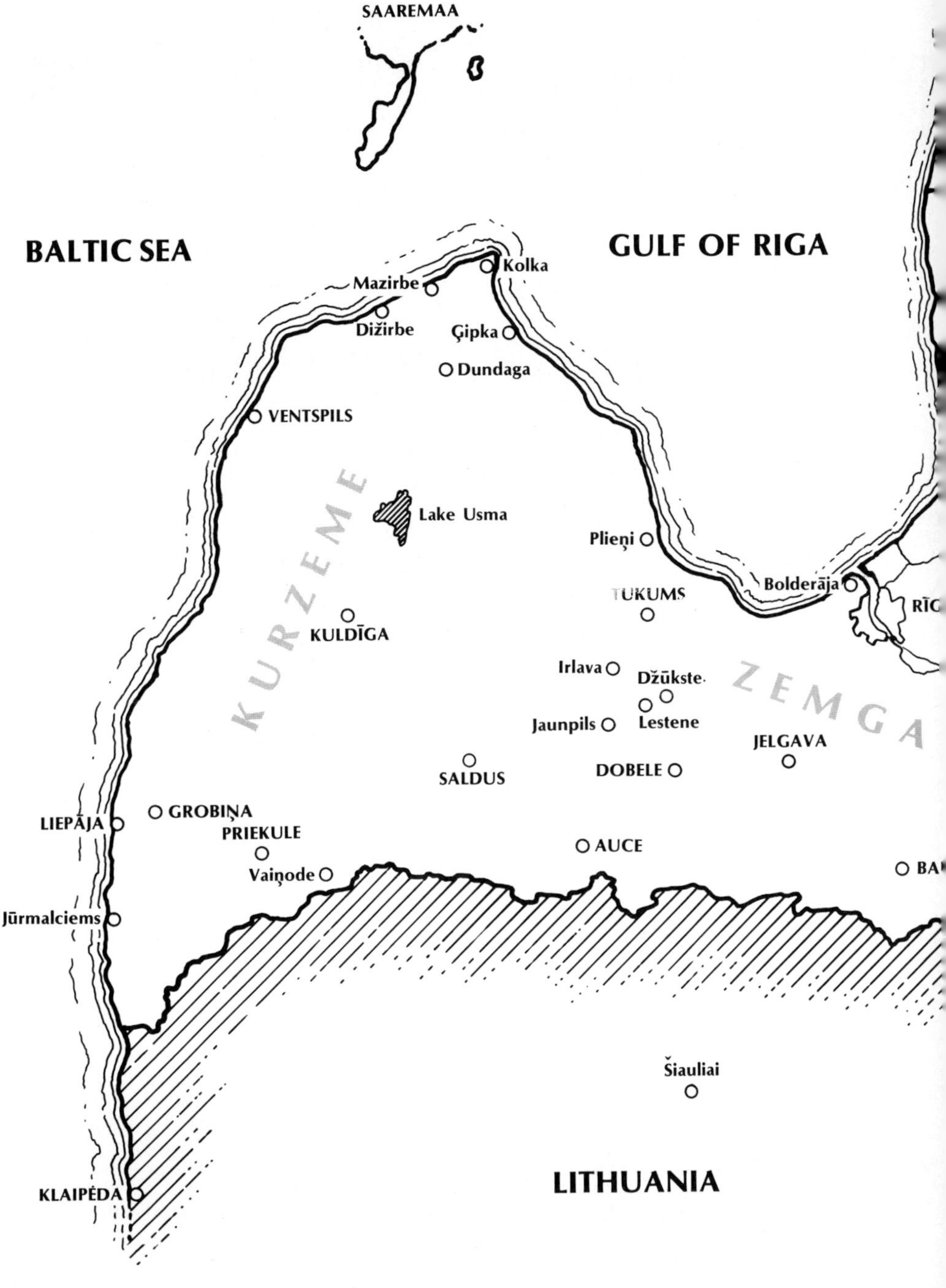
SAAREMAA
BALTIC SEA
GULF OF RIGA
Kolka
Mazirbe
Dižirbe
Çipka
Dundaga
VENTSPILS
KURZEME
Lake Usma
Plieņi
Bolderāja
TUKUMS
KULDĪGA
Irlava
Džūkste
Lestene
Jaunpils
ZEMGA
JELGAVA
SALDUS
DOBELE
LIEPĀJA
GROBIŅA
PRIEKULE
AUCE
Vaiņode
Jūrmalciems
Šiauliai
KLAIPĖDA
LITHUANIA

TARTU
ESTONIA
Lake Pihkva
VÕRU
PSKOV
Velikaya
Gauja R.
VIDZEME
OSTROV
CĒSIS
Jaunpiebalga
Tirza
Rugāji
SOVIET UNION
LDA
Nītaure
More
Mālpils
Zaube
Kārzdaba
Dzelzava
Vecpiebalga
Cesvaine
Lubāna
Tilža
KĀRSAVA
MADONA
LATVIA
Lake Lubāns
Mērdzene
Aiviekste R.
Daugava R.
RĒZEKNE
LATGALE
DAUGAVPILS
POLAND

The Red Army's offensive began on 22 June 1944, the third anniversary of Germany's surprise attack on the Soviet Union in Operation "Barbarossa," and attacks launched on 10 July 1944 were to force the whole of Army Group "North" relentlessly westwards to the Latvian border.

In July 1944 the 19th Division withdrew from its positions east of Opochka. It left behind its anitaircraft detachment which merged with that of the 15th Division to become SS-Flak-Abteilung 506 and thus had to rely on an antiaircraft company of its antitank battalion for protection against Russian air attack.[66]

JULY - OCTOBER 1944: RETREAT THROUGH LATGALE, VIDZEME & ZEMGALE:

The Russian offensive continued to force the already weakened Latvian divisions westwards, and on 16 July 1944 they were driven back over the old Russian border into Latvia. From then until the bitter end, every withdrawal meant more of their homeland falling back under Russian control, and in spite of the impossible odds, the Latvians' desperate determination increased. Pushed over the frontier onto their own territory, the 15th and 19th SS Divisions fell back westwards, and the VIth SS Army Corps was in the Kārsava-Mērdzene area on 17 July.

At this time the 19th Division had been so weakened during its withdrawal to Latvia and was thus so under strength that at an officers' meeting in the Mērdzene parish hall on 18 July the decision was taken to redesignate it as a battle group named after its commanding officer: Kampfgruppe "Streckenbach." What remained of the three infantry regiments were referred to as "battle group battalions."[67]

Kampfgruppe "Streckenbach" was then forced to retreat from Mērdzene to the original Latvian Army defense positions (as planned in 1939) north of Lake Lubāns. Thus the Kampfgruppe fell back through Tilža, Rugāji, Reibāni, Lauberti until it finally managed to check the Russian advance in the Dzelzava-Lubāna area.

During July and the first half of August 1944, the formation was obliged to use its replacement battalion (Waffen-Feldersatz-Bataillon der SS 19) as a combat unit, and during this period it was referred to as "Laumaņa bataljons" (in German, "Bataillon Laumanis") after its commander, Waffen-Sturmbannführer Ernests Laumanis.[68] In early August Streckenbach decided to convert the unit

---

[66]Ordered by V.O.SS 492, v. 2.7.44.

[67]Officially referred to by their former regimental numbers ("Kampfgruppen-Btl. 42, 43 and 44"), the Latvians, in fact, followed their normal practice by naming them after their commanders ("Galdiņš," "Stīpnieks" and "Kociņš" - Kažociņš, letter of 26.1.78 and Silgailis). The three battle group battalions consisted of 18 companies, antitank and grenade-launcher companies included (Silgailis).

[68]F.E.B. 19 had been formed in April/May 1944 from II./Ausb.Rgt. 2.

into an infantry reconnaissance battalion, and on 10 August 1944 it was pulled out of combat and sent to Jaunpiebalga for reforming.[69] A center was set up there and reinforced with volunteers, the battalion became "Waffen-Füsilier-Bataillon der SS 19" in mid-August. Well trained and led, this battalion soon gained a reputation for bravery and success in difficult missions where others had failed, and this was to earn it the nickname of "the Firebrigade." Streckenbach referred to the battalion as "excellent."

The Latvians fought well between 28 July and 4 August in the fierce battles in the Lubāna area, and SS-Obergruppenführer und General der Waffen-SS Walter Krüger, G.O.C. VIth SS Army Corps, thanked them for their bravery in his order of the day of 6 August 1944.[70]

But tough as their resistance was, it was impossible to withstand the Russian onslaught for long, and soon Kampfgruppe "Streckenbach" was forced to fall back over the Aiviekste river, the natural boundary between Latgale and Vidzeme. It managed to hold out for a time in the area between Madona and Cesvaine.[71]

Bangerskis and divisional commander Streckenbach near Tirza in Vidzeme, on 20 August 1944. Note that Bangerskis wears an Army breast eagle on his left upper sleeve.

---

[69] *Latviešu karavīrs otra pasaules kara laikā, Vol. 5, pg. 40.*

[70] *Ibid. Krüger, who had taken over the Corps on 25.7.44, in fact, addressed his order to the "19. Waffen-Gren.Div. d. SS (lett. Nr. 2)," whereas Kampfgruppe "Streckenbach" does not appear to have regained divisional status until later. Three days after Krüger's order (9.8.44), Streckenbach and the 19th SS Division (together with the 83rd Infantry Division) were mentioned in the Wehrmacht bulletin.*

[71] *Various descriptions of the area are to be found. "Modon in Livland" is German for "Madona in (the) Vidzeme (area)." "Livony" is another form for "Livland." The scenically beautiful area around Sigulda on the river Gauja was known as "Vidzeme Switzerland" (Vidzemes Šveice in Latvian and Livländische Schweiz in German) because it resembled Switzerland in miniature (Kažociņš & Silgailis).*

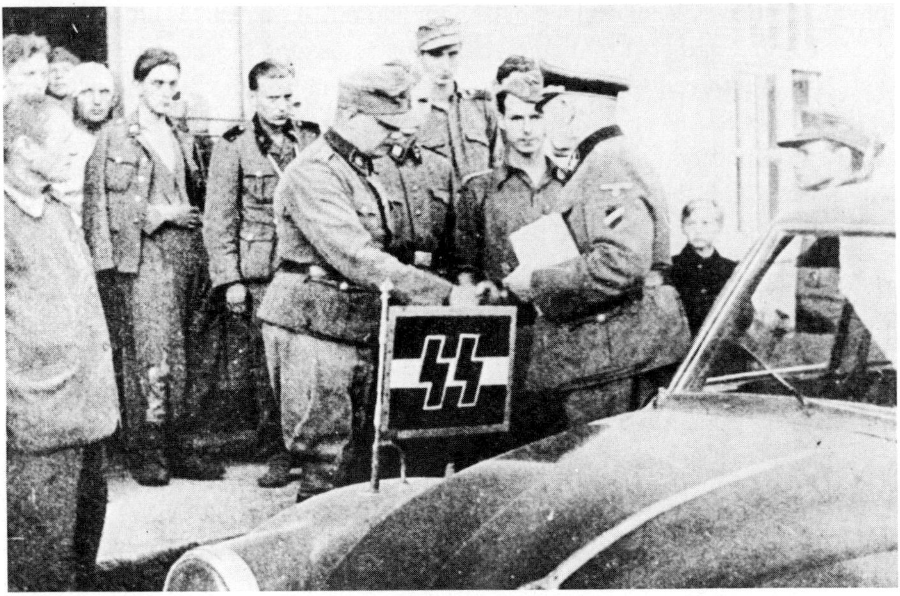

Waffen-Gruppenführer und Generalleutnant der Waffen-SS Rudolfs Bangerskis, Inspector General of the Latvian SS Volunteer Legion, visits the 19th SS Division's main dressing station (Hauptverbandplatz der 19. SS-Div.) in Jaunpiebalga on 20 August 1944. The Latvians referred to this station as "the 19th Division's hospital" although it was not technically a hospital. The officer greeting Bangerskis was the station's senior doctor, believed to have been named Osītis. Note the Inspector General's car flag (Kommandostandarte des Generalinspekteurs der lettischen SS-Freiwilligen-Legion).

Kampfgruppe "Streckenbach" fought a battle on the Cesvaine-Kārzdaba line in Vidzeme that lasted from 10 to 21 August 1944, following which it was reinforced and regained its divisional status.[72]

While the 19th Division was holding the front in Vidzeme to allow the 18th Army to withdraw from Estonia through Rīga to Courland (Kurzeme), further to the south the 15th Division had also been driven westwards after being virtually destroyed. The Germans decided to withdraw the 15th Division's cadres to Konitz[73] in West Prussia for reforming, but those of its men fit and equipped to soldier on in Latvia were used to fill in gaps in the by-now badly depleted 19th Division. This included the 15th SS Division's artillery regiment which having survived almost intact was taken over by the 19th and served with it to the end of the war.[74] These were required to replace the 19th's own

---

[72]As footnote 69, Vol. 5, pp. 24 and 42. According to Major Stīpnieks, Kampfgruppe "Streckenbach" was renamed as the 19th SS Division once the 43rd Infantry Regiment had been reinforced in early September, ibid., pg. 49.

[73]Verordnungsblatt der Waffen-SS, 5. Jahrgang, Berlin, 15.8.1944, Nr. 16, Z. 477 refers to SS-Samellager Konitz.

[74]Contrary to one report that only the IInd and IIIrd artillery detachments of the 15th Division's artillery regiment were taken over by the 19th, Silgailis (letter of 31.3.81) states it was the whole regiment with the exception of its Ist detachment, which was disbanded in November 1944, and its manpower taken to Germany as cadres for the newly raised artillery regiment of the 15th SS Division.

IIIrd and IVth artillery detachments, which between July and October 1944 were supporting German Army forces in an attempt to counter-attack the Russians in Zemgale.[75] In the late autumn of 1944, the Ist detachment of the 15th Division's artillery regiment and the IVth of the 19th's were disbanded and their equipment turned over to the remaining artillery elements, while their men were sent to the 15th Division as a base for a new artillery regiment.

The 19th Division had been driven back northwards towards Tirza and held positions there from 15 to 19 September 1944. On that day the Latvians obeyed

Žanis Butkuss, at left as a Legions-Untersturmführer wearing the Iron Cross Ist Class he received on 8 August 1943, and right as a Waffen-Hauptsturmführer soon after being awarded the Knight's Cross on 21 September 1944 as commander of 10th company, SS-Freiw.-Gren.Rgt. 43 (lett. Nr. 2) (NOTE: Schneider, op. cit., pg. 49, is incorrect in saying Butkuss won the Knight's Cross as a company commander of the 19th Division's field replacement battalion.)

---

[75] *At the end of July 1944, the Russians launched a drive through the Zemgale region of Latvia, towards the Bay of Rīga, and when they took the key town of Šiauliai on the Rīga-Tilzite railway, they effectively cut off the German and Baltic forces in Latvia and Estonia. The Red Army's initial success had been explained by the unexpected collapse of the German Army Group "Center," and the fact that there were hardly any trained and well armed troops in Zemgale. A vast and well prepared Russian assault with full artillery, tank and air support thrust a wedge bordered by the towns of Siauliai-Bauska-Jelgava-Tukums and all that faced them were hurriedly collected and insufficiently armed elements of the 15th SS Division's reserve battalion (Latviešu kaŗavīrs otra pasaules kaŗa laikā, Vol. 5, Pg. 71). The battalion's commander was a*

the order to withdraw and under constant attack from the Red Army retreated past Jaunpiebalga, Vecpiebalga and Skujene towards Nītaure. Arriving on 25 September 1944, the soldiers of the 19th Division immediately manned part of the "Cēsis position" in the area around Malpils, Zaube and Nītaure.[76] Particularly fierce fighting followed near Cēsis around the village of More, and the trenches became so filled with Russian dead that the Latvians simply filled them in with soil as mass graves. The 19th Division fought at More without losing ground from 25 September until 7 October 1944 and was thus fighting in Vidzeme under the VIth SS Army Corps when neighboring Estonia fell to the Russians at the end of September.[77]

In the night of 6/7 October, the Division, always part of the VIth SS Army Corps which was then under the 16th Army, withdrew unmolested from its positions at More as the Russians approached the Latvian captial.[78] It crossed the Daugava River by a military bridge south of Rīga on the 8th and reached the Džūkste area northeast of Dobele on 11 October. Here they took up posi-

---

senior German police officer with no tactical experience, and he sent his men to Šiauliai to face what he assessed as "only bandits." The German Army High Command (OKH) launched a desperate counteroffensive to try and re-establish contact with their troops in the two Baltic states, and a particularly fierce battle was fought at Šiauliai between 17 and 20 August 1944 in which large numbers of German and Russian AFVs were destroyed (600 Russian tanks and 250 German AFVs were destroyed according to the not always reliable Duprat, op.cit., pg. 363). The German forces managed to repulse the Russians and establish a front along the Rīga-Jelgava-Šiauliai line, and contact was re-established with Latvia and Estonia and their inevitable fall to the Red Army was postponed a little longer. Whereas the 19th SS Division as a whole was not involved in the counterattack in Zemgale (it was holding the front further to the east in Vidzeme), its IIIrd and IVth artillery detachments were sent and attached to German units. These two detachments rejoined their division in October 1944, when it took up positions in the Dobele area of Courland.

[76]Cēsis Position" - Cēsis pozicijas (Latvian) and "Wenden Stellung" (German). The area was also called the "Sigulda Position" (Siguldas pozicijas in Latvian and Segewold Stellung in German).

[77]A report that the 19th Division was part of the Lth Army Corps at this time is considered unlikely in the extreme - throughout the Vidzeme and later Kurzeme battles, divisional commander Streckenbach dealt exclusively with Krüger as his corps commander. Streckenbach and his division were mentioned in the Wehrmachtberichte of 30.9.44.

[78]Russian sources give Sigulda and Mālpils (the line held by the Latvians at More) being taken by the Red Army on 7 October (Indulis Kažociņš, letter of 22.5.81). There is a second report that the 19th SS Division left the VIth SS Army Corps for a time (see footnote 77 above). While remaining under the 16th Army in Courland, the 19th is said to have been attached to "Gruppe General von Kleffel" for a time in October 1944 (Tessin, op.cit., Vol. 4, pg. 127 and Vol. 5, pg. 161). Again the evidence would suggest this to be incorrect. KTB/OKW gives Gruppe General von Kleffel as composed of the 81st and 93rd divisions under the 16th Army, Army Group "North" on 16.9.44, and the Group had disappeared by 26.11.44 (it had been renamed "Korpsgruppe Generalleutnant von Mellenthin" by 20.10.44). Yet Haupt in Heeresgruppe Nord 1941-1945, pg. 327, states that the 19th SS Division was the sole component of "K.Gr.Kleffel" on 13.10.44. Philip Kleffel, who commanded the Lth Army Corps from 19.1.42 to 3.3.42, was G.O.C. XVIth Army Corps in October 1944 (note the coincidence: The other doubtful report of the 19th leaving the VIth SS Army Corps (see footnote 77 above) is that in July 1944 the survivors of the Division were part of the Lth Army Corps).

tions in the eastern sector of what became known as the "Courland Fortress" or "Courland pocket."[79] Rīga fell to the Red Army on 13 October 1944 and soon after the front line stabilized in Courland from Jūrmalciems on the Baltic Sea to the south to Plieņi, on the shore of the Gulf of Rīga to the north. The 19th SS was one of the many divisions[80] completely cut off from the rest of the eastern front, and with Hitler refusing to consider evacuation, the scene was set for one of the fiercest and costly battles of the Second World War.[81]

OCTOBER 1944 - APRIL 1945: "THE 6 GREAT BATTLES OF KURZEME": [82]

The 19th SS Division fought what remained of the war in the Courland region of Latvia (Kurzeme), resisting Russian assaults in the area roughly contained by the triangle having the towns of Tukums, Dobele and Saldus at its corners. During these months of bitter fighting, the Russians launched various assaults at different times and in different areas, but generally the period until early April 1945 can be divided into six battles, which Latvians remember as the "6 great battles of Kurzeme." A brief summary of each is given below, with comments on other aspects of divisional history that occurred in the respective periods.

1st Battle: 16 - 20 October 1944:

The 19th Division, exhausted from the bitter fighting in Vidzeme and Zemgale, had only just time to take up new defense positions between Dobele and Džūkste when the Russians launched their first attack on 16 October 1944. The Division was the focal point of the attack and although low in spirit (veterans stress morale was high!) was able to withstand the onslaught and win the first Courland battle. When it was over, the 19th SS Division and the 290th and

---

[79]*Courland is the English form of the original Latvian "Kurzeme" - it is "Kurland" in German, thus "Kurland Kessel" (Courland pocket). Courland had been a battlefield before - it was captured by the German Teutonic Knights at the beginning of the 13th century.*

[80]*After the 1st battle (21-22 October 1944) there were 34 divisions in Courland, three of which were Waffen-SS: the 19th under the VIth SS Army Corps in the Džūkste/Dobele area and the 11th "Nordland" and 23rd "Nederland" under the IIIrd (Germanic) SS Armored Corps far to the west around Priekule. Army Group "North" was composed of 399,500 men in January 1945, 12,000 of whom are said to have been SS and Police. During the Courland battles (to which the Russians committed 120 divisions according to Chabanier) a number of German formations were pulled out and shipped to Germany, and this fact coupled with the losses suffered during the fighting explains why a report drawn up after the last battle on 1.4.45 by the HQ of Army Group "Courland" shows only 19 divisions, some of which were reduced to mere battalion and even company strength (see footnote 128 on page 101 of this book).*

[81]*Heeresgruppenkommando "Nord" ordered that Courland should be held on 21.10.44 and the OKH repeated these instructions the following day. Hitler repeated the order again sometime in December 1944 (Haupt., Heeresgruppe Nord 1941-1945). Silgailis (letter of 31.3.81) says Hitler's order to defend Courland was made verbally to the assembled unit commanders of the 19th SS Division by G.O.C. Army Group "North," Generaloberst Ferdinand Schörner at the beginning of November 1944.*

[82]*See also Haupt, Heeresgruppe Nord 1941-1945, pp. 292 et seq.*

389th German infantry divisions made up the VIth (Latvian) Non-Germanic SS Army Corps.[83]

The Latvian soldiers had been low in spirits before this first battle, but in the respite that followed the situation deteriorated and the normally low level of desertions from the Division began to rise steeply. Various reasons have been given for this phenomenon. The Latvians had witnessed a succession of German defeats during the latter part of 1944, and with the greater part of the Baltic area retaken by the Red Army, regarded the war as lost and simply did not wish to continue sacrificing their lives for a lost cause. Others hoped for better treatment from the Russians were they to desert what was, after all, a Waffen-SS formation, rather than be taken prisoner at its now inevitable surrender (there was virtually no hope of surrendering to the Western Allies as the majority of the 15th Division was able to do, although some did try and a few succeeded). With most of the Latvian population trying to excape the advancing Russians, many Latvian soldiers did not know the whereabouts of their families and relatives and left their units in search of them among the refugees who had flocked to the one remaining part of Latvia still unoccupied, Courland. Other soldiers, mainly those with families in Russian occupied Latvia, were afraid of being parted from them forever by being transferred to Germany as the 15th Division had been, and many of these left their posts to join the "Organization of General Kurelis."[84]

The fear of being forced to leave Latvia and their families to the mercy of the Russians was probably the most common reason behind the large number of desertions that followed the first Courland battle.[85] Rumors spread that the 19th was, in fact, to follow the 15th in being evacuated to Germany, and large numbers decided to quit their posts. For the 500 soldiers who left their front line positions and the 2,000 who melted away from their reserve and training units, this was desertion with something of a difference, as one Latvian authority has described it:[86]

> "The result was numerous cases of men going absent without leave. I cannot describe the phenomenon in any other words. There was no slackness in the units, the men were tidy and dressed as smartly as the circumstances permitted. There was no slackness in fulfilling duty, and greeting and obeying their officers. The men simply disappeared singly or in small groups."

---

[83] *ibid., pg. 293.*

[84] *See pg. 98 of this book..*

[85] *Evacuation of the troops in Courland by sea to Germany remained a possibility until as late as March 1945 and was strongly recommended by the German High Command. Hitler simply refused.*

[86] *Kažociņš, letter of 26.1.78 - with which Silgailis agrees. See Kociņš in Latviešu kaŗavīrs otra pasaules kaŗa laikā, Vol. 5, pg. 124.*

It is easy to understand the motives behind this large number of desertions - these were not mutinies as one leading historian of the Waffen-SS would have us believe, as will be explained at the end of this chapter.

These cases of AWOL stopped when Hitler's order to hold out in Courland and so keep the 19th Division there became known.[87] Not only did a number of those who had gone AWOL return to the Division (some having succeeded in contacting their families), but also a considerable number of new volunteers stepped forward to swell the Division's depleted ranks.[88] Moreover, morale was strengthened within the formation by the many refugees from other regions of Latvia who had retreated with the Division and who now looked upon it as the last barrier against a return to Communist domination.

2nd Battle: 27 October - 7 November 1944:

The second Courland battle lasted from 27 October until 7 November 1944 and was fought around Priekule, southeast of Liepāja on Latvia's west coast and so some distance to the west of the 19th Division's positions. Since this Russian assault did not affect the sector defended by the VIth SS Army Corps, the 19th Division was not involved.

3rd Battle: 23 December 1944 - 9 January 1945:[89]

Known as the "Christmas battle," it followed the Russian assault launched on 23 December[90] in the area between Dobele and Džūkste, northwest of Lestene which breached the front lines between the left flank of the 19th SS Division and the 21st Luftwaffe Field Division. The battle raged until 9 January 1945, and with the Russians' attacks directed against the VIth SS Army Corps, it was the toughest battle the Latvians had to fight in Courland. On 31 December alone, the 19th Division withstood 27 separate major attacks without losing any ground. The Division withstood the onslaught of six well-equipped Russian regiments supported by artillery, rockets, tanks and aircraft, and throughout the whole battle lost very little ground.[91] The 106th Infantry Regiment of the VIth SS Army Corps under Waffen-Sturmbannführer Eduards Stīpnieks was particularly involved and suffered no less than 60 percent in casualties.[92]

---

[87]See footnote 81 above.

[88]See footnote 86 above.

[89]See R. G. Kuhrs: Zur dritten Kurlandschlacht in Der Freiwillige, Heft 1, Januar 1963, pp. 16-23.

[90]Kažociņš and Silgailis agree the 3rd battle began on 23.12.44 - according to Chabanier it was 21.12.44.

[91]Kociņš stresses that the main thrust was aimed at the 44th Waffen-Grenadier-Regiment (Latvian Nr. 6) which was under his command. According to Silgailis, the whole Division was involved and the 106th Regiment suffered the most.

[92]106. Waffen-Gren.Rgt. had been formed from the survivors of the 2nd and 5th Grenzschutz regiments. On 3.1.45, the Regiment took part in the counteroffensive of the VIth SS Army Corps north of Dobele and was disbanded at the end of the month.

That morale and esprit de corps should have survived at all, let along remained high during this desperate fighting, is all the more remarkable when one considers the increasing ferocity of the attacks, and the fact that there were simply no replacements to make up for the terrible losses sustained. The Latvians were mentioned three times in the Wehrmacht bulletins (Wehrmachtberichte) for their actions during the "Christmas battle" - on 27 and 29 December and again on 1 January 1945.[93]

Allied military intelligence[94] was quite wrong in placing the 19th SS Division on the Latvian coast in December 1944, and the theory that the formation "erupted in a series of mutinies" that month is a case of mistaken identity with an entirely different Latvian force and confusion with the desertions of the previous October.[95]

4th Battle: 23 January - 3 February 1945:

On 23 January 1945[96] the Russians launched their main attack in the direction of Liepāja and Saldus. They made simultaneous assaults elsewhere on the front to hold down German troops, and the 19th Division was successful in repulsing several such attacks in the Jaunpils area.

5th Battle: 12 February - 14 March 1945:

This time the Russians concentrated their efforts on smashing the German front line from Priekule to Tukums, close to the Bay of Rīga.[97] They launched five attacks during this battle:

- 12 February: in the direction of Džūkste/Irlava in the area of the VIth SS Army Corps
- 17 February: in the Auce area, to the southwest of the VIth SS Army Corps
- 19 February: in the Tukums area, north of the VIth SS Army Corps
- 20 February: near Priekule; this lasted until 6 March
- 5 March: near Saldus; lasting until 14 March.

As of 1 March 1945, the VIth SS Army Corps was composed of the 19th SS and 24th Infantry Divisions and was part of the 16th Army.[98]

---

93 *The entry for 27.12.44 referred to the 19th Division under Streckenbach's command and 205th Infantry Division led by Generalleutnant von Mellenthin. The entries of 29.12.44 and 1.1.45, although prompted by the 19th Division, referred to "lettische SS-Freiwilligenverbände" and "lettischer SS-Freiwilligen," respectively (Schill, op.cit., pg. 27).*

94 *MID, German OB, March 1945.*

95 *Stein, op.cit., pg. 194. See pg 98 below for full explanation.*

96 *Silgailis, letter of 28.12.78. Chabanier gives 24.1.45.*

97 *German Red Cross records are wrong in not mentioning the 19th SS Division's participation in the 5th Courland battle.*

98 *Schematische Kriegsgliederung 1. März 1945 (Bundesarchiv-Militärarchiv, Koblenz) and Haupt, Heeresgruppe Nord 1941-1945, pg. 328.*

99 *See footnote 152 on pg. 104 of this book. The report that Ancāns won the Knight's Cross as commander of 10th company, SS-Friew.Gren.Rgt. 43 (lett. Nr. 2) is unfounded (Silgailis, letter of 31.3.81).*

Jānis Jēkabsons

Waffen-Obersturmführer Roberts Ancāns, photographed in Courland sometime after being awarded the Knight's Cross of the Iron Cross on 25 January 1945.
Ancāns was appointed commander of the 180 man close-combat school ("Nahkampfschule," renamed simply "Kampfschule") when this was established by the 19th Division's HQ on 4 December 1944.[99] Having won the Knight's Cross in this capacity as a Waffen-Untersturmführer on 25.1.1945, he was later promoted to Waffen-Obersturmführer and finally to Waffen-Hauptsturmführer and led the school until it was disbanded on 14 March 1945.
Ancāns wears the badge of the platoon leaders course (Vada komandieru kursi) on his right breast pocket contrary to regulations, for it should have been worn on the left side as the right was reserved for badges of military staff colleges and universities. The badge was issued to members of the Schuma battalions who had attended the platoon leaders courses at the Rīga/Bolderāja training unit organized by the "Kommandeur der Ordnungspolizei Lettland" (Commander of the Order Police in Latvia) in 1942 and is the only known Latvian badge to have been issued specifically to Latvians in German service during the Second World War.
The words at the top of the badge translate as "fatherland and freedom" and the index finger of the hand in its design is pointing to a mobile Fire Cross.

6th Battle: 17 March - 4 April 1945:

The Russians began this attack on 17 March 1945[100] near Saldus and later followed it with an assault towards Saldus from Dobele. Again the VIth SS Army Corps with its 19th SS Division was heavily involved.

---

[100] *Silgailis, letter of 28.12.78. Chabanier gives 18.3.45.*

The Russians had to pay dearly for the destruction of the German, Latvian, Dutch and other forces in Courland, and the relatively small territorial gain that went with it.[101] Between October 1944 and May 1945, the Red Army is reported to have lost:[102]

90,000 men killed
300,000 wounded
4,000 taken prisoner
2,651 tanks
1,389 machine guns
1,091 artillery pieces
722 aircraft

During the whole time the 19th SS Divison was fighting in Courland, it was part of the VIth SS Army Corps, with only a short period in late March/early April 1945 when it was with the XXXVIIIth Armored Corps.[103] Its higher formation remained the 16th Army which in turn was a part of Army Group "North," renamed on 25 January 1945 as Army Group "Courland."[104]

While fighting in Courland, it was not always simple to distinguish between Latvian and German troops. They fought together as a whole, and while German armored artillery vehicles would be found supporting the 19th Division as and when necessary, so in turn the 19th sent whole battalions to counter-attack the Russians when they succeeded in piercing the German lines.

Given the late stage of the war, the bitter fighting and the fact that communications between Courland and Germany were cut, it is difficult to provide precise details of the Division's order-of-battle during the Courland battles. Charts from January and February 1945 show that its three infantry regiments were all short of their third battalions, and that there were two medical companies. A new field replacement battalion had been raised to replace that from which the highly successful infantry reconnaissance battalion (ex Laumaņa bataljons) had been formed. Cut off from the Division in Germany, an assault gun (Sturmgeschütz) company was being formed as well as a new heavy IVth artillery detachment for the Division's artillery regiment, but neither of these elements was completed before the war ended and so never reached the formation. The order-of-battle on 1 March 1945 was the following:[105]

---

[101]*See footnote 80 on page 89 above.*

[102]*Haupt: Kurland - Die letzte Front - Schicksal für zwei Armeen, pg. 128. These losses sustained during the relentless Russian attacks that lasted until almost the end of the war make Stein's reference to a "useless German enclave behind the Soviet lines" debatable (op.cit., pg. 178).*

[103]*At 1.4.45 the Division was with XXXVIII. Pz.Korps/16. Armee/H.Gr. Kurland - but on 6.4.45 was back with VI. SS-Armeekorps/16. Armee/H.Gr. Kurland.*

[104]*Haupt: Kurland, pg. 87 and Heeresgruppe Nord 1941-1945, pg. 306.*

[105]*Stellenbesetzungsliste der Waffen-SS, v. 1.3.45.*

19. WAFFEN-GREN.DIV. DER SS (LETT. NR. 2)

Waffen-Gren.Rgt. der SS 42 (lett. Nr. 1) "Valdemar Veiss"[106]
I. Btl.
II. Btl.
Waffen-Gren.Rgt. der SS 43 (lett. Nr. 2) "Hinrich Schuldt"
I. Btl.
II. Btl.
Waffen-Gren.Rgt. der SS 44 (lett. Nr. 6)
I. Btl.
II. Btl.
Waffen-Art.Rgt. der SS 19 (lett. Art.Rgt. Nr. 1)
I. Abt.
II. Abt.
III. Abt.
Waffen-Füsilier-Btl. der SS 19
SS-Waffen-Nachrichten-Abt. 19
SS-Waffen-Panzerjäger-Abt. 19
SS-Waffen-Pionier-Btl. 19
SS-Dina 19
SS-Feldersatzbataillon 19

The original two infantry regiments had been named after Veiss and Schuldt on 15 January 1945.

MAY 1945: THE END:

Events during the last few weeks of the fighting in Courland are confused, and conflicting reports are to be found in German, Latvian and Russian accounts as to precisely when certain towns were taken by the Red Army. After the 6th Courland battle, the Russians diverted their attention to the more momentous attack on Berlin, and the Courland pocket dwindled in importance. Army Group "Courland" nonetheless braced itself for a 7th Courland battle that never came, and during the spring mud period regrouped its forces and with Latvian support deliberately gave up some terrain in order to shorten and so strengthen its front.

According to Kociņš, the 19th Division was ordered to take up positions in the Saldus area during the 6th Courland battle at the end of March 1945, but the poor road conditions slowed down its transfer, and the formation did not reach Saldus until the middle of April.

On 30 April 1945, Hitler committed suicide in the Berlin bunker, and having assumed command of the ruins of the Third Reich, Grossadmiral Karl Dönitz ordered the long-awaited evacuation of the troops caught in the Courland pocket by radio at 1930 hours on 3 May 1945.[107] With virtually no transport available, it was far too late to avoid many falling into the hands of the Russians, but a few managed to escape in a Dunkirk-like evacuation with small

---

[106] *The Regiment's title appears to have been expressed so, not the correct Latvian spelling "Voldemārs Veiss."*

[107] *Haupt, Heeresgruppe Nord 1941-1945, pp. 309/310.*

and varied vessels being overcrowded to sinking point by tired and wounded soldiers. The survivors of the 19th Division were still at Saldus when the armistice was signed at 1400 hours on 8 May 1945, along with survivors of the 205th Infantry Division, they were all that remained of the VIth SS Army Corps. Divisional commander Bruno Streckenbach telephoned his unit commanders with the capitulation order and surrendered with most of his men to the Russians. Defiant even in defeat, the Latvian troops refused to accept that they had capitulated and disobeyed a Russian order to hoist white flags over their trenches. Of those who surrendered, only a few are believed to have survived the years of hunger, disease and forced labor that was to be their lot in Russian captivity close to the Arctic Circle. The first prisoners were released in 1953, but Streckenbach was not allowed to return to Germany until 10 October 1955, having spent nine years in solitary confinement in the Lubjanka prison. He died on 28 October 1977.

A large group that was taken prisoner by the Red Army after Germany's capitulation appears never to have had the opportunity to fight. On 29 March 1945 Himmler ordered that some 2,500[108] men selected from the original five construction regiments of the Field Replacement Depôt of the 15th SS Division should be made available to the 19th as replacements (an earlier plan to use these regiments as the basis for a third Latvian Waffen-SS division had to be abandoned following the Russian offensive of January 1945).[109] After working near Stettin digging trenches, they were grouped into Kampfgruppe "Rusmanis" under Waffen-Obersturmbannführer Nikolajs Rusmanis and shipped on 12 April 1945 from Swinemünde to Courland. When these untrained and unarmed men reached the VIth SS Army Corps, they were held back from the fighting and put into training near Irbe, to the very north of Courland on the Baltic coast.[110] They appear to have still been untrained and without weapons when they fell into Russian captivity.[111]

By no means all of the survivors of the VIth SS Army Corps and the 19th SS Division agreed to surrender to the Red Army. While their comrades were be-

---

[108]*The SS-FHA made 2,500 men available (Silgailis, letter of 28.12.78). Another report states that Himmler made 3,000/4,000 men available (PHB - the Archive of the Latvian Legion has no record of this).*

[109]*Kampfgruppe Rusmanis was made up mainly of men of the Waffen-SS Grenadier-Regiment 2 (unofficially called "Bauregiment") of the Field Replacement Depôt, which in turn had been made up from the former five construction regiments attached to the 15th SS Division (Silgailis, letter of 31.3.81).*

[110]*Latviešu kaŗavīrs otra pasaules kaŗa laikā, Vol. 6, pg. 283 and Silgailis (letter of 31.3.81) say the men were billetted around Irbe. Kažocinš (letter of 19.2.81) says they trained at Dundaga, adding that the whole Dundaga area (probably contained by the square having Dižirbe, Dundaga, Ģipka and Kolka at its corners) was designated a training area (Truppenübungsplatz) and all civilians were forced to leave their homes.*

[111]*One source suggests that Kampfgruppe Rusmanis did receive weapons of a sort and was sent to defend the coastline around Mazirbe-Dižirbe (Kažociņš, letter of 19.2.81).*

ing captured, they disappeared in groups of varying sizes. Some tried to escape to the West through Lithuania, East Prussia and Poland, and one such group, led by former Corps commander SS-Obergruppenführer und General der Waffen-SS Walter Krüger, and with members of his staff and a few soldiers, was captured by the Russians in East Prussia, having just crossed over the border from Lithuania. Krüger shot himself rather than be captured.[112]

Other former members of the Latvian Waffen-SS were among the large number who hid themselves in the dense forests to continue the fight against the Russian invaders as guerrillas. These men fought in separate groups[113] and estimates of their total numbers vary from 5,000 to 8,000[114] and it is probably not an exaggeration that they amounted to a third of all the Latvian soldiers in Courland.[115] These guerrilla groups, one of which was made up of former members of the tough infantry reconnaissance battalion still led by Major Ernests Laumanis,[116] were very active in the summer and autumn of 1945 and caused considerable hardship to the occupying Russians. But as time passed and the Russians adopted counter measures, the numbers and effectiveness of these guerrillas declined, and the last major guerrilla action seems to have taken place in 1948 in the Rēzekne area of Latgale. Combined Latvian-Lithuanian-Estonian guerrilla forces did, however, continue to harass the occupying powers and inflict considerable damage as late as 1952, and active resistance only ended with the suppression of the Hungarian Revolution in 1956.[117]

---

[112]Reports differ as to where and when Krüger committed suicide. "East Prussia" and "near the Lithuanian border" tally (Kažociņš and Silgailis respectively), but according to Stöber, it was in Lithuania. The German Red Cross are certainly premature in dating the capture/suicide at 9.5.45 - Silgailis suggests some ten days after the capitulation which supports both 20.5.45 (Krätschmer, op.cit., pg. 70 and von Seemen, op.cit., pg. 19) and the eye-witness testimony of SS-Sturmbannführer E. Rehmann: 22.5.45 (Stöber via Kažociņš).

[113]Duprat, op.cit., pg. 364, refers to these men as having joined "the Brothers of the Forest" - this should not be mistaken for an organization of that name, "meža brāļi" is a Latvian idiom meaning "people hiding in the forest" (Kažociņš, letter of 26.1.78). There were also "brothers of the forest" in Estonia - see following chapter.

[114]Kažociņš, letter of 19.2.81. According to Silgailis (letter of 31.3.81) there appear to have been around 5,000 guerrillas in the beginning, but with the passage of time, the numbers continually decreased, especially with the coming of winter. He estimates there to have been about 2,000 active guerrillas in the winter of 1945/46.

[115]The total number of Latvian troops in Courland at the time of the German capitulation (the Latvians maintain they never surrendered!) is estimated at between 14,000 and 23,000 (Kociņš in Latviešu karavīrs otra pasaules kara laikā, Vol. 5, pp. 231-232). The lower estimate of 14,000 could refer to just the Latvian Waffen-SS elements, but there were Police battalions. Aizsargi (Latvian National Guard), small remnants of the Kurelis force, construction battalions, individual Latvian policemen, young Luftwaffe auxiliaries, two-Abwehr groups and the pro-Nazi Wildkatze Group (Kažociņš, letter of 19.2.81).

[116]Laumanis was seen in 1948/1949 at the Vorkuta Gulag camp and after serving 25 years in prison died in Liepāja.

[117]Mag. iur. Ādolfs Šilde via Kažociņš, letter of 19.2.81.

EPILOGUE: THE MUTINY MYTH AND THE ORGANIZATION OF GENERAL KURELIS:[118]

In the spring of 1944 the sabotage section of German military intelligence ("OKW Abwehr II") approached General Kurelis over the raising of a camouflage guerrilla organization of Latvian patriots that would continue to wage a guerrilla war behind the Russian lines should the Germans be forced to retreat from the Baltic area. The retired general was really little more than a figurehead, and the organization's real leader was Kurelis' chief of staff, Captain Kristaps Upelnieks.[119] Also retired from the former Latvian army, Upelnieks was an ardent Latvian patriot, a fanatic convinced that with the help of the Western powers and support of Sweden, the organization would be able to restore Latvia's independence.

When the German Army did retreat from Latvia, the bulk of the "General Kurelis Group" (as it had by then become known) did not remain behind the Red Army as had been intended, but rather moved to the wooded area north of Lake Usma in northern Courland. There during October 1944, the Group was swelled by the many deserters who came to it from the Latvian Legion, especially from the 19th SS Division after the first Courland battle.

SS-Obergruppenführer und General der Waffen-SS und der Polizei Friedrich Jeckeln, Higher SS and Police Leader for the "Ostland," had never trusted the Kurelis organization and had tried in vain during 1944 to have it disbanded. These attempts failed since the Organization was a creation of Wehrmacht intelligence and the Abwehr shielded it from Jeckeln's attacks. However, this was to change at the beginning of November 1944 when Hitler decided to transfer from Wehrmacht jurisdiction all Abwehr activities other than in the immediate vicinity of the front. This left the Kurelis Group in Courland without protection and at Jeckeln's mercy, and he immediately ordered it to lay down its arms. Many refused to do so, and Jeckeln was obliged to use force. Six of the leaders of what was later reported as a mutiny, including Captain Upelnieks, were court martialled and executed, and General Kurelis himself was placed at the disposal of General Bangerskis, Inspector General of the Latvian Legion.

This affair within the General Kurelis Group was incorrectly reported on 14 December as a mutiny in a Latvian SS division,[120] and Professor George Stein in his history of the Waffen-SS assumed that it was the 19th SS Division that had been involved.[121] Probably making the double mistake of linking the

---

[118]*Special thanks to Artūrs Silgailis for providing this history of the Organization of General Kurelis (letters of 27.5.77 and 1.12.78).*

[119]*Known as "Krišs" for short, Upelnieks held the Latvian Army rank of "kapteinis."*

[120]*Straube - NO 1717 (via PHB).*

[121]*Stein, op. cit., pg. 194.*

SS-Obergruppenführer und General der Waffen-SS und Polizei Friedrich Jeckeln, wearing the Knight's Cross he was awarded on 27.8.44 as commander of a battle group made up of Latvian and German policemen that managed to halt Russian forces near Lake Peipsi. Jeckeln joined the SS as a Sturmbannführer in March 1930 and following Operation "Barbarossa" was Higher SS and Police Leader (HSSPF) first for South Russia in Kiev (1942) and then for the "Ostland" and North Russia in Rīga (1942/1945). In February/March 1942 he organized an operation known as "Action Marsh Fever" in which 389 partisans were killed, 1,274 persons shot on suspicion and 8,350 Jews liquidated. Jeckeln was G.O.C. Vth SS Volunteer Mountain Corps from March to May 1945 and was hanged by the Russians in Rīga on 3.2.46.

Kurelis episode with the flood of desertions that followed the first Courland battle in October 1944, he unjustly dismissed the heroism and sacrifice of what was undoubtedly one of the best foreign Waffen-SS divisions by saying it "erupted in a series of mutinies in December 1944."[122] The Germans, cut off as they were from what was happening in Courland, did not make the same mistake and praise for the Latvians fighting in the Courland pocket (meaning effectively the 19th SS Division) continued to appear in the Wehrmacht bulletins.[123] That the SS were also pleased with the Division's performance and sacrifice can be seen from a memorandum written on 15 February 1945[124] by SS-Obergruppenführer und General der Waffen-SS Professor Dr. Ernst-Robert Grawitz. In this, the supreme medical officer of the SS and Police[125] laid down that the wounded of the 19th SS Division should be afforded the same treatment as members of the SS in recognition of their formation's heroic performance.[126]

There was absolutely no connection between the Organization of General Kurelis and the Latvian Waffen-SS Legion. As a creation of the Abwehr, the Organization took great pains to avoid all contact with the General Inspection of the Latvian Legion, and one can only assume they were acting under orders. It was only after the execution of Captain Upelnieks and his five fellow officers that rumors about the Organization and what had happened began to spread among the men of the Latvian Legion.[127]

In conclusion, reference should be made to the one recorded instance of the Germans doubting the reliability and battleworthiness of the 19th SS Division. This unflattering assessment was made after the devastating Courland battles on 1 April 1945 when the HQ of Army Group "Courland" drew up a report in which the 19 divisions left in Courland were graded into four groups according to their battleworthiness.[128] The 19th Division failed to rate as "very good" (only the 11th Infantry Division so qualifying), nor was it among the eight infantry and one armored divisions considered "good." Together with five in-

---

[122] *How the single refusal by men of the Kurelis Organization to lay down their arms can have become a "series of mutinies" is not known, unless Professor Stein was further confused by the "disappearance" of "Btl. Rubenis" and the subsequent battle on 18.11.44 (Kažociņš, letter of 19.2.81).*

[123] *See Schill, op.cit., pg. 27 where extracts from the Wehrmachtberichte praising the Latvians from 29.10.44, 27.12.44, 29.12.44 and 1.1.45 are given (for English translations see Siegrunen, Vol. IV, No. 5 (23), January 1981, pg. 16).*

[124] *NO 777.*

[125] *Reichsarzt-SS und Polizei.*

[126] *The significance of Grawitz's memorandum is not entirely clear, since from the very beginning members of the Latvian Legion had enjoyed the same medical treatment as other members of the Waffen-SS and Wehrmacht. Silgailis (letter of 31.3.81) suggests that certain hospitals in Germany may have begun to treat the Latvian sick and wounded differently, so necessitating the memorandum.*

[127] *Recent reports suggest that the Kurelis force was really acting under the orders of the Latvian resistance leadership (Kažociņš, letter of 19.2.81).*

fantry and one armored division, it barely missed the lowest rating of "insufficient" (only the 563rd Infantry Division was so condemned), and so was deemed "sufficient." This low grading did not reflect its military qualities, however, for leadership was described as very good and morale and strength both high, but rather the Germans regarded the Latvians as politically untrustworthy if situated in a quiet area of the front. In fact, this was to a degree true and applied not only to the 19th, but also the 15th Latvian Waffen-SS division. Barely a month before the end of the war in Europe, many Latvians were planning to retreat to the West in an understandable attempt to fall into the hands of the Western Allies rather than to the Russians.

Order of Battle

(COMPOSITE)

Stab der Division/Div.-Kommando (ordered 7.1.1944 by reorganizing Stab 2. lett. SS-Freiw.Brig.[129])

SS-Kradmeldestaffel/Kradmeldezug[130]

SS-Div.-Kartenstelle (mot.)/SS-Kartenstelle 19 (ordered 7.1.1944)

SS-Musikzug

SS-Div.-Begleit-Kompanie[131]

Waffen-Grenadier-Regiment der SS[132] 42 "Valdemar Veiss"[133] (lettisches Nr. 1) (21., 19. & 16. Schuma-Btl. became respectively I., II. & III./Lettische Legion on 8.2.1943 at Krasnoje Selo. February 1943 became SS-Freiw.Rgt. der Lett. SS-Freiw.Legion. April 1943: SS-Freiw.Rgt. 1 (lettisch)[134] and on 18.5.1943 became SS-Freiw.Gren.Rgt. 1 (Lett. Brigade). Completed by June 1943. September 1943 numbered as SS-Freiw.-Gren.Rgt. 39.[135] Renumbered 12.11.1943 to SS-Freiw.Gren-Rgt. 42. 22. 1.1944: SS-Freiw.Gren.Rgt. 42 (lettisches Nr. 4). 16.5.1944: Waffen-Gren.Rgt. der SS 42 (lett. Nr. 1). July/August 1944: "Kampfgruppe-Btl. 42." III./42 missing in January/February 1945 and possibly until the end. Named on 15.1.1945.

---

[128]*Heeresgruppenkommando Kurland to the OKH, Ia Nr. 46/45 g.Kdos. Chefs (see Haupt, Heeresgruppe Nord 1941-1945, pp. 314-315).*

[129]*Not to be confused with "Aufstellungsstab der 2. lett. SS-Freiw.Brig." - Schupo Hauptmann Burkhardt being appointed its "Leiter" on 1.12.43.*

[130]*This motorcycle dispatch rider element appears to have disappeared in the course of expansion from Brigade to Division and Kažociņš believes that messages were thenceforth carried by a special and particularly brave detachment of Aizsargi (Latvian National Guard) volunteers on bicycles (letter of 19.2.81).*

[131]*This divisional escort company does not appear on the last organizational charts - it is not known for sure who protected the HQ at the end (Kažociņš suggests it was a detachment of the 106. Gren.Rgt. - letter of 19.2.81).*

[132]*The official names of the regiments included the phrase "der SS," although in internal communications between the divisional elements the Latvians omitted it (Silgailis).*

[133]*This spelling appeared in the Stellenbesetzungsliste der Waffen-SS of 1.3.45 - his first name should more correctly have been "Voldemārs" - Schill, op.cit., pg. 8, uses the spelling "Voldemars Veiss" when describing the proposed cuffband.*

[134]*Also (perhaps incorrectly) known as 1. and 2. lettisches Infanterie-Regiment.*

Waffen-Grenadier-Regiment der SS[132] 43 "Hinrich Schuldt"(lettisches Nr. 2) (24. & 26. Schuma-Btl. became I. & II./SS-Freiw.Rgt. 2 (lettisch)[134] in April 1943 at Krasnoje Selo and on 18.5.43 the regiment became SS-Freiw.Gren.Rgt. 2 (Lettische Legion). Completed on 12.6.1943 when 18. Schuma-Btl. became its III. Btl. September 1943 numbered as SS-Freiw.Gren.Rgt. 40.[135] Renumbered 12.11.1943 to SS-Freiw.Gren.Rgt. 43. 22.1.1944: SS-Freiw.Gren.Rgt. 43 (lettisches Nr. 5). 16.5.1944: Waffen-Gren.Rgt. der SS 43 (lett. Nr. 2). July/August 1944: "Kampfgruppe-Btl. 43." III./43 missing in January/February 1945 and possibly until the end. Named "Hinrich Schuldt" on 15.1.45.

Waffen-Grenadier-Regiment der SS[132] 44 (lettisches Nr. 6)[136] (ordered 7.1.1944 as SS-Freiw.Gren.Rgt. 44, the intention was to build it from III./42 & III./43, but its I. Btl. was formed from I./lettisches SS-Freiw.-Ausbildungs-Rgt. 2 (19. lett.Div.). March 1944 lettisches SS-Freiw.-Ausbildungs-Rgt. 1 (19. lett.Div) was disbanded, its men used to bring the new regiment to full strength and its field post numbers taken over.[137] 16.5.1944: Waffen-Gren.Rgt. der SS 44 (lett. Nr. 6). July/August 1944: "Kampfgruppe-Btl. 44." III./44 missing in January/February 1945 and possibly until the end.

Note:

Waffen-Grenadier-Regiment der SS 106 (lettisches Nr. 7) was part of the VI. Waffen-Armeekorps der SS (lettisches). This regiment is believed at times to have served under command of the 19th SS Division and was possibly administered by the Division for language and other reasons. (See footnote 92 on page 91.)

lett. SS-Füsilier-Bataillon 19/SS-Füsilier-Bataillon 19/Waffen-Füsilier-Bataillon der SS 19 (formed 10.8.1944 from SS-Waffen-Feldersatzbataillon 19, which had been reinforced with volunteers from the rear).

lett. SS-Panzerjäger-Abteilung 19/SS-Panzerjäger-Abteilung 19/SS-Waffen-Panzerjäger-Abteilung 19 (ordered 7.1.1944 on basis of 1. Kp. of SS-Panzerjäger-Abteilung 52 and by June 1944 had taken over field post numbers previously used by the whole SS-Panzerjäger-Abteilung 52)

SS-Fla.-Kompanie[138]

(Sturmgeschütz-Kompanie)[139]

Gren.Begleitzug

Waffen-Artillerie-Regiment der SS 19 (lettisches Artillerie-Regiment Nr. 1)[140] (ordered 7.1.1944 as SS-Freiw.Art.Rgt. 19[141] with SS-Art.Abt. 52 providing

---

[135] *Silgailis. This did not become official until publication of the 22.10.43 SS-FHA order (see footnote 2, pg. 56 of this book).*

[136] *The 3rd, 4th and 5th Latvian infantry regiments were in the 15th SS Division.*

[137] *All seven field post numbers for lett. SS-Freiw.Ausb.Rgt. 1 (19. lett.Div.) shown by the German Red Cross correspond with those given by Klietmann (op.cit., pg. 220) for SS-Freiw.Gren.Rgt. 44.*

[138] *The German Red Cross appears to have been confused by this unit. They list it incorrectly as existing in the summer of 1944 as "SS-Flak-Kp. 52." This is impossible and the result of confusion between a "Fla.-Kp." (part of infantry) and a "Flak-Bttr." (part of artillery).*

[139] *Charts indicate such an assault gun company was being formed for the Division's Panzerjägerabteilung in Germany in January/February 1945. Its Gren.Begleitzug existed but the assault guns had not yet arrived - and possibly never did (PHB, letter of September 1975). Silgailis knows nothing of this company.*

[140] *According to PHB (letter of 26.1.81) the regiment had been renumbered yet again to "Nr. 2" by February 1945 - the Stellenbesetzungsliste der Waffen-SS of 1.3.45 gives simply "Waffen-Art.Rgt. 19" without national numeration.*

[141] *Tessin, op.cit., Vol. 4, pg. 127. Also found listed without the adjective "Freiw."*

its I. Abt. Field post numbers listed for first time in April 1944. II. Abt. formed at the front during May/June 1944 and ready on 23.6.1944. III. & IV. Abt., as well as other regimental elements, formed in Vaiņode area of Latvia. 22.1.1944: SS-Freiw.Art.Rgt. 19 (lettisches Art.Rgt. Nr. 2). 16.5.1944: Waffen-Artillerie-Regiment der SS 19 (lettisches Art.Rgt. Nr. 1). III. & IV. Abt. served with German Army units in Zemgale July/October 1944 and so joined the Division for the first time at Dobele in October 1944. IV. Abt. disbanded in late autumn 1944[142] and Division fought the 3rd Courland battle with only its I. & III. Art.Abt. (its II. Art.Abt. was with 21. Luftwaffen-Felddivision). IV. Schw. Abt. was being formed in Germany in January/February 1945 but never joined the Division. SS-Art.Rgt. 15 (less its I. Abt.) was controlled by the 19th Division from August 1944 to the end of the war.)[143]

lett. SS-Freiwilligen-Flak-Abteilung 19/SS-Flak-Abteilung 19 (ordered 7.1.1944 from SS-Flak-Abt. 52.[144] Field post numbers listed in late March 1944. Detached July 1944 and added to SS-Flak-Abt. 15 to form SS-Flak-Abt. 506 for the VI. Waffen-Armeekorps der SS (lettisches)).[145]

SS-Waffen-Nachrichten-Abteilung 19 (ordered 7.1.1944 as lett. SS-Nachrichten-Abteilung 19 on basis of (gem.) SS-Nachrichten-Kompanie 52. Although the personnel were German and not Latvian throughout, the battalion was designated "Waffen-.")[146]

SS-Waffen-Pionier-Bataillon 19 (ordered 7.1.1944 and formed at SS-Pionierschule Beneschau/Hradischko from Latvians as lett. SS-Freiw.Pi.Btl. 19.[147] Ready by end March 1944 and field post numbers were first published in April 1944.)

Kommandeur der SS-Divisions-Nachschubtruppen 19 (formed March 1944 following order of 7.1.1944).

lettisches SS-Freiwilligen-Nachschub-Regiment 19 (existed in the summer of 1944 with the following elements:
SS-Nachschub-Kompanie
1. (& 2.)[148] SS-Kraftfahr-Kompanie (90t)
1. & 2. SS-Fahrschwadron (60t)
1., 2 & 3. SS-Fahrkolonne
SS-Werkstatt-Kompanie 19)

SS-Wirtschafts-Bataillon 19 (formed June 1944 and on 15.8.1944 became SS-Verwaltungstruppen-Abteilung 19)
SS-Bäckerie-Kompanie 19

---

[142] *IV./Art.Rgt. 19 and I./Art.Rgt. 15 were disbanded, their equipment turned over to the remaining artillery elements and their men sent to the 15th SS Division as a base for a new Art.Rgt. 15 (Silgailis, letter of 28.12.78).*

[143] *See Vol. 4, footnote 83, pg. 83.*

[144] *According to Tessin, op.cit., Vol. 4, pg. 127, SS-Flak-Abt. 52 was not reorganized, and it retained its number until its detachment in July 1944 (in fact, he gives September 1944, i.e., when the field post number lists were amended). German Red Cross shows separately for the summer of 1944 a lett. SS-Freiw.-Flak-Abt. 19 (FPNr. 57 966) and SS-Flak-Abt. 52 (Stab: 59 824, Einheiten: 48 296).*

[145] *V.O.SS 492 geh.Kdos., v. 2.7.1944. An SS-Fla.-Kp. was left for the Division's AA protection as part of its Panzerjägerabteilung.*

[146] *Silgailis, letter of 28.12.78.*

[147] *The 7.1.44 order laid down that the engineer companies of the 42nd and 43rd regiments should provide the 1st and 2nd of its three companies, but in practice the battalion was raised from men sent to Beneschau. The Pi.Kpn. did disappear and the Stabskompanien of the three infantry regiments each had a Pi.Zug (P H Buss, letter of September 1975).*

[148] *Only 1945 charts show two companies and in view of the German fuel shortage, it is probable that earlier charts showing only one were more realistic (P H Buss, letter of 26.1.81). Silgailis, in fact, remembers only one company (letter of 28.12.78).*

SS-Schlächterei-Kompanie 19

SS-Verwaltungstruppen-Abteilung 19 (formed 15.8.1944 by renaming SS-Wi.Btl. 19)

SS-Sanitäts-Kompanie 1/19 SS-Sanitäts-Kompanie 2/19
SS-Tr.Eg.Zug 1/19 (SS-Tr.Eg.Zug 2/19)[149]

SS-Krankenkraftwagen-Zug 19

SS-Veterinär-Kompanie 19 (supplied from Latvia by Aufstellungsstab der 15. SS-Division)

SS-Feldpostamt (mot.) 19

SS-Propagandakompanie 19/SS-Kriegsberichter-Trupp (mot.) 19/SS-Kriegsberichter-Zug 19[150]

SS-Feldgendarmerie-Trupp (mot.) 19/SS-Waffen-Feldgendarmerie-Trupp 19 (although the personnel were German and not Latvian throughout, the section was designated "Waffen-" in its final form).[151]

SS-Feldersatz-Bataillon 19 (ordered 7.1.1944 and in April 1944 formed by renaming II./lettisches SS-Freiw.-Ausbildungs-Rgt. 2 to SS-Freiw.Feldersatz-Bataillon 19. Received field post numbers in April 1944. July/August 1944 served as a combat element and known as "Laumaņa bataljons" by the Latvians after its commander Waffen-Sturmbannführer Laumanis. Reinforced with volunteers from rear areas, it became on 10.8.1944 Waffen-Füsilier-Btl. der SS 19.)

SS-Waffen-Feldersatz-Bataillon 19 (a new FEB formed after the original became Waffen-Füsilier-Btl. der SS 19 on 10.8.1944.)

Nahkampfschule/Divisions-Kampfschule der 19. SS-Freiw.Gren.Div. (lett. Nr. 2) (established 4.12.1944 for antitank, sniper, etc. training. Disbanded 14.3.1945)[152]

lettisches SS-Freiwilligen-Ausbildungs-Regiment 1 (19. lettische Division) (formed in Rīga January 1944[153] as SS-Ausbildungs-Regiment der 2. Lett.Brig. Nr. 1. Consisted of Stab, I(1.-4.), II(5.-8.), III(9.-12.),13., 14. & 15. and ready by February 1944. Disbanded March 1944 and its men used to bring 44. Rgt. up to strength.)[154]

lettisches SS-Frewilligen-Ausbildungs-Regiment 2 (19. lettische Division) (formed in Vaiņode January 1944[153] as SS-Ausbildungs-Regiment der 2. Lett.Brig. Nr. 2 with same composition as 1st but without the 15. Kp. Ready in February 1944 and in March 1944 its I. Btl. joined the Division at the front and used as I./44. Remainder joined Division April/May 1944. II.

---

[149]Charts show both medical companies having a Tr.Eg.Zug (Truppenentgiftungszug - personnel decontamination section) in February 1945, but according to Silgailis (letter of 28.12.78) the Division had only one.

[150]It was normal for a Division to have no more than a Kriegsberichter-Zug and so reference to SS-Propagandakompanie 19 in Verordnungsblatt der Waffen-SS of 15.9.44 at Hoffnungsstal is surprising and doubted by Silgailis (letter of 31.3.81). It is possible that the two KB-Züge of the 15th and 19th SS Divisions were collectively regarded as a company. These men belonged to SS-Standarte "Kurt Eggers" in any case. (P H Buss).

[151]SS-FG-Trupp 19 for some reason shared the same field post number (34 062) as SS-FG-Trupp 15 (P H Buss - no Waffen-SS listing is found for this number in Projekt Himmelblau).

[152]Led by Waffen-Obersturmführer (later Hauptsturmführer) Roberts Ancāns. Reported as part of the Feldersatzbataillon (P H Buss) but Silgailis remembers the school as directly subordinated to divisional HQ - the FEB being only responsible for the supply of pupils.

[153]Also said to have been ordered in February 1944 - possibly the date of an order issued after formation had in fact begun.

[154]Also reported to have been used to replenish losses in the 42nd and 43rd regiments.

Btl. became the original FEB 19. In February 1945 the regiment's field post numbers had been taken over by Ausbildungs-Regiment der 19. SS-Division.)

Ausbildungs-Regiment der 19. SS-Division/SS-Ausbildungs-Regiment 19 (in February 1945 took over field post numbers - and presumably surviving personnel - of lett. SS-Freiw.Ausbildungs-Rgt. 2 (19. lett.Div.)

SS-Baubataillon Zvaigzne (formed late 1944 from those men of the disbanded Grenzschutz-Regiment 5 who were unfit to be used for Waffen-Gren.Rgt. 106.)[155]

Arbeit-Kompanie Dolp[156] (with the Division in late August 1944)

Th. Rachsch-Kompanie[157] (with the Division in late August 1944)

Jagdkommando Herrmann[158]

KAMPFGRUPPEN:[159]

The following battle groups were formed from the 19th SS Division

- Kampfgruppe AIRA (see KG SCHULDT below)
- Kampfgruppe BOCK of the 4. SS-Polizei-Division became part of KG SCHULDT (see below)
- Kampfgruppe RUSMANIS (a large group of men[160] from the former construction regiments, they were shipped from Swinemünde to Courland on 12.4.1945 to serve as replacements for the Division. Apparently unarmed and untrained, they were captured by the Russians without having had a chance to fight.)
- Kampfgruppe SCHULDT (formed 29.1.1944 from the 2nd Latvian Brigade, KG BOCK, KG AIRA, Jagdkommando Hermann, 405. Inf.Rgt. of 121. Inf.Div. and some units of the 28. Jägerdivision. This KG was subordinated to the 21. Luftwaffen-Felddivision and disbanded 5.2.1944.)

---

[155] *Contemporary confusion arose from the Germans misspelling the name of Pulkvedis Zvaigzne, former commander of Grenzschutz-Rgt. 5 (e.g. "Zwaigsne," "Zwaigzne," "Zvaigne"). In December 1944 Bau-Btl. Zvaigzne was at the disposal of the 16th Army's HQ (Silgailis, letter of 28.12.78) and was listed that same month as "lett. Pol.Btl. Zvaigzne" (note conversion to a police battalion) - it had retained the same field post number as Stab/lett. Grenzschutz-Rgt. 5 (PHB, letter of 26.1.81).*

[156] *Listed in Feldpostübersicht Teil III Band 12 SS Einheiten 11. Neudruck Stand vom 25.8.1944. An "Arbeitskompanie" (labor company) is reported to have been organized by the Latvian Brigade in early 1944 and could have been a group of laborers possibly unarmed, working on fortifications, etc. in the Latvian sector. They could have belonged to the RAD, Org. Todt, a penal unit, the Latvian Legion itself or even have been civilians (P H Buss, letter of 26.1.81). Silgailis (letter of 28.12.78) knew nothing of it and doubted that a labor company could have been formed since there were no men available to form such an element. In the late autumn of 1943 a labor unit of Belorussian nationals under German command was attached to the Brigade for fortification work (Silgailis). Neither of these labor units can have been the mysterious Arbeits-Kompanie Dolp, which was attached to the Division much later (at least by 25.8.44). Dolp may have been the company's commander.*

[157] *Also given in the field post number list of 25.8.1944 (see footnote 156 above). Nothing is known of this company, possibly it was named after its commander - Th(eodor) Rachsch perhaps - or there may have been a misprint in the German document (Rachsch appearing rather than Nachschub - supply).*

[158] *During the retreat from the Volkhov, the German Jagdkommando Herrmann was attached to the Latvian Brigade and was a component of Kampfgruppe "Schuldt" that existed from 29.1.1944 to 5.2.1944. The Brigade is shown to have had a Jagdkommando in a chart dated 1.1.1944 (P H Buss, letter of 11.4.81).*

[159] *Neither the letters "SS-" nor the rank of the commander were used to name a Kampfgruppe (Silgailis, letter of 28.12.78).*

[160] *See footnote 108 on pg. 96 above.*

- Kampfgruppe SPEHT (on 12.2.1944 the Latvian Brigade was included in this KG.)
- Kampfgruppe STRECKENBACH (the whole Division itself was so called from 18.7.1944 until late August/early September 1944)

DIVISIONAL STRENGTHS:*

DATE	OFFICERS	NCOs	MEN	TOTAL
30.6.1944	329	1,421	8,842	10,592
20.9.1944	414	1,974	10,119	12,507
28.3.1945	275	1,699	6,222	9,396
8.5.1945				10,350

Notes:

1) At 29.3.1945, 4,019 men of the total 8,047 were combat soldiers.

2) With its three triangular infantry regiments, recce.battalion, field replacement battalion, six artillery detachments, etc., the 19th SS was one of the strongest divisions in the German forces in 1944.

*Actual strengths (including men in hospitals, on detachment or on leave)/Iststärke.

Brigade and Divisional Commanders

18 May 1943 - 5 September 1943 . . . . SS-Brigadeführer und Generalmajor der Waffen-SS Fritz von Scholz.

5 September 1943 - 15 March 1944[161] . SS-Standartenführer (promoted to SS-Oberführer on 9.11.43 and SS-Brigadeführer und Generalmajor der Waffen-SS on 15.3.44) Hinrich Schuldt[162]

15 March 1944 - 13 April 1944 . . . . . SS-Standartenführer Friedrich-Wilhelm Bock[163]

15 April 1944[164] - 12 May 1944 . . . . . SS-Oberführer Bruno Streckenbach

12 May 1944 - 19 May 1944 . . . . Waffen-Oberführer Artūrs Silgailis[165]

19 May 1944 - 8 May 1945 . . . . SS-Oberführer (promoted before 20.8.44 to SS-Brigadeführer und Generalmajor der Waffen-SS and before 21.1.45 to SS-Gruppenführer und Generalleutnant der Polizei und Waffen-SS) Bruno Streckenbach[166]

Notes:

1) SS-Brigadeführer und Generalmajor der Waffen-SS Fritz von Scholz may have commanded the Latvian Brigade from its formation until 5 September 1943.[167]

2) On 3 or 4 June 1944 Himmler told SS-Oberführer Gustav Lombard to take charge of the 19th SS Division. Lombard refused as he was on his way to the military academy and Himmler agreed.[168]

CHIEFS OF STAFF:

SS-Sturmbannführer Heckler (May 1944)[169]

Jost Schneider

Fritz von Scholz

Jost Schneider

Hinrich Schuldt

---

[161]*Killed in action by the Velikaya river and posthumously promoted and awarded the Swords to his Knight's Cross of the Iron Cross on 25.3.1944.*

[162]*See footnote 34 on page 68 of this book.*

[163]*Bock, an SS-Standartenführer since 9.11.1943, had previously commanded the artillery regiment of 4. SS-Polizei-Division. His (SS-) Kampfgruppe "Bock" of the Polizeidivision became part of Kampfgruppe "Schuldt," and as Bock is given as leading this battle group until 1 April 1944 (Klietmann, op.cit., pg. 132), it is possible that he did not, in fact, assume command of the 19th SS Division until early April 1944. In this case his tenure was very short indeed, for he left on 13.4.1944 to become artillery commander of the II. SS-Panzerkorps ("Arko II. SS-Pz.Korps"). Promoted to SS-Oberführer on 1.8.1944, he took command of 9. SS-Pz.Div. "Hohenstaufen" and led it until 10.10.1944 when he was reappointed "Arko II. SS-Pz.Korps."*

[164]*Although Klietmann, op.cit., pg. 222, gives 13 April as Bock's last day of command, he does not show Streckenbach in command until 15 April. German Red Cross on the other hand shows Streckenbach taking command on 13 April. Streckenbach himself stated he took over the Brigade at the beginning of April 1944. If there were a few days between Bock's departure and Streckenbach's arrival, then the Ia would presumably have taken temporary command.*

[165]*Silgailis was placed in temporary command of the 19th SS Division by the VIth Army Corps HQ while Streckenbach was away for a week. Silgailis, letters of 8.1.79 and 31.3.81.*

[166]*See footnote 58, pg. 75 of this book. Streckenbach received the Knight's Cross (17.8.1944) and Oakleaves (21.1.1945) while commanding the 19th SS Division.*

[167]*See footnote 34 on pg. 68 of this book.*

[168]*Lombard, letter dated 30.8.1976.*

[169]*Silgailis, letter dated 8.1.79.*

Friedrich Wilhelm Bock

Artūrs Silgailis

Bruno Streckenbach

Divisional and Unit Insignia

COLLAR PATCHES:

1) PLAIN BLACK:

Ordered for the Latvian Legion on 26.2.1943[170] and worn prior to issue of the Fire Cross.

This Waffen-Oberscharführer wears the plain black right and non-regulation four-pointed stars on his left collar patches. He wears the ribbon of the "Ostmedaille" (Medal for the Winter campaign in Russia 1941/1942) on a bar and not through his second buttonhole as was normal practice and has just been awarded the Iron Cross IInd Class. There is no reason to suspect that the plain collar patch indicated membership of the SD.

2) SS RUNES:

Widespread unofficial use throughout, especially before introduction of the Fire Cross.

---

[170]*Ziff. 10 of SS-FHA, Kdo.Amt der Waffen-SS, Org.Tgb.Nr. II/1501/43 geh., v. 26.2.1943.*

Waffen-Hauptsturmführer Kiršteins, permanent aide to the "Infanterieführer" of the 19th SS Division, in May 1944.

Waffen-Hauptsturmführer Atis Lukins of Waffen-Gren.Rgt. der SS 42 "Valdemar Veiss" (lett. Nr. 1), last heard of on 27.2.1945 while the 19th SS Division was fighting the 5th Courland battle near Priekule.

3) FIRE CROSS:[171]

Authorized for all ranks under Waffen-Standartenführer of the Latvian Legion on 11.3.1943[172] and later adopted by the 19th SS Division.

Notes:

1) The "Fire Cross" should not be confused with the "double-armed swastika" introduced in the second half of 1944 for former members of the German Army and Luftwaffe who were transferred to concentration camp staffs and guard units.[173]

2) Two post-war reproductions of this collar patch have been found that should not be confused with originals:

a) the metal cap badge of the Germanic SS in Flanders pinned to a plain black patch

b) a woven upright swastika which, unlike the originals that had all the arms of the Fire Cross parallel to the sides of the collar patch, has only two of its arms parallel to the longer sides of the collar patch.

Six Latvian NCOs of the 19th SS Division wearing the Fire Cross collar patch. Note that the NCO in the foreground wearing a camouflage cap wears unmatching rank insignia - the left collar patch is for a Waffen-Oberscharführer but the shoulder straps are of a Waffen-Scharführer.

The "Fire Cross" collar patch

(a)

(b)

---

[171]*See pg. 33 of this book.*

[172]*SS-FHA, Kdo.Amt der Waffen-SS, Org.Tgb.Nr. 340/43 g.Kdos., v. 11.3.1943 Aufstellung der Lettischen SS-Freiw.Legion (T-175/111/2635261-6).*

[173]*On 27.6.1944 Himmler ordered that the "double-armed swastika" should be so allocated (Der RF-SS - RF/M 1960/44 geh.) - but the inspector of the concentration camps (SS-Gruppenführer und Generalleutnant der Waffen-SS Richard Glücks, Chef Amtsgruppe D WVHA) did not pass on the orders to the camp commandants until 8*

SLEEVE SHIELDS:

Various patterns of shield featuring the Latvian national colors were worn by this Division, officially they should all have included the word "LATVIJA" in their design, but in practice this was not always the case.[174]

At a date as yet unknown in 1944, possibly in June, the Germans introduced a "Waffen-SS pattern" on a black cloth backing (type "F") which was not at all popular with the Latvians.

CUFF BANDS:

A cuffband "LATTVIJA" (sic - it should have been spelled "LATVIJA") was listed in the SS-FHA order of 22.10.1943[175] for the 2. Lett. SS-Freiw.Brigade. This cuffband was cancelled in the subsequent SS-FHA order of 12.11.1943.[176] It is most unlikely that any were manufactured and none were ever worn. On 15.1.1945 the honor names "Valdemar Veiss" and "Hinrich Schuldt" were given to the Waffen-Gren.Rgt. der SS 42 & 43 (lett. Nr. 1 & 2) respectively, but it is again considered unlikely in the extreme that cuffbands were worn, manufactured or even intended since it was too late in the war and the Division was cut off and fighting desperately in the Courland pocket.

Note:

The commanding general of Heeresgruppe "Kurland" recommended to Hitler in early 1945 that the men under his command be given some recognition for their services while undergoing siege in Courland. The recommendation was approved and a cuffband "Kurland" instituted on 12 March 1945. The band was manufactured in a weaving mill at Kuldiga in Courland and some of those that were issued in late April/early May 1945 may have found their way onto the left sleeve of men of the 19th SS Divi-

---

August 1944 (SS-WVHA, Amtsgruppenchef D, A V/4 Az.: Tgb.Nr. 759/44 geh., Uniformspiegel, Oranienburg). In theory, therefore, only Latvians transferred from Army or Luftwaffe service in the Latvian Legion to concentration camp staffs or guard units should have worn this collar patch. See page 38 of this book, however, for a clear photograph proving the as yet unexplained wear of such "double-armed swastika" by a Latvian member of the 15th SS Division.

[174] Der HSSPF für das Ostland, H./Gy., Riga, den 13. Sept. 1943 Lettische SS-Freiwilligen-Legion. See pg. 42 of this book.

[175] See footnote 2 on pg. 56 of this book.

[176] See footnote 37, pg. 70 of this book.

[177] Angolia: For Führer and Fatherland - Military Awards of the Third Reich, Bender Publishing, California, 1976, pp. 295-297. See also Klietmann in Feldgrau of August 1959 and Ärmelband "Kurland," Ordenskunde Nr. 15, "Die Ordens-Sammlung," Berlin, 1960. Kažociņš (letter of 19.2.81) is doubtful over Angolia's description of the manufacturing of the cuffband as he believes there was no silver-grey thread available at the weaving mill in Kuldiga at that time. He believes the band was woven in white thread with some sort of border, while the lettering and insignia on both ends were sewn on by hand at the homes of Latvian needlewomen. Bands were also made from any available material and the better made and more regular a specimen, the more likely it is to be a post-war reproduction.

sion. The 4cm wide cuffband has a silver-grey field upon which the shield of the Grand Master of the Teutonic Knights Order and the coat of arms of Jelgava are placed in black thread on either side of the word "KURLAND" in block capital letters.[177]

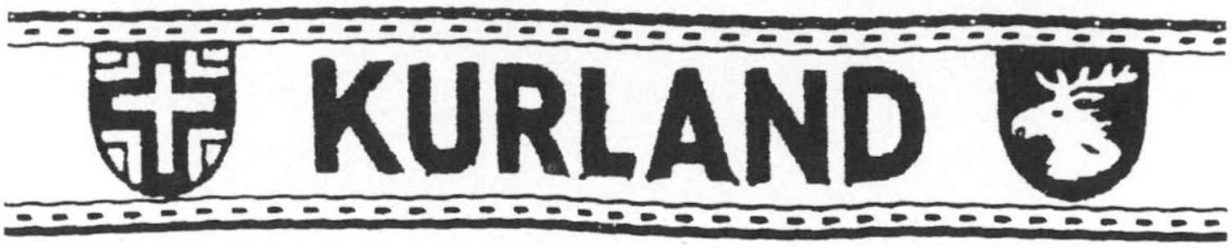

DIVISIONAL VEHICLE SYMBOLS:

(1) A capital letter "L" (to denote "lettische" - Latvian) with a Roman numeral "II" (to denote it was the 2nd Latvian Division) was assigned to the Division, but no copy of the corresponding order ever reached the General Inspection of the Latvian Legion or the divisional elements, and so the symbols were never painted or stencilled onto vehicles.[178]

(2) A variation of the above but having an oak leaf superimposed.[179]

(1)

(2)

(3) Rough drawing or stencil of the Latvian sleeve shield.[180]

---

[178]*Silgailis, letter dated 3.2.1978. This explains why no symbol had been identified for this Division by Allied Intelligence as late as 1 March 1945 (German Divisional Emblems, Military Research Section, London, MIRS(D)-EMB, January 1945 and 2nd supplement, MIRS(D-1)-EMB/3/45, 1 March 1945.*

[179]*This design was illustrated but then deleted from a HIAG draft chart on Waffen-SS divisional symbols. It is possibly a post-war fantasy.*

[180]*Such was unofficial - photographic evidence confirms it was done at least once (J. P. Petersen, 1.5.81).*

Legions-Obersturmbannführer Kārlis Lobe, commander of the 2nd Regiment of the Latvian Legion (later Waffen-Grenadier-Regiment 43 (lett. Nr. 2) of the 19th SS Divison) and Legions-Unterscharführer Viburgs outside a company HQ bunker on the Volkhov front. Note the badge Lobe is wearing on his left breast pocket - its design had also been engraved onto his Volkhov walking stick by a Latvian soldier who had been a wood carver before the war. This was the badge of the "Imanta Regiment" ("Imantas pulks"), which Lobe had commanded for a time during its short existence 1918-1920. Imanta is a name from ancient Latvian history and legend and was given to this regiment of Latvian riflemen that was raised at Vladivostok on 7.11.1918. It was one of the first armed elements of the Latvian Republic and came under the higher command of the French General Janin. After commanding the Regiment as a Captain, Lobe returned to Latvia and named his only son Imants. When Lobe was later appointed to command the 2nd Regiment of the Latvian SS Legion at the Volkhov front, he promptly named his regiment "Imantas pulks" and ordered his HQ to be built in the Volkhov marshes to resemble an ancient Lettish castle, which he called "Imantas sēta" ("Imanta's Farmstead"). Lobe was very popular with his men, and his only son was killed in action with the Legion. The Germans never recognized the name "Imanta" (few probably even knew of it, let alone its meaning), and it remained a purely internal Latvian designation until the 43rd Regiment received the name "Hinrich Schuldt" on 15.1.1945.
(Information kindly provided by Indulis Kažociņš and Colonel Kārlis Lobe, who survived the war and is still in possession of his Volkov walking stick! See Krätschmer, op.cit., pg. 397, and Stöber, Die lettischen Divisionen, footnote on page 136.)

The majority of the original "Imanta" Regiment's men came from Latvians whose families had lived on Siberian farms since the middle of the 19th century. The badge, designed in Siberia and worn officially throughout the period of Latvian independence, consisted of inverted upper white and lower green chevrons. These represented the white snow and green fields of Siberia, and by superimposing the shield in Latvian national colors on the lower green chevron is supposed to have symbolized how the Latvians were prepared to fight for independence. The letter "I" for "Imanta" and the crossed (silver?) clubs formed part of the original design worn during the life of the "Imanta" Regiment itself, but the brass bar must have been added later since it records not only the year in which the regiment was raised (1918), but also when it was disbanded (1920).

THE MEMORIAL STANDARD OF THE LATVIAN LEGION
(Latviešu leģiona piemiņas standards)

The following description of the standard is taken from the history of the Daugavas Vanagi organization over its first 25 years, LAIKS, TELPA, ĻAUDIS ("Time, Space, People"), editor Vilis Hāzners, 2nd Volume, 1976, kindly translated and commented upon by Indulis Kažociņš:

The Memorial Standard was made in Australia by the members of the Daugavas Vanagi organization in Australia after the design by a former member of the Latvian Legion, painter Ojārs Bisenieks, and it was presented to the Daugavas Vanagi organization on the occasion of its 25th anniversary. It was received by Vilis Hāzners - then the President of the organization - at Toronto on 4 July 1971, where it had been brought by the delegation of the members from Australia. The Standard was then left with the Daugavas Vanagi in Canada for five years until the next jubilee of the organization, when it was taken over by the Latvian Welfare Fund in England (1976). Thus the Standard travels from one country to another at each Daugavas Vanagi global rally. The last was in Australia in 1981, and the next will be in Germany, perhaps in 1984.

The motto of the Standard is: "Par Latvijas brīvību!" which translates as "For the Freedom of Latvia!" An album that accompanies the Standard, which contains a full description of it and the regulations governing its treatment, contains also an inscription: "Presented by Ojārs Bisenieks to his comrades in battles of their young days, 7.3.1970." This is a rather poor translation, since the actual Latvian idiom used is very difficult to translate. What is meant is that Ojārs presents this Standard to his friends in memory of the battles they fought together against a common enemy when they were all young.

The symbols embroidered onto the Standard are a mixture of ancient Lettish ornamental symbols and modern designs. The author explains them as follows:

The right hand side of the Standard is black, symbolizing war. On the black background the Latvian Army sun emblem is depicted, surrounded by oak branches. Although no exact explanation is given, it obviously symbolizes the hidden idea that the Latvian Legion was a continuation of the tradition of the Latvian Army. This is naturally what Ojārs Bisenieks and his friends all felt when they were conscripted into the Latvian Legion, even if they wore German uniforms. As one of the legionnaires said, when told that they had not chosen the right comrades-in-arms: "Our allies (i.e. the Germans) might not have been

the right ones, but the enemy was the right one indeed.'' Under the sun emblem is the inscription "TĒVZEMEI UN BRĪVĪBAI" - "For Fatherland and Freedom,'' and the figures "1940 - 1945'' indicating the years of the active battle service. It is to be noted that the period has been dated as beginning in 1940, that is with the Bolshevik occupation, and has nothing to do with the German occupation in 1941, nor with the formal extablishment of the Latvian Legion in 1943. Ideologically, the Latvian Legion was already in existence with the first resistance fighters against the Russians. The rôle of the Germans was only the arming of these resistance fighters.

The left hand side of the Standard is white, symbolizing peace. In the middle of the white field is the traditional symbol of the Latvian Legion - the shield in Latvian national colors, again surrounded by oak branches. At the top of the shield is the inscription "LATVIJA" continued below with the motto "MANS GODS IR UZTICĪBA,'' which together translated is construed as "Latvia, my honor is loyalty (to

thee).'' The author has heard several critical remarks for incorporating the motto of the Waffen-SS into the Standard. The author's answer constantly has been that he had meant loyalty to Latvia only, and nothing else. Below the figures ''1945 - 1970'' indicate the continued struggle for the freedom of Latvia by the Daugavas Vanagi organization - in 1970 already for 25 years.

The corner symbols of the Standard are the same on both sides. Top right is a combination of ancient Latvian ornament elements traditionally called: The Cross of Crosses, the Auseklītis (morning star), and the Saulīte (sun), symbolizing strength, loyalty to the Fatherland, and the welfare of the people. Below left is one of the numerous Firecross variants, symbolizing the fervor for the Fatherland. Below right are two crossed swords over a red sun ornament, symbolizing battle. Top left, next to the Standard's pole is the badge of the Daugavas Vanagi - a white falcon carrying three stars of Latvian freedom on a blue field.

The pole and pole top are made of oak, which symbolizes strength. The top of the pole is hand carved, with a number of ancient Lettish battle symbols, some of them dating back to the 10th century A.D. A ribbon (prievīte) is attached to the top of the pole, woven in the ancient "body-loom" technique. On this ribbon are the names of fifteen major battle grounds of the Latvian Legion, which for some unknown reason appear in reverse sequence, that is beginning with Berlin and ending with Leningrad:

"X BERLĪNE X MEKLENBURGA X POMERĀNIJA X RIETUMPRŪSIJA X KURŽEME X ZEMGALE X RĪGA X VIDZEME X LATGALE X OPOČKA X OSTROVA X VEĻIKAJA X STARJARUSA X VOLHOVA X ĻEŅINGRADA X"

* * * * * * * * * * *

Ojārs Bisenieks, author of the idea as well as the design of the Standard, was an NCO in the 15th SS Division and participated in the battles of Kurzeme.

* * * * * * * * * * *

Authors' note: Sincere thanks to the President and Chairman of the Central Board of the Daugavas Vanagi (Latvian Welfare Association, Inc.), Mr. Jānis Frišvalds, for permitting us to illustrate the Memorial Standard of the Latvian Legion, and to Mr. Indulis Kažociņš, Assistant archivist of the Archive of the Latvian Legion, for providing the information about the symbolism of the Standard's design. Our only comment to this very detailed description is that "My Honor is Loyalty ("Meine Ehre heisst Treue" in German) was the motto of the whole SS, not just the Waffen-SS.

Reichsführer-SS Heinrich Himmler dines with German and Estonian officers of the Estonian SS Volunteer Brigade in September 1943. Both plain black and SS runes collar patches can be seen, the latter probably being worn by the German majority.

20. Waffen-Grenadier-Division der SS (estnische Nr. 1)

EVOLUTION AND TITLES OF THE 20. WAFFEN-GRENADIER-DIVISION DER SS [estnische Nr. 1]

1 October 1942[1] - 5 May 1943	Estnische SS-Legion[2]
5 May 1943[3] - 22 October 1943	Estnische SS-Freiwilligen-Brigade
22 October 1943[4] - 24 January 1944 .	3.[5] Estnische SS-Freiwilligen-Brigade
24 January 1944[6] - 26 May 1944 . . .	20. Estnische SS-Freiwilligen-Division[7]
26 May 1944[8] - 8 May 1945[9]	20. Waffen-Grenadier-Division der SS (estnische Nr. 1)[10]

Note:
At no time did this Division ever officially have a name ("Estland," "Narwa," "Rebane," etc.)[11]

---

[1]*Creation of the Legion was authorized by Hitler in early August 1942, and the raising of the Legion was officially proclaimed in Estonia on 28 August 1942, the first anniversary of the liberation of the Estonian capital of Tallinn from the Russians by the Germans. This is the date that the Estonians take as the birth of the Legion (H. Rüütel, letter of 23.8.81). The men were to assemble at SS-Tr.Üb.Pl. Debica on 1 October 1942 by order of SS-FHA, Kdo.Amt der Waffen-SS, Org.Tgb.Nr. 5960/42 geh., v. 29.9.42, Aufstellung der Estnischen SS-Legion (T-175/111/2635437-8). Formation is given as November 1942 in Abschrift, Einheiten-Archiv, Estnische Einheiten, München, den 19. Juli 1954 (Eesti riik ja rahvas II Maailmasõjas - "The Estonian Nation and People in the Second World War" - Vol. VII, pg. 166). Allied Intelligence was premature in stating the "Estonian SS Legion" was formed "end summer 1942" (OSS, Public Orders, Police, & the Elite Guard, 13.11.1942) in that the regiment-sized Legion was only completed in the spring of 1943. To be noted that the term "Legion" was not at first used generically to describe all Estonians in German service - as was to be the case in Latvia.*

[2]*Formed as a motorized infantry regiment, the Legion was referred to as "1. Estn. SS-Freiw.Gren.Rgt." on 23.3.1943. Kleitmann is wrong in omitting "SS-" and calling the element "Estnische Legion" (op.cit., pg. 223).*

[3]*SS-FHA, Kdo.Amt der Waffen-SS, Org.Tgb.Nr. 600/43 g.Kdos., v. 5.5.1943, Umgliederung der 1. SS-Inf.Brig. (mot.) in die Estnische SS-Freiw.Brigade (T-175/111/2635256f). Manpower Study gives an unsupported 10.7.1943.*

[4]*SS-FHA, Amt II, Org.Abt. Ia/II, Tgb.Nr. 1574/43 g.Kdos., v. 22.10.1943, Bezeichnung der Feldtruppenteile der Waffen-SS, Anlage 3, III Brigaden und Sturmbrigaden.*

[5]*No number is given in Gesamtstärke der Waffen-SS am 31. Dezember 1943 (see Klietmann, op.cit., pg. 506).*

[6]*SS-FHA, Amt II Org.Abt. Ia/II, Tgb.Nr. 180/44 g.Kdos., v. 24.1.1944, Umgliederung bzw. Neuaufstellung der 3. Estn. SS-Freiw.Brig. zur 20. Estn. SS-Freiw.Div. (T-175/141/2669355). Finke gives an unsupported 16.5.1944. Difficulties in forming the Division while its men were in action at the front meant that formation took longer than expected. On 14.5.1944 it was 5,000 men under strength, and Himmler ordered it up to full strength by 15.6.1944. It was not, in fact, complete until July 1944.*

[7]*Although already numbered as the 20th Division of the Waffen-SS in the SS-FHA order of 24.1.1944 (see fn. 6 above), some early sources omit the divisional number from its title.*

[8]*It is difficult to give a precise date for the final naming of this division and dates before and after Klietmann's 26.5.1944 (op.cit., pg. 223) could originate from different people, agencies and divisional elements being informed of the change at different times. Himmler used the final designation in his letter of 14.5.1944 (see fn. 104 on page 172 of this book). Whereas Tessin's estimate of June 1944 (op.cit., Vol. 4, pg. 150) is generally considered unrealistically late because it is based on field post data, Riipalu wrote that his regiment was told of the change in the summer of 1944 (Kui võideldi kodupinna eest; Eesti Hääl, London, 1951, pg. 109).*

History

Estonia (Eesti in Estonian and Estland in German) is a northeast European country to the north of Latvia, bounded on the north by the Gulf of Finland, on the east by Russia, and on the west by the Gulf of Rīga and the Baltic Sea. The Estonians belong to the Finno-Ugrian family of nations and are considered "cousins" of the Finns. The Estonian and Finnish languages are very similar and, although not exactly the same, are like two dialects of the same tongue and Estonians and Finns can converse with one another without much difficulty.

As with the other Baltic States, the Estonians' history has been one of foreign invasions and domination since the Vikings first stormed through their country in the mid-9th century. The German Conquest of Latvia begun in 1180 was extended to Estonia when the Estonian forces were defeated in 1217 and was completed with the help of the Danes in 1227. Successive Russian, Polish and Swedish invasions reduced Estonia to a battlefield during the 16th and 17th centuries, and an end was put to the relatively benevolent Swedish rule when Tsar Peter I defeated Charles XII of Sweden at Poltava in 1709, and the Swedes ceded all their Baltic provinces to Russia by a peace treaty signed in 1721. Russian influence upon Estonia was then increased with their municipal constitution introduced in 1882 and Russian becoming the language of instruction in 1887.

The Russian revolution of March 1917 brought autonomy to the long-suffering Estonians and a provisional government was appointed on 12 October 1917. This change for the better was soon reversed when a puppet Communist government was imposed upon the Estonians following the November 1917 coup-d'ētat in Russia, but as German troops marched on the Estonian capital of Tallinn (Reval) the Communists fled the city, and on 24 February 1918 the Estonian provisional government declared the independence of the Republic of Estonia.[12] The following day the German Army entered Tallinn

---

[9]Date the main body of the Division surrendered to the Russians north of Prague.

[10]Rebuilt at Tr.Üb.Pl. Neuhammer by order of SS-FHA, Amt II Org.Abt. Ia/II, Tgb.Nr. 3572/44 g.Kdos., v. 6.10.1944, Verlegung 20. Waffen-Gren.Div. der SS (estn. Nr. 1) (T-175/141/2669112). The Division's final title in the Estonian language was "20. SS-Relvagrenaderide Diviis (Eesti Esimene)." In February 1945 the formation was so weakened that it had to be referred to as a battle group (SS-Kampfgruppe), possibly named "Augsberger" after its commander.

[11]Many sources (e.g., Duprat, Histoire des SS, pg. 364 and Deutsches Rotes Kreuz, Suchdienst, Divisionsschicksale, Band II, pg. 804) quite incorrectly name this Division "Estland" (German spelling of "Estonia"). Dr. Masing, an Estonian who served with the Division, recalls it being called "Division "Narwa" and "Division Rebane," but this was unofficial practice (B. Brooks, letter of 29.8.1976).

[12]All promotions in the Estonian Army were traditionally made on the 24th of February in commemoration of independence, and this practice also appears to have been followed within the Estonian Waffen-SS.

Soomepoiste Klubi Torontos

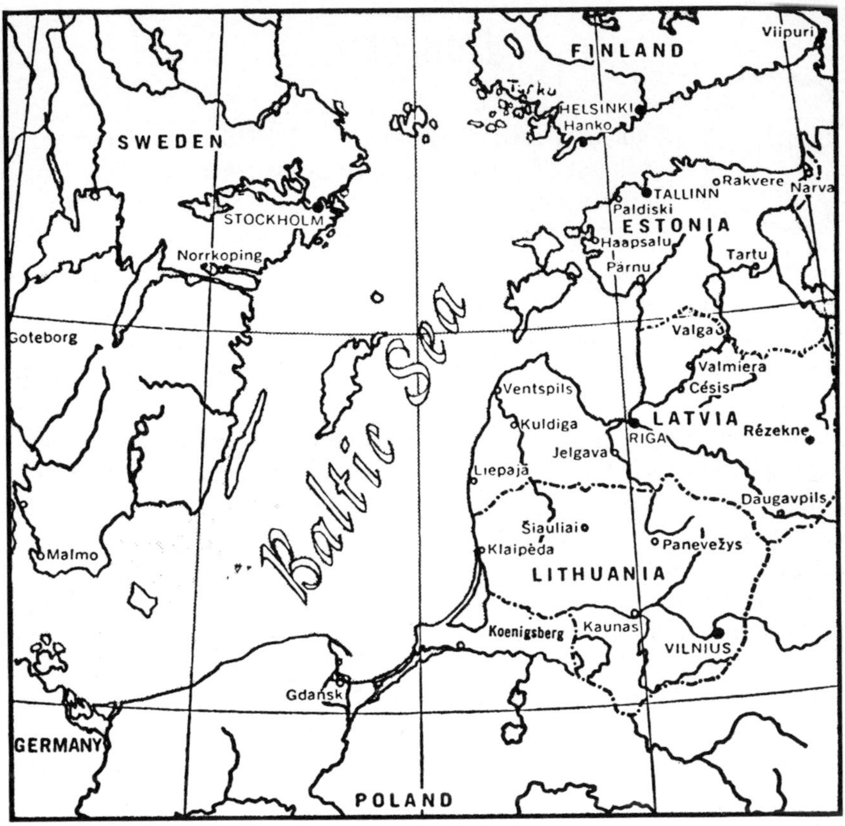

and on 3 March 1918 the Treaty of Brest-Litovsk was signed, but World War I was into its closing year and on the same day as Germany's capitulation (11 November 1918) the provisional government met in Tallinn and once more proclaimed Estonian independence. With Germany no longer in a position to block Russian intervention, the Soviet government declared the Treaty of Brest-Litovsk null and void on 13 November and on the 28th of that month the Red Army took the northeastern city of Narva and began to invade the rest of Estonia.

The Estonian government ordered general mobilization and the war of liberation was begun in which the British and Finns assisted the Estonians in driving out their Russian oppressors. On 2 February 1920 a peace treaty was signed in the university town of Tartu (Dorpat) under the terms of which the Russians renounced their sovereign rights over Estonia "voluntarily and forever." The long-awaited independence was not to see political stability, and in the fourteen years between May 1919 and May 1933 the country was ruled by no less than twenty coalitions. The Estonian Communist Party was outlawed following their unsuccessful coup d'état of 1 December 1924 in Tallinn.

Estonia's precious yet short-lived freedom was to die with the outbreak of the Second World War. The German Foreign Minister, Joachim von Ribbentrop, traveled to Moscow and on 23 August 1939 signed a so-called non-aggression treaty with his Russian counterpart, V. M. Molotov.[13] In fact they had agreed on a monstrous plan of aggression, and a secret clause to the treaty divided the spoils that would follow their planned take-over of Poland and the Baltic States. Finland, Estonia and Latvia were assigned to Russia, Lithuania to Germany, and Poland was to be split along the line of the Narev, Vistula and San Rivers to give the eastern part to Russia, the remainder to Germany.[14] Russia then followed Germany's earlier example by invading Poland on 17 September

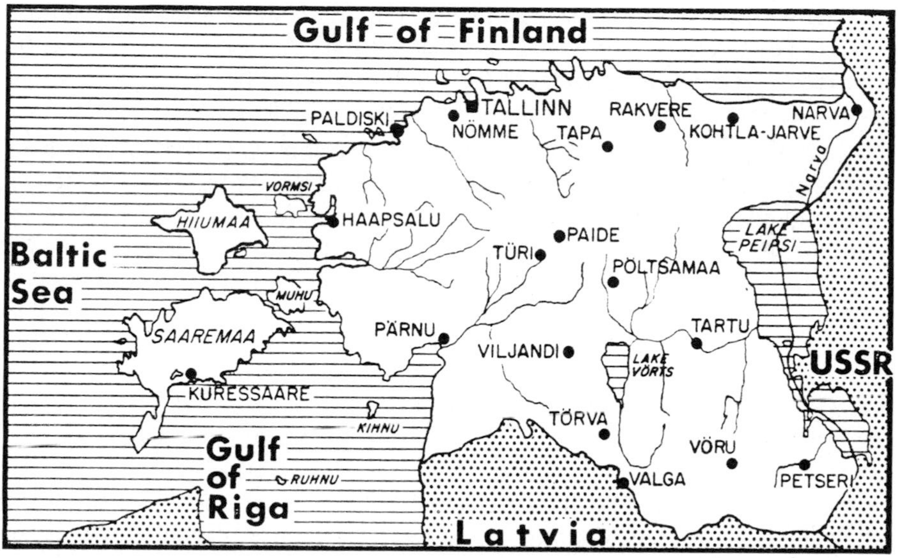

Soome Poiste Klubi Torontos

1939, and on 23 September, exactly a month after the non-aggression treaty had been signed, Molotov used the escape of the Polish submarine "Orzel" from an Estonian port as a pretext to impose upon the Estonians a Mutual Assistance Pact. In fact Molotov's suggestion was an ultimatum for massed Russian troop concentrations on the Estonian frontier, and Russian aircraft flying menacingly low over Estonian towns were clear indications that Russia would not hesitate to use force should the Estonians fail to accept. Estonia was in no position to resist, and the Mutual Assistance Pact was signed in Moscow on 28 September 1939. Apart from containing hollow promises, the Pact effectively put Estonia at Russia's mercy and gave Russia the right to maintain naval and air bases on Estonian territory.[15] This so-called Mutual Assistance Pact was nothing more than a calculated step towards the total Russian eclipse of Estonia and the other Baltic States. A secret appendix

---

[13] *Vyacheslav Mikhaylovich Molotov (real name Skryabin) was chairman of the Council of People's Commissars (prime minister) from 1930 to 1931 and from 1939 to 1949, and again from 1953 to 1956 was Commissar for Foreign Affairs. He was expelled from the Communist Party in 1963.*

[14] *A revision was made on 28 September 1939 by a secret supplementary clause to the Treaty whereby Germany ceded eventual control of Lithuania to Russia in exchange for the Lublin Province and part of the Warsaw Province in Poland.*

[15] *Latvia was forced to do the same in October - see Vol. 4, pg. 64.*

limited the number of Russian troops allowed into the country to man the bases at 25,000, but since the Estonians had no way of controlling these numbers, the agreed limit was grossly exceeded. The Pact also gave Russia the right to refuel and shelter her war ships in the capital port of Tallinn.

The Russians waited until Germany's victory over France to complete their occupation of Estonia. Unjustly claiming that she had contravened the Mutual Assistance Pact with alliances with Latvia and Lithuania, Russia gave Estonia a bare eight and a half hours on 16 June 1940 to accept their ultimatum demanding the forming of a new government "able and willing to secure the honest application of the Soviet-Estonian Mutual Assistance Pact" and the granting of freedom of movement for Russian troops "to be stationed in sufficient numbers in the most important centers of Estonia."

The following day, 17 June 1940, the Red Army troops already stationed in Estonia (who alone outnumbered the entire Estonian Army) were joined by others flooding over the frontier, and the country was occupied without opposition. On 21 June 1940 a puppet Communist government as demanded in the Russian ultimatum took over the country, and a totally false picture of "voluntary" incorporation of Estonia into the Soviet Union was projected by rigged elections, blackmail and intimidation. The outside world was expected to believe that the Estonian people had expressed their "fervent desire" to become a Soviet Republic and join the USSR, in reality nothing could have been further from the truth.[16] In a three-day session begun on 21 July 1940, the Communist Chamber of Deputies unanimously declared Estonia to have become a Soviet Republic and its request to the Supreme Soviet of the USSR for the incorporation of Estonia into the Soviet Union was granted with effect from 6 August 1940.

Once Estonia had become a Soviet Republic, its regular Army was absorbed into the Red Army and redesignated the 22nd Territorial Rifle Corps. It consisted of the 180th and 182nd Rifle Divisions. The vast majority of the Estonian officer corps were naturally unhappy by these events, and a number went into hiding rather than serve in the Red Army. The Russians in turn rejected a number of Estonian officers they considered unsuitable, and a sinister and uncertain fate befell a group of senior Estonian officers. Summoned to a meeting in south Estonia, they were sent to Russia and never heard from again. It is little wonder that when the Germans drove through Estonia a year later, many Estonian soldiers in the Red Army did their best to surrender to the Wehrmacht.

JULY 1940 - JULY 1941: A YEAR OF RUSSIAN OCCUPATION:

There followed in Estonia the same kind of "year of horror" as has already been described for Latvia. This was characterized by economic exploitation while private industry, banking and trade were all nationalized. But far worse were the loathsome activities of the Russian secret police (then known as the NKVD) which set about preparing lists of "undesirables" as soon as they arrived along with the Red Army in July 1940. Their task in persecuting what

---

[16] *Uustalu, The History of Estonian People, pg. 243.*

they considered "enemies of the people" was legalized by the retroactive application of Russian laws in Estonia for this automatically branded as criminals and thus fair game for the NKVD all Estonians who had fought against the Russians in the War of Liberation 1918-1920, as well as former judges who had tried cases of Communist subversive activities against the independence of Estonia.

Virtually no one was safe from the NKVD's terrifying "knocks on the door" policy, even some fellow-travelers fell victim to the system they outwardly supported. Whereas some 2,000 Estonians are known to have been executed during the Russians' year of occupation,[17] far larger numbers were arrested by the NKVD and deported to Russian slave labor camps in remote areas of northern Russia and Siberia. As fate would have it, the NKVD waited until just a week before Hitler unleashed Operation "Barbarossa" on the Soviet Union to make their first mass deportation. During the single night of 13/14 June 1941, they arrested 10,205 of the 11,157 Estonians appearing on their lists. The country fell into a state a shock and as all normal life ground to a halt, large numbers of Estonians left their homes fearful of arrest and deportation. While 490 railway cattle trucks carried the unfortunate 10,205 on long and nightmarish journeys to Russia, many escaped to the forests and formed themselves into groups of varying size known collectively as the "Brothers of the Forest" (metsavennad).[18] Many more joined them at the news of Germany's surprise attack on the Soviet Union on 22 June 1941, for the Russians had reacted by rounding up a further 22,200 Estonians under the guise of conscription, but rather than arm and use them against the onrushing Germans, they were deported to work in lumber camps in the frozen north of Russia. The "Brothers of the Forest" began to arm themselves by surprise attacks on individual Russian soldiers and small elements of the Red Army, and as will be seen below, were helpful in softening-up the Russian forces in southern Estonia even before the Germans crossed over and into the country from Latvia in July 1941.

In the single year the Russians occupied Estonia, 59,732 Estonians were either executed, deported, or in some other way forced to leave for Russia and almost certain doom. In the small country of Estonia, that is a staggering 5.3 percent of the pre-war population, and it is not surprising that their first reaction was to welcome the Germans as liberators. But other than giving Estonia the opportunity of fighting the Russians, the three years of German occupation were to allow the Estonians little real advantage, and all their pleas for independence fell on deaf ears.

JULY - OCTOBER 1941: THE GERMAN INVASION OF ESTONIA:

Germany attacked the Soviet Union at 3:15 in the morning of Sunday, 22 June 1941, along a front that stretched all the way across eastern Europe from the Baltic to the Carpathians.

---

[17]1,741 were found to have been executed and buried in mass graves when the Wehrmacht drove the Russians from Estonia in 1941.

[18]The Estonian equivalent of the Latvian "meza brali" (see fn. 113 on page 97 of this book). The singular form is "metsavend."

Operation "Barbarossa" involved three major assaults delivered by as many German army groups. While von Rundstedt's Army Group "South" and von Bock's Army Group "Center" drove towards the Ukraine and north of the Pripet Marshes, Field Marshal Wilhelm Ritter von Leeb's Army Group "North" was to thrust towards the key objective of Leningrad. It was thus von Leeb's Army Group "North" that was to smash through the Baltic States and drive the Red Army from Estonia.

Von Leeb's force was in turn divided into three parts, the central and major of which was General Erich Hoepner's formidable 4th Armored Group (Panzergruppe 4) which drove directly for Leningrad. It passed through Lithuania, eastern Latvia and missing the southeastern corner of Estonia broke the heavily defended "Stalin Line" which ran south from Lake Peipsi (Peipus) through Pskov (Pleskau), Ostrov and Opochka after bitter and costly fighting lasting from 6 to 11 July 1941. Pskov was taken on 8 July and Opochka fell to units of the Waffen-SS "Totenkopf" Division and the German Army's 30th Infantry Division of the 16th Army on 11 July.

While the left wing of the spearhead captured Gdov on the eastern shore of Lake Peipsi on 17 July, the main force pushed northwards past Luga to the east Estonian city of Narva on the Gulf of Finland close to the Russian border. The Wehrmacht was only 13 kilometers south of Narva by 21 July but had to overcome stubborn Russian resistance before the strategic town fell on 17 August, and the Germans were able to push their advance further east into Russia herself.

Estonia was crowded with elements of the Red Army who had been using the open sea route from Tallinn to Leningrad for the transport of military equipment westwards and the deportation of Estonian civilians eastwards.[19] The task of crushing these Russian forces fell upon the left wing of Army Group "North," made up of Generaloberst Georg von Küchler's 18th Army. This Army had taken Kaunas (Kovno) in southern Lithuania on the second day of the attack (24 June 1941) and crossing into Latvia took the southern Latvian town of Liepāja (Libau) the next day. According to plan, von Küchler's men drove northwards across central Latvia, took the capital of Riga on 2 July and on the 7th crossed the Latvian/Estonian border.

The German advance through southern Estonia was greatly assisted by the efforts of Estonian guerrillas, those men who had started to go into hiding as "Brothers of the Forest" during the latter stages of the Russian occupation, especially following the mass deportation of 13/14 June and the beginning of the German-Russian war on 22 June 1941. Armed with weapons stolen from the Russians, these men had formed themselves into groups of varying size along military lines. So even before the Wehrmacht entered Estonia in early

---

[19]In the days following the launching of Operation "Barbarossa," the Russians had proclaimed a general mobilization in Estonia. Such was only feasible in the north, and fearful of the 22,200 mobilized men turning against them rather than fighting the Germans, the Russians deported them to lumber camps in the far north of the Soviet Union.

July 1941, the Estonian guerrillas had risen up against the occupying Red Army and actually managed to inflict severe losses and virtually drive them from the southern half of the country.

Estonians had begun to fight the Russians from the very beginning of Operation "Barbarossa." Groups were raised throughout the country and every town and village had its local resistance unit. Collectively they formed a sort of partisan army, which the advancing German unit commanders were only too pleased to let carry on fighting. The Germans referred to them as "Selbstschutz" (self-defense) and many such units were attached to the advancing Wehrmacht divisions.

In the wake of the German advance, special action groups of Security Police and Waffen-SS efficiently and systematically carried out the mass killing of whom were considered enemies of the "New Order": political commissars, Communist partisans, Jews, NKVD agents, traitorous ethnic Germans. Sanctioned by the C-in-C of the Army, Field Marshal von Brauchitsch, two months before Operation "Barbarossa" was launched, Einsatzgruppen A, B, C and D were responsible for mopping-up and security in the eastern territories left behind by Army Groups "North," "Center" and "South."[20] It was thus Einsatzgruppe A that followed the progress of Army Group "North" through Estonia in July and August 1941, and it was this Action Group that assumed control of the Estonian guerrilla units left behind, their job done, as the front moved further east. Einsatzgruppe A was composed of Sonderkommandos 1a and 1b and Einsatzkommandos 2 and 3. The commander of Sonderkommando 1a was SS-Sturmbannführer Dr. Martin Sandberger, who took over as Chief of the Security Police and SD for Estonia in Tallinn in December 1941 and was later to play a major rôle in the raising of the Estonian SS Legion.[21]

Thanks to the Estonian guerrillas, von Küchler's 18th Army of Army Group "North" had little difficulty in driving up through southern Estonia and reaching the central town of Viljandi (Fellin) and the western port of Pärnu (Pernau) by 9 July 1941. Here the Germans met with stronger Russian resistance and their rapid advance was checked along the whole Estonian

---

[20]Einsatzgruppen A and B followed Army Groups "North" and "Center," respectively, while C and D both served "South."

[21]A former assistant judge and administrator in southern Germany, Sandberger joined the SA in 1931 and the SD in 1936. When the RSHA was formed on 22 September 1939, he served in it for a year and a half, becoming deputy head of Department I (RSHA I - Personnel), handling training matters. At the beginning of the war with Russia in July 1941, he left Berlin and took command of Sonderkommando 1a of Einsatzgruppe A under the Higher SS & Police Leader (HSSPF) in Rīga (Prützmann then Jeckeln). This special action group saw to 'security' matters in the area to the rear of Army Group "North" and was responsible for the mass killings of "undesirables," including 125,000 Jews. Once the front had moved eastwards out of Russia, Sandberger was placed in charge of the Security Police & SD in Estonia (Kdr. Sich.P. u. SD Reval) in December 1941 and held this position until the end of 1943, when Schellenberg summoned him to Berlin to run Group A (Administration) of RSHA VI. After the war Sandberger had to answer for his crimes as leader of Sonderkommando 1a, and at the conclusion of the two-year "Action Group Trial" in 1948, he was sentenced to death. He was pardoned three years later in 1951 and released. (Kahn, Hitler's Spies, pp. 263-264; Mollo, Uniforms of the SS, Vol. 5, pg. 19; Brown Book, pg. 100).

SS-Sturmbannführer Dr. Martin Sandberger, Security Police and SD Leader in Estonia 1941-1943. This photograph was taken at Tartu on 25.7.1942.

front from 9 to 12 July.[22] The center of the advance was held up at Viljandi for about a week and resumed on 22 July, whereas the left wing at Pärnu on the west coast was blocked for over a month. This respite allowed the Russians time to bring in reinforcements and brace themselves for the coming attack and so prolonged the German conquest of Estonia and rendered it more difficult and costly. The Russians also had time to carry out a general mobilization in the northern part of the country, but fearing the Estonians would turn against them rather than fight the invading Germans, promptly deported those they could lay hands on to labor camps in the Soviet Union.

There were also many officers and men of the former Estonian Army, since June 1940 a part of the Red Army, who preferred to surrender to the Wehrmacht rather than fight for their country's Russian oppressors. Many who found the opportunity went over to the Germans and apart from reservists and veterans of the War of Liberation these were the only trained and experienced Estonian soldiers available to the Germans. At first they were afforded no special consideration, but later these men, after a year's service in the Red Army behind them, were to provide experience and expertise to the Estonian battalions raised by the German Police and Army.

The German advance was resumed at first in central and eastern Estonia around Viljandi and Tartu and later at Pärnu further to the west. Encountering tough resistance the Wehrmacht proceeded to fight its way through Türi

[22]*One source (Uustalu, For Freedom Only, pg 16) suggests the Germans deliberately suspended their hitherto successful advance, but is unable to provide a reason.*

and Rakvere towards the Gulf of Finland. The Red Army was forced to retreat from its line along the Emajõgi River, and on 7 August the German column which had driven north from Tartu reached the Gulf of Finland at Kunda, midway between the capital of Tallinn to the west and the besieged eastern city of Narva close to the Russian border. When the Germans reached the coast they effectively cut off all Russian troops in northwestern Estonia and the Estonian islands. The Wehrmacht then split once more into two groups. The larger veered eastwards at the coast and advanced through Tapa to link up at Narva with the other spearhead of Army Group "North" that had been laying siege to the city from the south. A smaller force turned westwards at Kunda to clear northwestern Estonia of the now-trapped Russian troops. This fighting was to last for several months. The attack on Tallinn was launched on 20 August, and the city fell to the Germans and Estonian guerrillas after eight days of hard fighting. At the end of August the taking of Haapsalu on the west coast completed the German conquest of mainland Estonia, and there remained only the crushing of Russian resistance on the islands. Saaremaa (Ösel) was taken on 4/5 October and Hiiumaa (Dagö) on 21 October.

Just as had happened earlier in the south, as the Wehrmacht forced the Red Army back through northern Estonia, a large number of guerrillas who had been hiding in the woods and marshes rose up and joined the German troops in driving out the hated Russians. In the summer of 1941 the "Company of Captain Talpak" and the "Battalion of Major Hirvelaan" were among various groups who linked up with German units liberating northern Estonia.[23] These groups joined those in the south in forming what was considered a partisan army which assisted the Germans by taking over entire sectors of the front line. They were particularly active in eastern Estonia, capturing the southern part of the city of Tartu and repelling continued Russian efforts to cross the River Emajõgi between Lakes Võrts and Peipsi for a week until the German offensive from Viljandi forced the Russians to abandon their positions along the river on 25 July.

Help for Estonian guerrillas operating in areas of northern Estonia still held by the Red Army came from their countrymen who had managed to escape Russian occupation by crossing the Gulf of Finland and a group code-named "ERNA"[24] was organized in Finland with German support and trained and equipped by the friendly Finns. "ERNA" numbered 65 officers and men and an advance party of four with radio transmitters was parachuted into northern Estonia behind the Russian lines. Having established contact with the local resistance, they radioed back for "ERNA" to be put ashore by boat on the northern coast. During the crossing some of the boats were discovered by the Russians and had to turn back, and so only a first group of 38 men succeeded in landing during the night of 9/10 July 1941. On the 19th the Russians were surprised to find themselves being attacked from the rear by Estonians in Finnish uniform and the activities of "ERNA," strengthened as time passed by

---

[23] *See below for more details of the Talpak and Hirvelaan units.*

[24] *"ERNA" was merely a code name and had no meaning in Finnish, Estonian or German. See Uustalu, The History of Estonian People, pg. 251 & especially For Freedom Only, pp. 26-27.*

Alfons Rebane as a Captain (Kapten) in the prewar Estonian Army. Following the German attack on the Soviet Union of 22 June 1941, Rebane led a partisan group raised at Viru and in July/August commanded the local Viru self-defense group (Omakaitse or Selbstschutz).

new volunteers, boosted the morale of the Estonian guerrillas fighting behind the front line.[25] Those members of "ERNA" who had been unable to land by boat with the first party were parachuted into Estonia on 26 July. On 4 August "ERNA" was advised that it had fulfilled its mission and should join the Germans by breaking through the Russian lines. The Germans then formed the veterans of "ERNA" and other resistance fighters on 18 August 1941 into "Battalion ERNA II" under Kolonel Hans Krug, which fought in the liberation of Tallinn (20/28 August) and with Finnish support took part in the conquest of the Estonian islands. When this job was done, most men of the "ERNA II" battalion returned to Finland (some to return to join the Estonian Waffen-SS division in 1944), others joined the Omakaitse (self-defense league - see below and box) or the police battalions.

---

[25]ERNA, a unit of Estonian volunteers in the Finnish Army, wore Finnish uniforms but with a badge depicting a dagger piercing the letter "E" on a shield on their caps instead of the usual Finnish cap badge. This could have inspired the first German pattern collar patch for the Estonian Waffen-SS - see below.

THE ESTONIAN SELF-DEFENSE ORGANIZATION

Partisan groups rose up throughout Russian-occupied Estonia as soon as Germany attacked the Soviet Union on 22 June 1941.

These groups, based on the "Brothers of the Forest" (metsavennad) who had already started to go into hiding before the German attack, were at first called Kaitseliit (literally "defensive line") and then "Omakaitse" ("self-defense" - abbreviated "O.K."). The Germans referred to them as "Selbstschutz" ("self-defense").

In the confusion of the German advance across Estonia, these units were raised at different dates, but officially the O.K. is given to have been formed on 2 August 1941, when it was organized to guard bridges, buildings and installations and fight against pro-Russian partisans.

O.K. groups took on the occupying Russians alone before the Wehrmacht arrived in their area, fought alongside the German soldiers to drive the Red Army out, and once the front was pushed eastward came under Einsatzgruppe A and saw to mopping-up and general security matters.

Most of the Estonian partisan combat units were disbanded in July and August (three were allowed to carry on fighting at Tallinn and to free the islands - see main text) and their men taken into a new O.K. (also known by the Germans as "Selbstschutz") which was organized on a territorial basis under the control of the local Army Feldkommandant.[1] The O.K. was maintained throughout the German occupation of Estonia and in July 1942, following an unsuccessful attempt by the SD to gain control of the organization, was organized into thirteen regions, each led by a Regional O.K. Leader (Selbstschutzgebietsführer), who answered to the local police prefect.[2]

As the situation on the Eastern front worsened for the Germans, the Commander-in-Chief of the O.K., Kolonel A. Sinka, prepared his organization for the desperate fight that was to come. In February 1944 he ordered the raising of O.K. combat battalions (Omakaitse Lahingpataljon) and six months later, in August 1944, with the Red Army about to smash its way past Narva and into Estonia itself, Sinka ordered the grouping of these combat battalions into combat regiments (Omakaitse Lahingrügement - Selbstschutz Regiment).

These O.K. combat units fought desperately to halt the Russian advance between lakes Peipsi and Võrts and were all destroyed, the vast majority of their men killed.

The O.K. units were led entirely by Estonian officers, and the only German influence was a liaison officer (Verbindungsoffizier) and a few German NCOs in every battalion.[3]

All of the O.K. units are believed to have provided men for the 20th SS Division.

---

[1]A Feldkommandant commanded a Feldkommandantur, a field HQ established in rear areas and occupied countries, approximately equivalent to an Area Command.

[2]Amtlichter Anzeiger, Nr. 13, v. 31.7.1942, Art. 53, Anordnung über Organisation der Ordnungspolizei und des Selbstschutzes. See Mollo, Uniforms of the SS, Vol. 5: Sicherheitsdienst und Sicherheitspolizei 1931-1945, 1971, pg. 25.

[3]H. Rüütel, letter of 23.8.1981.

Useful at the front to the Wehrmacht, and at the rear to Einsatzgruppe A, as the Estonian partisan army may have been, the Germans were wary of this highly nationalistic, indigenous and entirely Estonian-led force and to the dismay of the Estonians set about disarming and disbanding it. No sooner had Tartu been taken in a combined effort by Estonian irregular forces and the Wehrmacht, a group of Estonians hoping to gain independence for their country from the German liberators presented the local Wehrmacht area commander with a memorandum on 29 July urging the establishment of a national Estonian government and the raising of an Estonian army from the guerrilla units that had fought the Russians in and around Tartu.[26] Some days later the group presented a copy of the memorandum to Generaloberst George von Küchler, G.O.C. 18th Army based in Viljandi, but were never to be given the courtesy of a direct reply from either German general. The Germans had no intention of tolerating the spread of nationalism in what they had called the "Ostland," let along the formation of national governments, and at that stage mistakenly believed they could gain victory on the Eastern front without a military contribution from the Baltic States. So it was that the proud Estonian guerrillas who had played such a vital rôle in liberating southern Estonia and had helped the Germans take Tartu were ignominiously disarmed when they broke ranks after the "victory parade" in Tartu on 29 July 1941.

All the other units of the Estonian partisan army were then systematically disbanded by the Germans, with the known exception of just three (two of battalion and one of company strength), which the Wehrmacht let carry on fighting intact for a few more months.[27] These were the already-mentioned "ERNA II," "Battalion of Major Hirvelaan" and "Company of Captain Talpak," all three of which were allowed to shed their blood and play important rôles in the successful capture of Tallinn in August 1941. The Hirvelaan battalion (its commander had been killed on the opening day of the attack) was then sent to the west of the capital to ward off any Russian attempts to land on the mainland from the islands they still held and to start organizing local self-defense (Omakaitse/Selbstschutz) groups. The battalion did in fact repel two Russian landing attempts and having successfully organized and trained the self-defense, was disbanded on 8 November 1941.

Captain Karl Talpak's company had been attached to a Germany Army division, and he fell from favor with the divisional commander when he refused to allow his men to follow the formation's eastern drive out of Estonia and on towards Leningrad. Talpak's refusal was typical of so many Estonians who agreed to fight with the Germans for the liberation of their country, but not as

---

[26]The group was centered upon Professor Jüri Uluots, last Prime Minister of the Estonian Republic before the Russian occupation. The memorandum was presented to the local Wehrmacht Feldkommandant.

[27]It is assumed that Uustalu (The History of Estonian People, pg. 251) was wrong in stating that all three units were of battalion size. If he was correct, then the identity of the third battalion-sized unit disbanded after the taking of Tallinn in late August 1941 remains a mystery.

Kapten Karl Talpak, in Finnish Army uniform.

a part of Hitler's war beyond the Estonian frontier. He wanted his men to continue fighting for the liberation of the Estonian islands and when after the capture of Tallinn on 28 August 1941 the Germans in turn refused his request to be allowed to do so, he ordered his company to hand its transport and heavy weapons over to the German division. Each member of the company was allowed to keep his rifle, 100 rounds of ammunition and was issued with a firearms certificate and a written statement of his service with the company signed by Talpak and a German officer. They were then ordered to report to their local self-defense units.[28]

The "ERNA II" battalion was allowed to continue fighting as an Estonian-led element of the partisan army after the capture of Tallinn and with Finnish help it played its part in driving the Red Army from the Estonian islands before being disbanded in October 1941.

Having disbanded the tough Estonian-led partisan units they feared they could not control and realizing they still needed Estonian help to destroy the Russian troops holding out in the north of the country, the German Army decided to raise new units from the many Estonians still anxious to fight, but under German rather than Estonian command. In the autumn of 1941, Generaloberst von Küchler, who earlier had received and ignored the request for the raising of a national army, instructed General Hans Knuth to raise Es-

---

[28]*Talpak went on to organize the flight of numerous Estonians to Finland and played a leading rôle in the training of J.R. 200 (see below pp. 179-181 & fn. 116).*

tonian combat units for his 18th Army.[29] These were to be the Estonian "Security Groups," later "Detachments," of which six were formed and numbered in the 18th Army's '180' series from 181 to 186.[30] The first (Julgestusgrupp 181 to the Estonians, estnische Sicherungs-Abteilung 181 to the Germans) was raised in Tartu on 29 August 1941, and the Estonians were so anxious to join that 2,000 men stepped forward for a unit requiring only 700. The Estonians would certainly have preferred joining units commanded by their own rather than German officers, but there was simply no choice. This desire to fight stemmed from nationalism and a wish to wreak revenge upon the Russians for their crimes during the unforgettable year of occupation - these volunteers, as Captain Talpak, had no interest in waging Hitler's war.

The six Estonian security detachments fought alongside the German Army and casualties, the failure of some men to sign on again at the expiration of their original year's contract, and general reluctance to cooperate with the Germans who refused to create an Estonian army, forced the Germans to merge them into three "East Battalions" and one "East Company."[31] The 181st, 182nd and 184th security detachments became the 658th, 659th and 660th "East Battalions" respectively, and the 13th company of the 184th was detached to become the 657th "East Company" (Ost-Btl. 657 (estn.)). The other three detachments were disbanded and their men absorbed into the three new battalions. Later, on 1 January 1943, these three East Battalions were to be renamed "Estonian Battalions" and in 1944 they were all incorporated into the Estonian Waffen-SS division (the 658th and 659th as complete units).[32]

The German Army was not, however, alone in enrolling Estonians into its service, and a rivalry was to begin between the military and Heinrich Himmler's

Men of the 658th and 659th East (after 1.1.1943 called Estonian) Battalions of the German 18th Army pose for photographs at the Tartu railway station on their way to the Narva front. These men wear German Army uniforms with type "A" (see page 217) sleeve shields on their upper right sleeves (note the same shaped shield with battalion

SS and Police.[33] Einsatzgruppe A had followed closely behind the Wehrmacht as it drove the Red Army from Estonia and had originally taken over control of the partisan groups. The SS and Police at once set about recruiting for Estonian "Schutzmannschafts-" battalions, and within the end of that first month of July 1941, an initial group of 396 Estonian volunteers was handed over to the Higher SS and Police Leader North Russia for police duties.[34] The SS and Police formed a number of Estonian "Schuma" battalions which, although originally intended for police duties at home, were committed to the front during the Russian winter offensive of 1941-42 where they were attached to Wehrmacht and Waffen-SS formations. Although inadequately trained and armed, these units fought well and suffered heavy casualties. It is no wonder the Estonians longed for the re-establishment of their own national army, or at least the chance to join closed Estonian units under their own officers. It is

---

[29]Knuth was Korück (Kommandant des rückwärtigen Armeegebietes - O.C. Army L. of C. area) 583 from 20 January 1941 to 20 June 1943.

[30]Estnische Sicherungsabteilung in German and Julgestusgrupp in Estonian. There were also non-Estonian units in the "180" series. Stein (op.cit., pg. 174) incorrectly gives the number as 8 and says that 4 of them were sent to fight with Army Group "North."

[31]The units were called Ost-Bataillon (estn.) and Ost-Kompanie (estn.) in German and Idapataljon and Idakompanii in Estonian. This conversion to "East Battalions" was also due to the German policy of standardizing Ost units.

[32]Estnische Bataillon in German and Eesti pataljon in Estonian.

[33]Estonia became a military district (Generalbezirk Estland) of the German Army, which in 1943 was commanded by General der Infanterie Kuno-Hans von Both, who was based in Tallinn. Von Both's immediate superior was General der Kavallerie Walther Braemer, Military C-in-C (Wehrmachtsbefehlshaber) Ostland with HQ in Riga (German Order of Battle, MIRS, The War Office, London, January 1944).

numbers fixed to their railway trucks). On 24.4.1944 these battalions became the IInd and Ist battalions of SS-Freiw.Gren.Rgt. 47 and upon issue of Waffen-SS uniforms may have retained their Army issue sleeve shields.
Source: Eesti riik ja rahvas II Maailmasõjas, Vol. IX, pp. 12 & 13.

perhaps ironic that the opportunity to attain this goal should not have been offered by the Wehrmacht, but by the military arm of Himmler's empire, the Waffen-SS.

JULY 1941 - SEPTEMBER 1944: THREE YEARS OF GERMAN OCCUPATION:

Hitler had decided how to rule Estonia and the other "occupied eastern territories" even before he ordered the Wehrmacht to turn on their bewildered former Russian allies at dawn on 22 June 1941. Estonia was to be a component of the "Ostland," controlled by a Reich Commissariat under Alfred Rosenberg's Reich Ministry for the Occupied Eastern Territories.[35]

Establishment of such civilian administration naturally had to wait for the total conquest of Estonia by the German armed forces and so was preceded by a period of martial law. Then SA-Obergruppenführer Karl-Sigismund Litzmann, a high-ranking veteran of the Nazi Party's "Kampfzeit," was brought in to rule the country as Governor-General (Generalkommissar), supported by a Provincial Governor (Gebietskommissar) in each country.[36] To give the impression that the local political leaders had some say in the running of their countries' affairs, indigenous "Self Administrations" (Landeseigene Verwaltungen) were set up in each of the Baltic States, and thus an all-Estonian Self-Administration was established under Dr. Hjalmar Mäe.[37] If anything, this had even less influence than its Latvian counterpart and was a mere puppet of the German occupiers, a powerless body used as a vehicle for the passing of orders and decrees.

In fact, who exercised most power in German-occupied Estonia was neither the military hierarchy nor politically appointed Governor-General Litzmann.

---

[34]HSSPF Russland-Nord. SS-FHA, Einberufungen zur Waffen-SS (T-175/110/2634485ff.) In November 1941 Hitler agreed to raise the Schutzmannschafts-Bataillonen, in which 9,000 Estonians were to serve. At first they were unnumbered and were known by the name of the place where they were stationed. Two groups of numbers were then allocated to these battalions, at first 29 to 42 and later 286 to 292. On 22.12.1943 the Estnische Schutzmannschaftsbataillone were renamed "Estonian Police Battalions" - the same had happened to the Latvian "Schuma" on 24 May 1943. Although the abbreviation "Schuma" does not appear to have been used officially, it is used in this book for the sake of convenience. The Estonians called the Schutzmannschaftsbataillon a Kaitsepataljon (literally a "defense battalion") and the Estonian Polizei-Bataillon an Eesti Politsei pataljon.

[35]Reichskommissariat für das Ostland - Reichsministerium für die besetzten Ostgebiete (R.M.f.d.b.O.), or Ostministerium. It is of interest that Rosenberg was born in Estonia (H. Rüütel, letter of 23.8.81).

[36]Karl-Sigismund (also found as Karl Sigmund, and even just Sigmund) Litzmann rose to high rank within the SA even before Hitler came to power (SA-Gruppenführer in 1931 and SA-Obergruppenführer in 1933). He was leader of SA Group "Ostland" (Führer SA-Gruppe Ostland) in 1932, but, of course, this had nothing to do with what was later called the "Ostland," and this Group covered East Prussia and Danzig (it was later renamed SA-Gruppe "Tannenberg"). By 1934 he was leader of SA-Obergruppe II (based in Stettin, this controlled three SA Groups) and responsible for horse-breeding and control (Leiter der oberst. Behörden für Pferdezucht und Prüfung). By late 1937 he was national training inspector for riding and driving (Reichsinspekteur für Reit- und Fahrausbildung) with his HQ in Berlin, a post he held until his appointment as Governor of Estonia in 1941.

[37]Mäe's title in German was Landesdirektor (local director), in Estonian "Eesti Omavalitsuse Juht" (Estonian Self-Administration Leader).

(above) SA-Obergruppenführer Karl-Sigismund Litzmann, Governor-General of Estonia.

(right) Governor-General Litzmann (at right) in conversation with Alfred Rosenberg, Reich Minister for the Occupied Eastern Territories. In the center in a dark suit is the leader of the Estonian Self-Administration, Dr. Hjalmar Mäe. Tallinn, 1942.

It was the misleadingly junior SS-Sturmbannführer (Major) Dr. Martin Sandberger who, after leading Sonderkommando 1a of Einsatzgruppe A into Estonia in the summer of 1941, had been installed in Tallinn in December of that year as commander of the German Security Police and SD in Estonia.[38]

---

[38]*Sandberger held no military rank and, having been an SS-Sturmbannführer since 9 November 1938, was promoted to SS-Obersturmbannführer on 9 November 1942. Maasing was, therefore, premature in referring to Sandberger as such at the time of his first meeting (Eesti riik ja rahvas II Maailmasõjas, Vol. VII, pg. 17).*

With the Russians driven from their country, Estonians settled down to the lesser evil of a German occupation that was to last for three years. For the majority, gone was the terror of arrest, deportation and an uncertain fate at the hands of the secret police, but it did not take the Estonians long to realize that the Germans had as little intention of granting them any degree of independence as had the Russians. The first pleas to the German Army to allow the establishment of an Estonian government and national army made after the liberation of Tartu at the end of July 1941 had been ignored, and the same pointed lack of interest and sympathy met all further attempts. Among the Estonian officers at home and abroad (mainly in Finland) there was a great desire to see the re-establishment of the former Republic's National Army, an Estonian force led by Estonian officers which they felt could serve its country infinitely better than the badly trained and inadequately armed German-raised battalions, scattered as they were among German formations at the front. The realists feared the turning of the tide for the Germans in the East and how this could lead a retreating Wehrmacht to abandon Estonia, undefended and without a national force to face the vengeful returning Red Army.[39]

A chance to put the Estonians' case to the Germans came in early February 1942 when Colonel Richard Maasing, who had recently been sent from the staff of the Finnish Commander-in-Chief to the German military control center in Tallinn,[40] was invited to the office of the commander of the German Security Police and SD in Estonia on Tõnismäe. Sandberger, in office for only two months, proceeded to explain to Maasing his views on security arrangements in Estonia.

First, the front line had moved east and so Estonia could be considered a rear area. This meant that the German Army no longer had any say in the territory which was now under Sandberger's jurisdiction and he, as commander of the Security Police and SD, was the highest German authority in the country with sole responsibility for the organizing of internal security of the country and its border areas. Sandberger went on by saying that he would be making all appointments of Estonians, especially of Estonian military personnel to administrative posts and that he invited all former Estonian officers still in the country (for, as has been seen, many had fled to Finland) to work for him - he would give them posts in the SD, police, the self-defense organization, and so on.

Colonel Maasing bravely took the opportunity to counter the German's demands with the views he shared with the majority of Estonian soldiers and people as a whole. He could not accept that the front had moved sufficiently far from Estonia to allow it to be considered a rear area: hard and bitter fighting was being waged as they spoke around Leningrad, and Soviet partisans were active east of Narva and around Lake Peipsi. In Maasing's view there was precious little time for the Germans to give the Estonians, who

---

[39] *In reality, it was to be combat regiments of the Omakaitse who made the last desperate stand against the Red Army in 1944.*

[40] *OKW Abwehrstelle Estland, located near the HQ of Admiral Burchard on Freedom Square (Vabadusplats) in the EKA Building.*

found it unpleasant to serve in the SD, police and "Schuma" battalions, permission to reorganize their national army. He urged the Germans to allow Estonian military units under the leadership of Estonian officers to assume the internal and border defense of Estonia and that of the area between Lake Ilmen and Leningrad.

Sandberger was doubtless surprised and not a little displeased by this outburst of views so conflicting with his own. He curtly informed Colonel Maasing that the re-establishment of an Estonian national army was totally out of the question and dismissing him brought the fruitless meeting to a close.

Unwilling to give in to what he considered unreasonable demands, Maasing flew to Finland and made a personal appeal to Marshal Gustaf Mannerheim to intervene to try and pursuade the Germans to allow the Estonians to raise a national army. But the proud old Finnish Commander-in-Chief said he could not assist Estonia in this way, and a downcast Colonel Maasing returned to Tallinn.

In early March 1942 Maasing had his second and last meeting with Sandberger. When asked whether he had changed his mind, Maasing replied that he was more convinced than ever of the need for a national army. Sandberger brought the encounter to an end by declaring that there was nothing left to discuss.

Unaware of the unproductive meetings between Colonel Maasing and Dr. Sandberger and Litzmann's relative impotence in such matters, the Estonian people had great hopes that the Governor-General would take the opportunity of the festive assembly at the "Estonia" theatre in Tallinn on independence day, 24 February 1942, to make an announcement about the Estonian military question. The hopes of many that Litzmann would actually announce that the Germans had agreed to the re-creation of their national army were dashed when, in anticlimax, all he authorized was the wearing of the Cross of Freedom by Estonians who had fought in the war of liberation 1918-20.[41]

Realists within the German Army were becoming more aware of the growing need for military support from the people of the "Ostland" and the German military leaders in Estonia were consequently far more tactful and diplomatic than Governor-General Litzmann and the more sinister and influential Dr. Sandberger. Rather than alienating the Estonians by openly crushing their aspirations for the rebirth of a national army, generals such as Otto Schneider, military commandant of the key northweatern city of Narva, paid tribute to the efforts and sacrifice of the Estonians in driving the Russians from their land. Here is what Schneider said to the people of Narva on that same independence day, 24 February 1942:[42]

---

[41]*The central motif of the Cross of Freedom provided the design for collar patch and vehicle sign for the Estonian Waffen-SS - see below, pp. 210.*

[42]*Eesti riik ja rahvas II Maailmasõjas, Vol. VII, pp. 18-19. Otto Schneider, a Generalmajor from 1.12.1941, had been put in charge of Feldkommandantur (FK or administrative sub-area HQ) 189 in mid-May 1941. In this capacity he became military commandant of Narva when FK 189 was established there after the town's capture from the Russians. Schneider left Narva on 20.7.1943 and went on to command FK 298 (10.3.1944 - 1.12.1944).*

Today on 24 February the Estonian people celebrate the day of regaining their freedom. The German soldiers who have seen with their own eyes the tyranny of the Bolsheviks, must express their respect and honor to these Estonian men who led Estonia to freedom. German soldiers have seen the vast difference between the cultural and economic achievements in Estonia and the Soviet Union. German soldiers have a good picture of the progress which was possible in Estonia because it was a free country. Two years ago Estonia fell once again under the terror of the Soviet Union. Again the attempt to regain their freedom cost the Estonians new blood and material losses. The help received by the German soldiers from the Estonian people serves as proof of the fact that they, the Estonians, want to protect themselves from the Soviet terror. The events which have taken place in the past few years should make us conclude that the fight against Bolshevism should not be left to a few nations. A unified Europe should join in this fight under a unified leadership. Only a united Europe's joint power under a unified leadership can keep this danger in check which threatens the whole world. The German Army is forced to suffer still more losses, still the Estonian people, and especially in the border region of Narva, must suffer and bring many sacrifices. Our goal must be to give the world a longer lasting peace which results from new ideas, to create a world based on cultural and economic wellbeing. Today the German Army hopes that the Estonian people will be happy again in the very near future.

Such fighting talk from the soldiers who, aided by Estonian freedom fighters, had driven the Russians from their land naturally appealed more than anything the German civilian authorities, SS and Police were prepared to say at the time, but the German Army had no say in the political problems in the East for this was the domain of Rosenberg's "East Ministry," Governor-General Litzmann and Himmler's powerful representative in Estonia, Dr. Sandberger.

In July 1942, Colonel Ludvig Jakobsen, who had been the Estonian military attaché in Berlin before the war, visited Tallinn and appraising the highly unsatisfactory situation sent a secret letter to the head of the Abwehr (German military counter-intelligence), Admiral Wilhelm Canaris. Openly critical of the use the Estonian volunteers were being put to, he urged the establishment of an "Estonian National Division":[43]

14 July 1942
SECRET

Your Excellency Admiral Canaris:

I consider it my duty to present to you some observations concerning the Estonian voluntary soldiers.

---

[43] *ibid, pp. 19-20. Colonel Ludvig Jakobsen KS dipl. died on 11.12.61 (H. Rüütel, letters of 23.8.81 & 30.9.81).*

Today 20,000 Estonians are fighting side by side with the Germans east of Lake Peipsi, partly at the front and partly behind the lines against the parachutists and Soviet guerrilla forces.

The Estonians are grouped in single battalions and are subordinated to the SD and SS. Most of these voluntary soldiers are young. The Estonian battalions lived through a difficult winter. They were poorly dressed. Their welfare is poor. The pay which they receive in the so-called "Schutzmanschafts-" battalions is absolutely irregular. The Estonian officers are not given credit for their former ranks. In some battalions they are known as "Sonderführer." The food rations in these battalions are smaller than in the German Army. The battalions are extremely poorly armed. Worst of all is the fact that there is no central unified leadership. Often the actual commanders are German lieutenants and sergeants.

The circumstances mentioned above have caused the morale in the Estonian units to be very low. There are cases of breaches in discipline, something unknown in the Estonian Army. The men complain that the promises that were made to them upon mobilization have not been kept. It was promised that the Estonian units would defend the Estonian border, but they are being sent elsewhere.

I must emphasize that the Estonian officers and the young soldiers do not want to serve in the "police battalions," but want to enter into action as an "Estonian unit."

The SD in Estonia is now planning to gather some Estonian "Schutzmannschafts-" battalions into units of regimental size. This neither improves the situation nor satisfies the Estonians.[44]

The only way to remedy the situation would be to form an "Estonian National Division." This should be clearly an Estonian military formation.

Sincerely,
L. Jakobsen
Colonel of the former
Estonian Army

The situation had certainly changed in that first year of German occupation. The Wehrmacht, who upon arrival in July 1941 had scoffed at the need for military help from the Balts, had learned bitter lessons in the 1941/1942 winter campaign on the Russian front and realized that the war in the East was going to be a long and difficult one and that Germany would need all the help she

---

[44] *This happened later. The 1st Estonian Police Regiment (1. Estnische Polizei-Regiment) was formed from the 37th, 38th and 40th Schuma battalions and a specially formed antitank company (Estn. Pol.PAK-Kp.). It was disbanded (August 1944?), the 40th battalion and antitank company being absorbed by the 38th battalion and sent to the front along with the 37th battalion. Both battalions were later absorbed by the 20th SS Division.*

German and Estonian officials salute at a march past in Tartu on 25 July 1942, celebrating the first anniversary of the liberation of the town from the Russians. Second from left, with his arm raised in the Nazi salute, is SS-Sturmbannführer Dr. Martin Sandberger, commander of the Security Police and SD in Estonia. In light-colored dougle-breasted suit with his arms by his sides is Paul Keerdoja, Mayor of Tartu. The stout figure with moustache in dark suit and holding a hat is the puppet leader of the Estonian Self-Administration, Dr. Hjalmar Mäe, following Sandberger in giving the Nazi salute. The German Army general (giving a military salute) to Mäe's left is unidentified, but to his left is Nikolaus Graf von Üxküll, the Baltic German military commandant (Feldkommandant) of Tartu. The German Political Leader, second from right in this photograph, is the adjutant to the Provincial Governor (Gebietskommissar) of Tartu.

Source: Eesti riik ja rahvas II Maailmasõjas, Vol. VIII, pg. 143.

could get. Many officers disagreed with Hitler's eastern policy and favored increased autonomy within the Baltic States, including the freedom to raise national armed forces. But the German civilian and police authorities on the other hand had either no idea of the real difficulties facing the Wehrmacht or simply refused to face facts: they acted as if the war was as good as won and their high-handed behavior lost them what little sympathy they may have had with the Estonian people.

In spite of their more realistic attitude towards the employment of Estonian volunteers, and an overwhelming preference on the part of the Estonians to join a military rather than para-military force, the German Army was continually out-maneuvered by Himmler's SS and Police when it came to authority over the Estonian military situation. After German troops entered Estonia in July 1941, the Army and Police set about raising their own and quite separate units of Estonian volunteers. The Army had raised just six "Estonian Security Detachments" by the autumn of 1941 and rather than raising more was soon obliged to concentrate their Estonian volunteers into a meagre three "East Battalions" and an "East Company." The SS and Police on the other hand had enrolled far more men into their "Schuma" battalions and continued to do so during 1942 and 1943. Moreover, Dr. Sandberger did his best to wrestle control of the Army's "East Battalions" away from the local Army field commanders during the summer of 1942 - for a while he failed and the Army retained control, but eventually these battalions were to come under the dominion of the SS.[45]

AUGUST 1942 - MAY 1943: THE ESTONIAN SS LEGION:

The Estonians viewed with increasing dismay the swing in power and influence away from their Wehrmacht liberators towards the SS, and when at last in early August 1942 Hitler authorized the raising of an "Estonian Legion" this was, at Himmler's request, to be an element of the Waffen-SS and not of the German Army.[46] Orders were passed from Berlin to Governor-General Litzmann in Tallinn, and he issued a corresponding proclamation on 28 August 1942, exhorting the Estonians to step forward and join the Estonian Legion. The date was significant and had been chosen deliberately: it was the first anniversary of the German liberation of the Estonian capital of Tallinn from the Russians.[47]

Sandberger had handed out appointments to a group of Estonian officers he felt he could trust, and it was through them in September 1942 that he made quite clear to the Estonian officer corps that the new Legion was to be an element of the SS rather than the Wehrmacht. Perhaps the Estonians were unaware of the distinction between the para-military "SS and Police" on the one hand that had so inefficiently run the unpopular "Schuma" battalions, and the predominantly military Waffen-SS on the other to which the new Legion was to belong, for Estonia was the first Baltic country to be allowed to raise a Waffen-SS formation (German Waffen-SS troops had fought in the liberation of their country, however). In any case, the news was received with opposition

---

[45]*An early attempt by the SS to gain control of the "East Battalions" was blocked by the Army (SS-FHA, v. 31.7.1942 geh., Einberufungen zur Waffen-SS - T-175/110/2634485ff.). KTB/OKW 2.12.1943, IV, 1328f. records how the Army was forced to turn its "Estonian Battalions" over to the Waffen-SS (see Stein, op.cit., pg. 174). The SD tried to gain control of the territorial Omakaitse (self-defense organization) in the summer of 1942, but failed. Survivors of the O.K. went to the Waffen-SS.*

[46]*The following is probably an incomplete listing of the SS establishments in Tallinn:*
- SS Fürsorge Kommando Estland (welfare HQ - reported at 7.9.1944)
- SS-Fürsorgeoffizier/Fürsorgeoffizier der Waffen-SS Estland (welfare officer - reported in February 1944)
- part of SS Funkschutz Abteilung (wireless protection battalion)
- Branch of SS und Polizei Gericht, XVI Rīga (court)
- Ersatz-Kommando der Waffen-SS Ostland, Nebenstelle Reval (Tallinn branch of the Ostland replacement training command - reported as such on 1.4.1944 - name changed in the summer of 1944 to Ersatz-Inspektion der Waffen-SS Ostland - SS-Ersatzkommando Estland also reported)
- Truppenwirtschaftslager der Waffen-SS (supply depot).
The Estonian Waffen-SS training and replacement element was moved from Heidelager in Poland to Klooga near Tallinn and was reported there on 15.4.1944. (Installations and Establishments of the SS, April 1945, MIRS/OCC-C1/34/45, London).

[47]*Reports that Litzmann made his proclamation on 26.8.1942 are wrong - this may have been the date he received instructions from Germany (H. Rüütel, letter of 23.8.81).*

and dismay, especially by those Estonian officers already serving in the battalions raised by the 18th Army, and strenuous attempts were made to try and reverse the decision. Estonian officers took pains to explain to the German High Command how they and their men would much prefer to fight in an Army-controlled force, and a Captain Kurgvel was a particularly bold and straightforward spokesman in this respect. The German Army sympathized and would undoubtedly have preferred having dominion over the new Legion, but they had far less influence in these matters, and in any event there was no question of changing Hitler's decision.

The Waffen-SS had looked to the Baltic States as a suitable new source of manpower for some time, and its recruiting chief, Gottlob Berger, had proposed the raising of Baltic Waffen-SS formations to Himmler as early as May 1942.[48] Estonia was chosen to provide the first Waffen-SS contingent for it was felt that the Estonians were the most pro-German and according to Himmler's confused racial theories, they were of "purer" racial stock.

The SS-FHA order of 29 September 1942 provided that men for the Legion should assemble on 1 October 1942 at the SS training area (SS-Truppenübungsplatz) Debica in the General Government (as Poland had become) and that training and the raising of the required elements should begin.[49] The uniform was to be that of the Waffen-SS, but recruits should wear plain black collar patches on both sides of the collar.[50] The language of command was to be German, and the oath to be taken read as follows:

"Ich schwöre bei Gott diesen heiligen Eid, dass ich im Kampf gegen den Bolschewismus dem Obersten Befehlshaber der deutschen Wehrmacht, Adolf Hitler, unbedingten Gehorsam leisten und als tapferer Soldat bereit sein will, jederzeit für diesen Eid mein Leben einzusetzen."

"I swear by God this holy oath, that in the struggle against Bolshevism I shall give the C-in-C of the German Armed Forced, Adolf Hitler, absolute obedience and as a brave soldier I will always be ready to lay down my life for this oath."

Contrary to what was soon to happen in Latvia, in the case of Estonia the term "Legion" was not used at first generically to describe all indigenous elements serving with the German forces (Army, Luftwaffe, Kriegsmarine, Waffen-SS, Police, etc.) but rather it signified a specific military unit, at first planned with the composition of a motorized infantry regiment.[51]

[48]Waffen-SS recruiting chief and head of the SS Main Office Gottlob Berger had favored the establishment of Baltic Waffen-SS formations and submitted such a proposal to Himmler in May 1942 (Stein, op.cit., pg. 175).

[49]See fn. 1 on page 122 of this book.

[50]This only applied to new recruits and NCOs; officers were permitted to show their rank on the left collar patch.

[51]Evidence suggests that the meaning of the term "Legion," when applied to Estonia, was later changed to take on the same generic significance as had been used in Latvia all along. On 14.5.1944 the HSSPF Ostland & Russland-Nord laid down orally

On 23 November 1942 a German formation staff (Aufstellungsstab) and a group of assistant instructors arrived at the Debica training grounds from the IIIrd SS "Totenkopf" Infantry Replacement Battalion at Brno.[52] They had come to instruct the Estonian volunteers, but lack of enthusiasm to join the Legion had resulted in difficulty in raising the required number of men. In the first two months of the recruiting drive, only 500 Estonians had stepped forward, and half of these had come from a previous tour of duty in the Schuma battalions.[53] The Legion was at once strengthened by 200 Germans (by citizenship or racial origin) and so from the very beginning was never to be a purely Estonian force.

In the winter of 1942/1943 the Estonian Legion's composition was:[54]

Stab mit Stabs-Kp.	HQ with HQ company
I. Btl. (1. - 4.)	Ist battalion (1st - 4th companies)
II. Btl. (5. - 8.)	IInd battalion (5th - 8th companies)
III. Btl. (9. - 12.)	IIIrd battalion (9th - 12th companies)
schwere Granatwerfer-Kp.	heavy mortar company
Infanterie-Panzerjäger-Kp.	infantry antitank company

Such a regiment should, in fact, have had an infantry gun (13th) company, but shortage of infantry guns obliged the unit to use heavy mortars and be designated accordingly. The infantry antitank company should have been numbered the 14th from the very beginning.

Propaganda was then stepped up and every prefecture was obliged to send a certain number of policemen as "volunteers" for the Legion (action doubtless prompted by Dr. Sandberger). Even so, as was also to happen in Latvia, all did not go smoothly with the raising of the Legion. Equipment and barracks were inadequate and the recruiting program was mismanaged. In spite of these problems and the Estonians' wariness of the SS and definite preference to serve with the German Army, sufficient numbers did eventually come forward. The Legion numbered 37 Estonian officers, 175 NCOs and 757 other ranks at the end of March 1943.[55] 1,280 men had enrolled before the spring of

---

that individual indigenous policemen in Estonia as well as in Latvia belonged to the respective SS legions. This was put on record by Oberstleutnant der Schutzpolizei Flick in an order he signed in Rīga on 17.5.1944 on behalf of the Chief of Staff of the Order Police (Der Befehlshaber der Ordnungspolizei für das Ostland, KdO. Abt. V 28.13/44, Riga den 17. Mai 1944 - reporduced in Latviešu karavīrs Otra pasaules kara laikā, Vol. 2, pg. 379.

[52] *SS-Totenkopf-Infanterie-Ersatz-Bataillon III, Brno (Brünn), Czechoslovakia. Klietmann, op.cit., pg. 225.*

[53] *According to Uustalu (For Freedom Only, pg. 18) only 500 Estonians volunteered for the Legion in the first two months of the recruiting campaign. When giving 700 Estonian volunteers for the same period, Stein (op.cit., pg. 176) may possibly have made the mistake of including the 200 Germans in this number - although he does give 700 Estonians plus 200 Germans.*

[54] *Klietmann, op.cit., pg. 225.*

[55] *Divisions-Stammtafel 31.3.1943, BAMA, S15 - 20/1.*

1943, and this number was to rise to 6,500 Estonians within the first six months of the Legion's existence. Deficiencies in the recruiting program however led to only 2,850 of these 6,500 having been called up for service by 15 April 1943.[56]

Recruiting poster for the Estonian SS Legion, 1943. The soldier being offered flowers by an Estonian girl in traditional national costume wears the SS runes on the collar patch, a practice at first forbidden. The text reads: "PRIDE OF THE ESTONIAN PEOPLE: ESTONIAN LEGIONNAIRE!"
Source: Eesti riik ja rahvas II Maailmasõjas, Vol. IX, pg. 164.

Heinrich Himmler had been keeping an eye on progress in Estonia and in January 1943 visited a group of 54 Estonian legionnaires undergoing training at a Waffen-SS NCO school and came away impressed - this was the same month that he visited Latvian Schuma battalions in action on the Leningrad front and ordered the raising of a Latvian SS Legion around them.[57]

It has already been seen how the Legion comprised a large number of Germans from the beginning, 200 having joined in the first two months. The German influence was strengthened further on 21 January 1943 when the two officers, 24 NCOs and 62 men of the disbanded 1st company of the Waffen-SS Battalion for Special Employment were taken into the Estonian SS Legion at Debica. Under their company commander, SS-Hauptsturmführer Fritz Störtz, many of these men had participated in the mass killings carried out by Einsatzgruppe A in the wake of Army Group "North's" drive through the Baltic States in the summer of 1941 and had assisted the Security Police and SD in dubious 'security' operations to the rear of the front in the "Ostland."[58]

---

[56]Klietmann, op.cit., pg. 223; Uustalu, For Freedom Only, pg. 18; Duprat, Histoire des SS, pg. 364; Stein, op.cit., pg. 176. Duprat gives 6,500 in the first four months - Stein gives the same number after six months.

[57]The SS-Unterführerschule has not been identified (Stein, op.cit., pg. 175). See Vol. 4, pg. 68 in this series, and this book, pg. 60.

[58]1. Komp./Batl. der Waffen-SS z.b.V. (zur besondere Verwendung) was formed from Sonderbataillon "Dern" under SS-Obersturmführer Rosenow and had been a part of Einsatzgruppe A that had carried out mass killings in the wake of Army Group "North" as it drove the Red Army back through the Baltic States. After serving under the C-in-C Security Police & SD (Befehlshaber der Sipo u. SD) "Ostland" in Riga and

On 22 February 1943 a training and replacement battalion was formed for the Estonian Legion at Debica, and two days later on 24 February 1943 the Reichs Commissar for the Ostland ordered the drafting of men born between 1919 and 1924.[59] In theory the draftees were free to choose between the Legion and special labor companies, but in practice poor conditions in the latter and pressure brought to bear on the men by the staff of the draft boards drove many to choose the Legion. Thus of the 12,100 Estonians recruited between March and August 1943, 5,300 opted for the Waffen-SS Legion, the other 6,800 chose to serve as support elements of the Wehrmacht.[60]

The order of battle of the Legion, built as a motorized infantry regiment, was the following in early 1943:[61]

---

then the Higher SS & Police Leader & C-in-C Rear Area of Army Group "North," the company was ordered to the SS "Totenkopf" Division with effect from 1.10.1941 and was actually incorporated in SS-Totenkopf-Infanterie-Regiment 3 in mid-October 1941 (see SS-FHA, Org.Tgb.Nr. 4057/41 geh., Kompanien des Bataillons der Waffen-SS z.b.V., v. 24.9.1941 - T-175/109/2633183 & Sydnor, Soldiers of Destruction, pg. 323 & fn. 19). In fact, it remained with "Totenkopf" for only a short time and soon reverted to the orders of the C-in-C Security Police & SD, fighting partisans and carrying out executions in the rear areas, from time to time placed under the command of Wehrmacht units. The company's IIIrd platoon (III. Zug) did see proper front-line duty and was reduced to five survivors in the 1941/1942 winter battle at Cholm as a part of Kampfgruppe "Scherer." Estonians and Latvians were then used to bring the unit back up to strength, and it provided two groups that served in SD-Jagdkommandos in White Russia under the C-in-C of the Security Police & SD, while men from the Ist platoon served in a Jagdkommando under the C-in-C Security Police & SD in Estonia, Dr. Martin Sandberger. Following Störtz's repeated entreaties to the C-in-C Security Police & SD "Ostland" that he and his company be allowed to serve as a combat unit of the Waffen-SS, on 19.12.1942 the SS-FHA ordered the whole company to go through the SD to Debica to be disbanded and incorporated into the Estonian SS Legion (Kommandoamt der Waffen-SS, Org.Tgb.Nr. 8699/42, v. 19.12.1942 - T-175/140/). Klietmann is wrong in identifying this company as 11. Komp./Batl. der Waffen-SS z.b.V. and in saying that only a group of NCOs went to the Estonian Legion (op.cit., pg. 225). P. H. Buss points out that the Batl. der Waffen-SS z.b.V. (ex Sonderbataillon "Dern") was not the same Batl. der Waffen-SS z.b.V which was formed in September 1942 by redesignating SS-Sonderkommando Künsberg.

[59]The battalion appears at first to have been called simply "replacement battalion of the Estonian SS Legion" (Ersatzbataillon der Estn. SS-Legion). It was renamed "SS-Grenadier-Ausbildungs- und Ersatz-Bataillon 33" when the Legion achieved brigade status, and "SS-Grenadier-Ausbildungs- und Ersatz-Bataillon 20" when it became a division. The unit was transferred from Debica to Klooga near Tallinn and was reported there on 15.4.1944 as "SS-Panzer- (sic!) Grenadier-Ausbildungs- und Ersatz-Einheit 20" by Allied Intelligence (Installations and Establishments of the SS, April 1945, MIRS/OCC-C1/34/45, London). A new training and replacement battalion (SS-Ausbildungs- und Ersatz-Bataillon 20) was formed from the Division's original SS-F.E.B. 20 and was expanded to a regiment (SS-Ausbildungs- und Ersatz-Regiment 20 - also called SS-Ersatz-Regiment 20) on 6.12.1944. The regiment was sent by rail from Forst/Neisse to Odense in Denmark on 15.2.1945 and remained there until the end of the war.

[60]Uustalu, For Freedom Only, pg. 19.

[61]SS-FHA, Kommandoamt der Waffen-SS, Abt. Feldpostwesen, Geheime Kommandosache, Feldpostübersicht der Waffen-SS, I. Teil, Vorliegende Ausgabe enthält Blatt I und 1 - 30, Berlin, 1943 (Bundesarchiv-Militärarchiv, 593/64).

ESTNISCHE SS-LEGION	ESTONIAN SS LEGION
Rgt.Stab	regimental HQ
Stabs-Kompanie	HQ company
schw. Granatw.Kompanie	heavy mortar company
Panz.Jäg.Kompanie	antitank company
Pionier-Kompanie	engineer company
I. Btl.	Ist battalion
Stab	HQ
1. - 4. Kompanie	1st - 4th companies
II. Btl.	IInd battalion
Stab	HQ
5. - 8. Kompanie	5th - 8th companies
III. Btl.	IIIrd battalion
Stab	HQ
9. - 12. Kompanie	9th - 12th companies

This order of battle is virtually the same as given above for the winter of 1942/43, except for the addition of the three battalion HQs and engineer company and the deletion of the adjective "infantry" from the title of the antitank company. Availability of only heavy mortars prevented the renaming of the heavy mortar company to an infantry gun (IG-) company such a regiment required, but the guns did eventually arrive and the company's title changed.[62] The regimental heavy mortar (later infantry gun), antitank and engineer companies should and were soon after numbered 13th, 14th and 15th respectively.

In March 1943 the Germans decided upon a number of changes to the Legion, the most significant of which was far from popular with the Estonians. Con-

This poster outside a recruiting office for the Estonian SS Legion reads "Waffen-SS 'Estonian Legion' volunteer registration."

---

[62]*It is possible that separate infantry gun and heavy mortar companies existed contemporaneously. If so, then the IG company would have been intended to replace the heavy mortar company, which would eventually have been wound up.*

An Estonian private soldier and German NCO of the Estonian SS Legion at the Debica SS training grounds in early 1943. The recruit at left wears the plain black collar patch as laid down by regulations, and from the ribbon of the Medal for the Winter Campaign in Russia 1941/1942 on his tunic one can tell that he served in Russia with either the German Army or Schuma battalions. The upper arrow sign points to the Ist battalion of the Estonian SS Legion, which was detached from the rest in April 1943 and served with the "Wiking" Division as SS-Panzer-Grenadier-Bataillon "Narwa."

trary to assurances that the Legion would only be used in or near Estonia, it had been decided to detach its senior, Ist, battalion, made up of the 800 Estonians most fluent in the German language and who were considered by the Waffen-SS to be the racial élite, and send them to the already multi-national "Wiking" Division fighting in the Ukraine.[63] This was ordered on 3 March 1943 and put into effect on 4 April.[64] The battalion was detached, renamed an SS-

[63]*The battalion strength of 1,280 given by Jüri Remmelgas in Kolm kuuske (Kirjastus EMP, Stockholm, 1955, pg. 130) presumably applied to a later date.*

[64]*Tessin gives 3.3.1943 (Vol. 14, pg. 69) and Klietmann 23.3.1943 (pg. 225). as the date the Ist battalion was detached. In fact, "Narwa" left Heidelager on 4.4.1943 (H. Rüütel, letter of 4.10.1981).*

Estonian Combatants Association in GB

Two officers of the Estonian SS Legion (at right Legions-Hauptsturmführer Harald Riipalu with buttons on his sleeve) wear the plain black right hand collar patch at the SS training area (SS-Truppenübungsplatz) Debica in Poland, 1943.

Grenadier-Bataillon (mot.) and joined "Wiking" at first as "Estnisches SS-Freiwilligen-Bataillon 'Narwa,' " later as "SS-Pz.Gren.Btl. 'Narwa,' " named after the town of Narva close to the Russian border which had been the scene of such bitter fighting in 1941 and was to be so again in 1944.[65] The battalion was to be away for 16 months and when its survivors were to return they were used as the foundation of an infantry reconnaissance (Füsilier-) battalion for what had in the meantime become the Estonian Division of the Waffen-SS.

When its Ist battalion was detached in April 1943, the remainder of the Legion was used as the basis for what was named the 1st Estonian Volunteer Regiment (1. Estn. SS-Freiw.Gren.Rgt.), made up of HQ, three battalions and 13th (infantry gun) and 15th (engineer) companies.[66]

Whether by coincidence or design, Estonian officers serving with the German Army chose Hitler's 54th birthday (20 April 1943) to submit through the Ger-

---

[65] *SS-Grenadier-Bataillon (mot.) & Estnisches SS-Freiwilligen-Bataillon "Narwa" are given by Klietmann (op.cit., pg. 225) - SS-Panzergrenadier-Btl. "Narwa" by Tessin (op.cit., Vol. 14, pg. 184). SS-Gren.Btle. (mot.) were renamed SS-Pz.Gren.Btle. throughout the Waffen-SS. This battalion should not be confused with Estnisches Ersatz-Bataillon "Narwa" (also called Estnische Ost-Ersatz-Bataillon "Narwa") which was formed at Narva in the spring of 1943 and was commanded by the German Oberleutnant Fischer.*

[66] *Klietmann (op.cit., pg. 225) does not list the 14th (antitank) company. According to Tessin (op.cit., Vol. 14, pg. 69) only 400 men were left when the Ist battalion was detached in 1943.*

man Fregattenkapitän Cellarius in Tallinn to the Wehrmacht High Command (OKW) their stand on the question of the Estonian Legion. This document read as follows:[67]

20 April 1943
Tallinn

Re: The Estonian Legion

After Tallinn was captured in 1941, many Estonian voluntary units were disbanded. This disappointed the Estonians. Later when the front line stopped before Leningrad, the mobilization of Estonians into the police and defense battalions began. In the beginning a great number of officers joined in the belief that these units would go into action as Estonian units. These battalions became famous because of their bravery. Unfortunately, these units were dispersed and used for various tasks, especially in the winter battles of 1941/1942. The achievements and victories of these units went unacknowledged; no mention was made of the fact that the "Estonian battalions" took part in these battles.

In the autumn of 1942 permission was received for the formation of the "Estonian Legion." The Estonians wanted clarification on the following matters above all else:

1) who would be appointed to lead the Legion;
2) the strength of the Legion;
3) the Legion's armament.

For a time no information was received at all. This led the Estonians to be extremely cautious. At last it was announced that the German SS-Obersturmbannführer Augsberger had been appointed as commander of the Legion. At the same time it was announced that Estonian officers would be appointed to the posts in the Legion if they were found capable of leadership. And finally, it was announced that the Legion would be a modern motorized element which could also be used outside Estonia.

This proved to be of no help. There were no volunteers for the Legion.

Now the forceful sending of "volunteers" to the Legion began. "Volunteers" are also transferred from the Estonian police and SD units to the Legion. In order to remedy the situation the SD has formed from better known Estonians a society - "The Friends of the Legion."

Rumor has been spread that the Estonian officers are the real leaders of the Legion and the Legion will be placed in the defense of the Estonian frontier.

To date six classes of Estonian youngsters have been registered and each of them personally notified that they must report for duty in the Labor Service (Arbeitsdienst). These youths have been told that if they

---

[67]*Eesti riik ja rahvas II Maailmasõjas, Vol. VII, pp. 20-21.*

volunteer for the Legion they will be released from their Labor Service obligation. These youths are being forced into the Legion.

With all kinds of pressures 8,000 men have been mobilized into the Estonian Legion.

Great harm was done to the Legion when its Ist battalion was sent to the Ukraine to strengthen a German SS regiment. A promise was thus broken. It is clear that following this Estonians do not want to join the Legion.

Estonian Landesdirektor Mäe and some of his closer subordinates have openly accused the Estonian officers of having forgotten their duty when they refused to join the Legion. Landesdirektor Mäe demands that all Estonian officers and NCOs report as volunteers for the Legion. The Estonian officers consider this accusation as strange. What the Estonian officers want first is more information about the nature of the Legion. The position of the Estonian military personnel is as follows:

1. We do not want an SS Legion, we want the creation of an Estonian army.
2. The formation and training of Estonian elements must take place in Estonia.
3. The Estonian elements must be engaged near Estonian territory.
4. The leaders of the Estonian military elements (one or two divisions) must be Estonian officers.
5. The Estonian military elements should be under the command of the German Wehrmacht High Command (OKW).
6. Estonians serving in the German Army and other organizations in Germany and occupied territories will be given freedom to return to Estonia should they so desire.
7. Germany will supply the arms, technical equipment and all other supplies and ammunition for the formation of the Estonian elements.
8. The German Army will supply the instructors for the training of the troops in the use of the new weapons.

Once more the Estonian officers' call for the formation of a national force, at the disposal of the German Army rather than the Waffen-SS, met with no success, and the Legion remained the main Estonian fighting force, very much a part of the Waffen-SS. After almost two years of German occupation, a clear distinction does not seem to have been made between the para-military "SS and Police" and the Waffen-SS and as a result of the unpopularity of the former, the Legion was mistrusted.

Cellarius' reference to SS-Obersturmbannführer Franz Augsberger having been appointed (albeit with considerable delay) to command the Legion prior to 20 April 1943 is the earliest mention found so far of this appointment, since the SS-FHA order of 29 September 1942 raising the Legion made no mention of its commander.

An Austrian by birth, Augsberger had distinguished himself in the pre-war SS-Verfügungstruppe by passing out as an SS-Untersturmführer with the first

This bilingual sign outside a local reporting office of the Estonian SS Legion is decorated with the symbols of Nazi Germany and the Republic of Estonia. "Legion Estland" (literally "Legion 'Estonia' ") was an improper designation for what should have been called the "Estonian Legion."

class (1935) from the SS Officer Cadet School at Brunswick on 1 June 1935 and going on to be the school's senior graduate when promoted SS-Obersturmführer on 1 July 1936 and SS-Hauptsturmführer on 1 June 1937.[68] As an officer Augsberger stayed on as a member of the school staff at Brunswick throughout the pre-war years and having seen active service must have been chosen to lead the Estonian Legion some time after 29 September 1942, because the SS-FHA order of that date raising the Legion made no reference to its commander.[69] The Estonians, who so desperately wanted to see one of their own officers lead the Legion, had been told of the choice of Augsberger by 20 April 1942 and so the German decision, although perhaps not yet final, had been made even earlier.

Cellarius' plea was ignored as had all those made previously, and on 1 July 1943 Augsberger was promoted to SS-Standartenführer and formally given command of the Legion.[70] He arrived at the Debica SS training area in east Poland in July and was there the following month when the Estonian hero of the War of Liberation, Johannes Soodla, was named by the Germans as commander of the 1st Regiment of the Estonian Legion with the rank of a Legions-

[68]Shown as "B35" in the SS officers lists (Dienstaltersliste der SS der NSDAP), the first course began in the spring of 1935 and lasted ten months. At first known as SS-Führerschule Braunschweig, the title was changed to SS-Junkerschule Braunschweig on 1.2.1935.

[69]No record has yet been found of Augsberger's previous service in the Second World War, but he won the Iron Cross 2nd and 1st Class on 4 July and 15 September 1941 and the German Cross in Gold on 30 May 1942 (Schneider, op.cit., pg. 19).

[70]This is the date given by Klietmann (op.cit., pg. 228). Quite apart from any merit, Augsberger had to be promoted to Colonel for otherwise he would have been out-ranked by two of his Estonian subordinates, Soodla and Tuuling.

Standartenführer.[71] Soodla was not to hold operational command for long, however. Appointed Inspector General of the Estonian SS Legion and promoted to Legions-Oberführer, he handed over command of the nascent regiment to Legions-Standartenführer Hans Kurg and left Debica to set up his new office in Tallinn.[72]

Eesti riik ja rahvas II Maailmasõjas

Johannes Soodla, here in the uniform of a Waffen-Oberführer, speaks on the telephone from his office in Tallinn. Soodla, born on 14.1.1897, was one of the 28 national heroes from the Estonian War of Liberation, one of the 28 recipients of the Estonian Cross of Liberty VR II/2 (he also had the VR II/3). Promoted to Colonel on 24.2.1940, he was commander of the Estonian Military Academy when the Russians invaded Estonia in July of that year. Forced by the Russians to leave the Army, Soodla managed to escape to Germany thanks to his wife Irene's German extraction. When the Germans ousted the Russians in 1941, Soodla was able to return, and in early 1943 he was one of the two senior Estonian officers in the Estonian SS Legion (he and Juhan Tuuling had both had their previous Estonian rank of Colonel recognized as Legions-Standartenführer). In August 1943 Soodla was given command of the 1st Regiment of the Estonian SS Legion, and as the Legion only consisted of one regiment at the time, the mistake has often been made to consider Soodla as the commander of the Estonian SS Legion (even of its successor formation, the Estonian SS Volunteer Brigade). But this was neither possible nor intended, and at about the same time as the German Franz Augsberger was appointed commander of the Estonian SS Legion, Johannes Soodla gave up his regimental command to become Inspector General of the Estonian SS Legion, based in Tallinn. Promoted first to Legions-Oberführer and on 15.9.1944 to Waffen-Brigadeführer und Generalmajor der Waffen-SS, Soodla became Inspector General of all Estonian elements in the Waffen-SS and was involved in the raising of the six Frontier Guard regiments in early 1944. After the capitulation of Germany, he managed to escape falling into the hands of the Russians via the French-occupied zone of Germany and made his way to Florida, USA. He later returned to settle in West Germany and died there at Goslar on 26 May 1965.

---

[71]*The fact that at the time the Legion was composed entirely of this regiment has led some mistakenly to believe that Soodla (of equal rank to Augsberger) commanded the whole Legion, even the Brigade it later became. This is not so, and the Germans would never have allowed it. (Duprat refers to "Soodla's 3rd SS Brigade" in* Historie des SS, *pg. 365 and the later* Les Campagnes de la Waffen-SS, *Vol. 2, pg. 165.)*

[72]*Soodla went on to become Inspector General of all Estonian Waffen-SS units and, promoted to Waffen-Brigadeführer und Generalmajor der Waffen-SS on 15 Sep-*

MAY 1943 - JANUARY 1944: THE ESTONIAN SS VOLUNTEER BRIGADE

The Legion, by now consisting of and therefore rather confusingly known as the "1st Estonian SS Volunteer Grenadier Regiment" (1. Estnisches SS-Freiwilligen-Grenadier Regiment), had not even time to complete its basic training when the Germans decided in the spring of 1943 to expand it to a brigade. The second infantry regiment and other necessary brigade elements were also raised as the Legion itself had been at the SS training area east of Debica in the General Government of Poland, which since 15 March 1943 had been renamed from "Debica" to "Heidelager."[73] Many more Germans and Russian Hiwis were brought in from the 1st SS Infantry Brigade to complete the formation, and so its already diluted national character was weakened still further.[74] By order of 5 May 1943 the SS-FHA in Berlin redesignated the Estonian Legion as the Estonian SS Volunteer Brigade (Estnische SS-Freiw.Brig.).[75]

The new Brigade's original order of battle was as follows:[76]

ESTNISCHE SS-FREIWILLIGEN-BRIGADE	Estonian SS Volunteer Brigade
1. Rgt./SS-Freiw.Gren.Rgt. 1 (Estn.Brigade)	1st regiment/SS volunteer grenadier regiment 1 (Estonian Brigade)
I. Btl. (1. - 4.)	Ist battalion (1st - 4th companies)
II. Btl. (5. - 8.)	IInd battalion (5th - 8th companies)
III. Btl. (9. - 12.)	IIIrd battalion (9th - 12th companies)
IV. Btl. - Stab	IVth battalion (HQ only)
13. schw.Gr.W.Kp.	13th heavy mortar company
14. Pz.Jg.Kp.	14th antitank company
15. Pi.Kp.	15th engineer company
2. Rgt./SS-Freiw.Gren.Rgt 2 (Estn.Brigade)	2nd regiment/SS volunteer grenadier regiment 2 (Estonian Brigade)
I. Btl. (1. - 4.)	Ist battalion (1st - 4th companies)
II. Btl. (5. - 8.)	IInd battalion (5th - 8th companies)

tember 1944, was certainly the senior Estonian officer in the Waffen-SS, but never the Estonian Waffen-SS formation's commander. For his promotion to Waffen-Brigadeführer, see article in Postimees of 16.9.1944 - and for more biographical data, the photo caption on page 156 of this book.

73Klietmann, op.cit., pp. 223 & 452.

74Hiwi, short for "Hilfswilliger," a non-German conscripted laborer serving with a labor unit attached to the Wehrmacht or Waffen-SS. There were 566 in the Division on 15.9.1944.

75See fn. 3 on page 122 of this book.

76Tessin, op.cit., Vol. 14, pg. 69, who for some reason does not number the regimental companies.

III. Btl. (9. - 12.)	IIIrd battalion (9th - 12th companies)
15. Pi.Kp	15th engineer company

Henno Uus

Staff officers of the Estonian SS Volunteer Brigade at SS-Truppenübungsplatz Heidelager bei Debica, August 1943. The SS-Sturmbannführer with the German Cross in the center of the front row is Emil Rehfeldt, at the time this photograph was taken the Brigade's operations officer ("Ia" or 1. Generalstabsoffizier (Führung)). Promoted to SS-Obersturmbannführer on 9.11.1943, Rehfeldt continued to serve on the staff of what became the 20th SS Division until at least 1 October 1944. He was not listed as being on the Division's staff as of 1.3.1945 and in the last months of the war was commanding the divisional training and replacement regiment (SS-Ausbildungs- und Ersatz-Regiment 20) based in Denmark. The SS-Hauptsturmführer to Rehfeldt's left wears the Waffen-SS adjutant's cords and Odalrune collar patch indicating previous service in the "Prinz Eugen" Division. To be noted that of these 15 officers, only one (2nd from left in the center row wearing a plain black right hand collar patch) appears to have been an Estonian - all the others were Germans.

It is to be noted that originally the infantry guns were still unavailable, and so the 1st Regiment's 13th company was still armed with and designated by heavy mortars.

As was also the case in Latvia, the Estonian Brigade was at first unnumbered. The Germans then decided to number all Waffen-SS formations and infantry regiments in single numerical sequences according to their chronological dates of formation, and the Estonian Brigade became, by SS-FHA order of 22 October 1943, the 3rd Estonian SS Volunteer Brigade (3. Estn. SS-

Freiw.Brigade).[77] This same order renumbered the new Brigade's two infantry regiments from SS-Freiw.Gren.Rgt. 1 & 2 (Estn.Brigade) to SS-Freiw.Gren.Rgt. 42 & 43 and prescribed that the formation's support elements and services should be numbered "53."[78]

On paper at least the order of battle of the Estonian Brigade following the SS-FHA order of 22 October 1943 was as follows:

3. ESTN. SS-FREIW.BRIGADE	3rd Estonian SS volunteer brigade
Stab der Brigade	Brigade HQ
SS-Freiwilligen-Grenadier-Regiment 42	infantry regiment
Stab	HQ
I. - III.	Ist - IIIrd battalions
13. Infanteriegeschütz-Kp.	13th infantry gun company
14. Panzerjäger-Kp.	14th antitank company
SS-Freiwilligen-Grenadier-Regiment 43	infantry regiment
Stab	HQ
I. - III.	Ist - IIIrd battalions
13. Infanteriegeschütz-Kp.	13th infantry gun company
14. Panzerjäger-Kp.	14th antitank company
SS-Panzerjäger-Abteilung 53	antitank battalion
SS-Artillerie-Abteilung 53	artillery detachment
SS-Flak-Abteilung 53	antiaircraft detachment
SS-Nachrichtungs-Kompanie 53	signals company
SS-Feldersatzbataillon 53	field replacement battalion

The increase in the number of infantry regiments in the senior Waffen-SS divisions led to a need to renumber the whole series which was ordered by the SS-FHA on 12 November 1943.[79] This renumbered the Estonian infantry regiments from 42 & 43 to 45 & 46.

On 22 January 1944 the SS-FHA carried out Himmler's order that all non-German infantry regiments of the Waffen-SS (SS-Freiw.-Gren.Rgtern.) should have their nationality - and a progressive numeration within that nationality - added parenthetically after their titles and so the Estonian formation's regiments (only two of which were, in fact, in existence at that time) became "SS-Freiw.Gren.Rgt. 45, 46 & 47 (estnisches Nr. 1, 2 & 3)."[80]

These bureaucratic changes were being made while the Brigade was in action at the front, for while listed as "forming under the C-in-C Replacement Army," the Estonians had been sent to the central sector of the Eastern front in October 1943 and placed under Army Group "North."[81] To provide the ad-

---

[77]See fn. 4 on page 122 of this book.

[78]Waffen-SS brigade elements and services were numbered in the '50' series, that is, by adding the brigade number to a base of 50.

[79]SS-FHA, Amt II Org.Abt. Ia/II, Tgb.Nr. II/9542/43 geh., v. 12.11.1943, Bezeichnung der Feldtruppenteile der Waffen-SS.

[80]SS-FHA, Amt II Org.Abt. Ia/II, Tgb.Nr. 166/44 g.Kdos., v. 22.1.1944, Bezeichnung der SS-Freiw.Rgter. (T-175/141/2669368-9).

[81]Tessin, op.cit., Vol. 2, pg. 213 surprisingly gives the Brigade in November 1943 as forming under "BdE(SS)," or "C-in-C Replacement Army (SS)." This cannot have been correct because Himmler did not take over the Ersatzheer until after 20 July 1944.

ditional men still required to complete transition from regimental to brigade size - and to make up for the mounting losses being inflicted on the Brigade by the Russians - new pressures were brought to bear back in Estonia. Men born in 1925 were to be drafted according to a decree of the Self Administration dated 26 October 1943, but this drive in the last days of that month and during November led to only 3,375 of the 7,800 men drafted (just 43 percent) reporting to the Brigade and other assigned units. Even less success followed Hitler's wider-sweeping extension of the draft to the older Estonians born between 1915 and 1924. This had been ordered at the beginning of November 1943 and yielded a meager 900 men by the end of January 1944.[82] At 31 December 1943 the Estonian SS Volunteer Brigade numbered 178 officers, 864 NCOs and 4,057 other ranks with a total of 5,099.[83]

In November 1943 the Brigade was moved further north to the Nevel area where strong Russian partisan forces were active far behind the front line.[84] The Estonians set about the difficult task of tracking down and destroying these partisans and sustained many casualties in the process, including the loss of a regimental commander, Legions-Standartenführer Hans Kurg, commander of the Brigade's senior infantry regiment (Gren.Rgt. 45) who was blown up as his staff car drove over a mine between Idritsa and Sebezh about a hundred kilometers west of Nevel. Kurg died of his wounds a few days later and was replaced by Legions-Sturmbannführer Paul Vent.[85]

Formation of the Brigade was only completed in the last weeks of 1943 while the Estonians fought the Russian partisans around Nevel. In December the formation was transferred to the north of Nevel to face the impending Red Army's advance and as the year closed was at Staraja Russa under the VIIIth Army Corps, 16th Army, Army Group "North."[86] The Russian offensive came in mid-January 1944 and the Estonians fought to check the advance at Staraja Russa. They were driven back to the southwest to Opochka and by the end of the month had come under the Ist Army Corps. On 8 February 1944 the formation, which as will be seen below had been redesignated as a division on 24 January, was withdrawn northwards to face the Red Army on the Narva.

JANUARY - APRIL 1944: FROM BRIGADE TO DIVISION:

The final expansion of the Estonian Waffen-SS came in the first days of 1944 when Himmler decided to expand the Brigade to a division. On 24 January 1944 the SS-FHA ordered the raising of a division with immediate effect.[87]

Manpower Study is therefore more accurate when it gives simply "C-in-C North" ("Bfh. Nord"). MID, German OB, March 1945 gives the Division as forming in December 1943 on the central sector of the Eastern front. Klietmann (op.cit., pg. 223) gives the formation in the Nevel area in the northern sector of the Eastern front at the end of 1943.

[82] *Uustalu, For Freedom Only, pg. 19.*

[83] *Klietmann, op.cit., pg. 507.*

[84] *They were in the 'Republic of Rossona,' nick-named 'Soviet partisan stronghold' (H. Rüütel, letter of 23.8.1981).*

[85] *Harald Riipalu, Kui võideldi kodupinna eest, pp. 17-38 & Jüri Remmelgas, Kolm kuuske, pp. 161-172.*

[86] *Tessin, op.cit., Vol. 2, pg. 213.*

[87] *See fn. 6 on page 122 of this book.*

Franz Augsberger, who had led the Estonians since July 1943, was named as temporary commander of the new division but in fact was to lead it until his death in March 1945.

The former Brigade was to be reorganized as a "new type" (neuer Art) infantry division. This required the raising of a new third infantry regiment as well as divisional support elements and services. With the Russians driving the

Paul Vent, as a Legions-Sturmbannführer, probably in late 1943. Vent took command of the 1st Regiment (45th) of the Estonian SS Brigade in November 1943 when its commander, Standartenführer Hans Kurg, was killed behind the Nevel front. Promoted to Obersturmbannführer, Vent continued to lead the 45th SS infantry regiment until April 1944, when he assumed command of the newly formed 47th SS infantry regiment and handed over his command to Harald Riipalu. In August 1944 he was commanding a battle group (Kampfgruppe "Vent") made up of three battalions.

Source: Estonian Combatants Association in GB.

Germans ever closer to the Estonian border, the expansion to a division had to be carried out while the formation was in action at the front and so could not be accomplished easily and in a hurry. The following summary by branch of the service shows how true divisional status was really not achieved until the formation's third infantry regiment was completed in April 1944, and how other units were not even completed until as late as July 1944, when the division was on the point of being driven out of Estonia altogether.

INFANTRY:

The "new type" division was to be triangular and at first it was proposed that the necessary third infantry regiment (SS-Freiw.Gren.Rgt. 47 (estn. Nr. 3)) should be built by detaching the IIIrd battalions of the former Brigade's two infantry regiments, the 45th and 46th (1st and 2nd Estonian respectively).[88] In fact, this decision was changed (just as had been done over the expansion of the Latvian Brigade to the 19th SS Division) and the new regiment's Ist and IInd battalions came by transferring from the Army the 659th and 658th Estonian Battalions respectively.[89]

A new HQ and 13th (infantry gun) and 14th (antitank) companies were added and the Division's third infantry regiment was completed on 24 April 1944 - it still had no third battalion and in fact was not to get one until the formation was rebuilt in Germany at the end of the year.

In addition to the three basic infantry regiments, an infantry reconnaissance battalion was needed and SS-Divisions-Füsilier-Btl. 20 was ordered on 18 April 1944.[90] This battalion was in fact not formed until June/July 1944 when survivors of the Estonian battalion that had been serving with the "Wiking" Division since April 1943 were brought back to the Estonian formation and used as a base for SS-Füs.Btl. 20.

The existing field replacement battalion (SS-F.E.B. 53) was simply renumbered SS-F.E.B. 20 on 7 February 1944.[91]

ARTILLERY:

The existing artillery detachment (SS-Art.Abt. 53) was used as the Ist (light) artillery detachment for the required divisional artillery regiment (SS-Art.Rgt. 20). A new HQ and IInd and IIIrd (light) detachments were raised on 4 April 1944, while a IVth (heavy) detachment had begun formation at Benešov (Beneschau) in the Protectorate of Bohemia and Moravia on 31 March 1944.[92]

ANTITANK:

The (14th) antitank company of the 46th infantry regiment was detached and used as the 1st company of SS-Panzerjäger-Abteilung 20. This battalion was not complete until 10 July 1944. The (14th) antitank company of the 45th infantry regiment was broken up and used to provide new antitank companies for all three of the new Division's infantry regiments.

ANTIAIRCRAFT:

Formed from the old SS-Flak-Abt. 53. Unlike the A.A. detachments of the two Latvian divisions, which were detached and merged to form a corps A.A. detachment, the 20th SS Division retained its A.A. detachment until it was destroyed in the fighting in Estonia in September 1944.

ENGINEERS:

SS-Freiw.Pi.Btl. 20 was formed from the (15th) engineer companies of the 45th and 46th infantry regiments.

SIGNALS:

The Brigade's signals company (SS-Nachr.Kp. 53) was at first renumbered as SS-Nachr.Kp. 20 and then used as a base for SS-Nachr.Abt. 20 (HQ, telephone and wireless companies) which was formed on 13 April 1944.

The Estonian Division's principal elements can thus be summarized as follows:[93]

20. ESTNISCHE SS-FREIWILLIGEN-GRENADIER-DIVISION

Stab der Division	HQ
SS-Freiw.Gren.Rgt. 45 (estn. Nr. 1)	volunteer infantry regiment with HQ, two battalions of four companies each, 13th infantry gun and 14th antitank companies and an unnumbered heavy mortar company
SS-Freiw.Gren.Rgt. 46 (estn. Nr. 2)	As above but it had no heavy mortar company
SS-Freiw.Gren.Rgt. 47 (estn. Nr. 3)	Volunteer infantry regiment with HQ and two battalions of four companies each
SS-Freiw.Div.Füsilier-Btl. 20	Volunteer divisional infantry reconnaissance battalion
SS-Panzerjäger-Abt. 20	Antitank battalion
SS-Freiw.Art.Rgt. 20	Volunteer artillery regiment with HQ and four detachments
SS-Freiw.Flak-Abt. 20	Volunteer antiaircraft detachment
SS-Freiw.Pionier-Btl. 20	Volunteer engineer battalion
SS-Nachrichten-Abt. 20	Signals battalion with HQ and two companies
SS-Feldersatz-Bataillon 20	Field replacement battalion

The fact that the antitank and signals battalions were not prefixed with the adjective "Freiwilligen-," (strictly speaking meaning "volunteer" but effectively

[88]*Tessin, op.cit., Vol. 4, pg. 150.*

[89]*OKH, Gen.St.d.H., Org.Abt. II/17893 geh., v. 21.7.1943 provided that the 657th Estonian Company and 658th, 659th and 660th Estonian Battalions should be transferred from the Army to the Waffen-SS, but actual transfer was staggered. The 658th and 659th Estonian Battalions, previously called "East Battalions" and before that the 181st and 182nd "Estonian Security Detachments," had been raised by the German Army and their last commanders were Alfons Rebane and Georg Sooden, respectively. According to Klietmann (op.cit., pg. 226) the 658th and 659th became the Ist and IInd battalions of the 47th SS infantry regiment, respectively; whereas according to H. Rüütel they became the IInd and Ist, respectively. The 660th Estonian Battalion (previously 660th East Battalion and before that the 184th Estonian Security Detachment) was not absorbed as a unit but broken up and its men spread among the Division. The independent 657th Estonian Company (formerly the 13th company of the 184th Estonian Security Detachment) was similarly broken up and absorbed by the Division.*

[90]*Klietmann, op.cit., pg. 227.*

[91]*ibid.*

[92]*ibid. The IVth (heavy) artillery detachment was formed at SS-Artillerie-Schule II Beneschau.*

[93]*Klietmann, op.cit., pp. 226-227 & Tessin, op.cit., Vol. 4, pp. 150-152.*

indicating "non-Germanic"), suggests that they were entirely composed of Germans.

More men were required and Himmler ordered compulsory military service in Estonia as elsewhere in the "Ostland." So all men born between 1915 and 1924 became liable for conscription into the Waffen-SS. During 1944 this conscription was widened to include older Estonians born between 1904 and 1914 (so that men under the age of 40 had to join) and the classes of 1925 and 1926 (so Estonian youths of 18 and over were also eligible for service). In addition, all former Estonian Army officers and NCOs up to the ages of 60 and 65 respectively became liable for military service.

FEBRUARY - SEPTEMBER 1944: THE NARVA FRONT AND WITHDRAWAL FROM ESTONIA:

Having examined the gradual expansion from Brigade to Division that effectively lasted from January to April 1944, we must return to developments on the Eastern front that involved the men of the Estonian Waffen-SS during this same period.

The three years of German occupation were drawing to their inevitable close and the return to Russian domination was imminent. German defeats in the East had led Wehrmacht and Waffen-SS to be driven steadily westward, and by the end of January 1944 the Red Army was forcing its way towards the whole north/south Russo-Estonian frontier. To the north the Red Army's offensive on the Leningrad front had driven the German 18th Army back and across the Narva River. The Germans thus held positions running along the west bank of the Narva from Hungerberg to the extreme north. Only opposite the strategically crucial Narva City itself had they established a strong bridgehead on the eastern bank of the river.

From Narva to the south, along the western shore of Lake Peipsi and down to Petseri (Petschur) in the southeastern corner of Estonia, German divisions waited for the inevitable assault.

With the Red Army massing on the eastern bank of the Narva River, poised to continue their drive westward, a new Russian invasion of Estonia was inevitable. On 1 February 1944 a final and eleventh-hour general mobilization was ordered, and three days later the Higher SS and Police Leader for North Russia ordered the raising of six regiments of Estonian frontier guards (Estn. Grenzschutz-Rgter. 1 - 6) as well as a replacement regiment.[94] The fact that this mobilization succeeded where previous attempts had failed can be attributed to the Estonians' fear of the return of the Russians and support given to the German initiatives by Professor Uluots and other patriotic leaders who had previously found so little sympathy from the Germans for their appeals

---

[94]Six infantry and one replacement regiments were formed as a result of the 1.2.1944 mobilization. Thrown into battle ill-equipped and with virtually no training, they were all destroyed by the Red Army's drive through Estonia in 1944. When raised, G.O.C. XXVIth Army Corps, Generalleutnant Anton Grasser, ordered the 2nd & 4th and 3rd & 6th to be paired to form battle groups "North" and "South," respectively, of a newly-formed 300th Infantry Division. Survivors of these frontier guard regiments were used to rebuild the 20th SS Division at Tr.Üb.Pl. Neuhammer in late 1944/early 1945.

Henno Uus

Major Alfons Rebane is the guest of honor at a reception held in the Kadriorg Palace in Tallinn on 24 February 1944 to celebrate his becoming the first Estonian recipient of the Knight's Cross of the Iron Cross (23.2.1944). At left in dark civilian suit is Dr. Hjalmar Mäe, Leader of the Estonian Self-Administration (Der Erste Landesdirektor). To Rebane's left is Legions-Oberführer Johannes Soodla, Inspector General of the Estonian Waffen-SS, and the bald figure at right is SA-Obergruppenführer Karl-Sigismund Litzmann, Governor-General of Estonia.

Alfons Rebane in the uniform of a Major of the German Army, soon after his award of the Knight's Cross of the Iron Cross on 23 February 1944. Rebane had joined the Wehrmacht on 1 September 1941 and was given command of the 15th (ski) company of the 184th Security Group (later renamed Security Detachment). Promoted to Hauptmann on 1 January 1942, he was given command of the 658th East Battalion in September 1942 (the unit was renamed 658th Estonian Battalion with effect from 1 January 1943). Rebane was promoted Major in June 1943 and led his battalion with skill and distinction at Volkhov and Novgorod following the Russian offensive of January 1944. For this he became the first Estonian to receive the Knight's Cross of the Iron Cross. In the photograph above, Rebane clearly wears the type "A" sleeve shield on his upper right sleeve.

for independence and the raising of a national army.[95] Professor Uluots made a radio broadcast calling his compatriots to rally to the national cause, and his appeal was answered by no less than 45,000 Estonians. Most of these men were used for the new frontier regiments, and serving under Estonian officers led the Germans to fear that they had in fact sanctioned the forming of a sort of national Estonian army, precisely what they had taken such pains to prevent happening ever since the liberation of Estonia in the summer of 1941. Himmler felt that Johannes Soodla had acted improperly over these regiments and set about gaining full control of them and arranging their absorption into the 20th SS Division.

Three Estonian officers of the 20th SS Division pose with their hand-carved "Volkhov swamp" walking sticks during a lull in the fighting on the Narva front in the spring of 1944. From left to right: Legions-Hauptpsturmführer Tepner, Legions-Hauptsturmführer Paul Maitla, and Legions-Obersturmführer Heine. Maitla, a Hauptsturmführer since 30.1.1944, commanded the IInd battalion of the 45th SS infantry regiment throughout 1944 and the first months of 1945, and in August 1944 led one of the three battalions of Battle Group "Vent." Recommended for the Knight's Cross by the "Nordland" Division (together with the 20th SS Division in the IIIrd (Germanic) SS Armored Corps in Army Group "North" on the northern sector of the Eastern front), he received this decoration on 23 August 1944. Maitla, who wore the SS runes on the collar after winning his Knight's Cross, disappeared without trace in Czechoslovakia in May 1945.

The Estonian Waffen-SS formation, in name a triangular division but in fact still only a bi-regimental brigade, was only allowed a short period for reorganization and reforming under the VIIIth Army Corps, 16th Army, Army Group "North," before it was decided to add its weight and natural determination to the defense of Narva.[96]

The Division left Opochka by rail on 8 February 1944 and having traveled northwards to the east of Lake Peipsi arrived the following day. For the first ten days, its 45th infantry regiment was short of its Ist battalion, for this had

---

[95]*See above, pg. 134.*

[96]*Tessin, op.cit., Vol. 2, pg. 213 gives the Brigade under the VIIIth Army Corps of the 16th Army at Staraja Russa in December 1943 and January 1944.*

stopped off at Tartu on the journey north and had successfully repelled Russian attacks in the Meerapalu-Mehikoorma area on Lake Peipsi. Having helped stabilize the front in this area, the battalion continued its journey north and rejoined its regiment on the Narva front. Before leaving Tartu, this old university town's mayor presented the men of the battalion with specially made collar patches in gratitude for their efforts.[97]

The Russians had launched their first attack on Narva on 2 February 1944, and on that day all German troops on the Narva front were grouped into Army Detachment "Narva" (Armeeabteilung "Narwa"), controlled by what had previously been the HQ of the LIVth Army Corps. Thus upon the Estonians' arrival on 9 February 1944, they too joined Army Detachment "Narva," a strong and multi-national body which was to make a stubborn stand against vastly superior Russian forces that were to hammer it for over seven months in an attempt to take Narva.[98] During this time the main strength of the Detachment was provided by the Waffen-SS formations making up the IIIrd SS Armored Corps.[99] These were the Estonian and "Nordland" divisions and the "Nederland" Brigade throughout, with the Belgian SS Brigades "Langemarck" and "Wallonien" joining the fight in August 1944.[100]

The advance elements of the Estonian Division reached positions opposite the Russian bridgehead at Vepsküla on 20 February 1944, and the Estonian SS battalions took up positions among the other elements of Army Detachment "Narwa" on the line running north from Narva City to Hungerberg in the extreme north. At this time the Division had only two infantry regiments (the 47th was still forming) and Augsberger gave instructions to their commanders for deployment. The Division's senior regiment (the 45th) was under command of Legions-Sturmbannführer Paul Vent, who deployed his men to the north of Narva City. His IInd battalion under Legions-Hauptsturmführer Paul Maitla held positions that stretched northwards from the outskirts of the city to Ssivertsi - the Ist battalion under Harald Riipalu held positions between Vasa and Vensküla. The rest of the line up to Hungerberg was held by Legions-Standartenführer Juhan Tuuling's 46th infantry regiment. Its Ist battalion under Legions-Hauptsturmführer Silvert was positioned south of Kudrukula and SS-Obersturmführer Weber's IInd battalion took up positions around Riigi.[101]

---

[97]*See under COLLAR PATCHES on page 211 below.*

[98]*The Russians attacked Narva with their 2nd Storm and 8th & 47th Armies. No evidence has been found to confirm the report in Manpower Study that the Estonian SS Division was under "Gruppe Scholz" in February 1944. (Generalmajor Erich Scholz was awarded the Knight's Cross on 26.12.1944 for his actions as commander of Kampfgruppe "Scholz").*

[99]*The IIIrd (Germanic) SS Armored Corps was a part of Armeeabteilung "Narwa" throughout. XXVIth Army Corps was a part until June, XXXXIIIrd Army Corps between April and July, and the IInd Army Corps in August and September. Tessin, op.cit., Vol. 14, pg. 171.*

[100]*The 5th & 6th SS Brigades "Wallonien" and "Langemarck" joined Armeeabteilung "Narwa" in August 1944, the former coming at first under the IInd Army Corps, before joining the other Waffen-SS formations in the IIIrd (Germanic) SS Armored Corps.*

[101]*Richard Landwehr, Siegrunen, Vol. III, No. 6 (18), January 1980, pg. 10. Harald Riipalu did not take command of the 45th regiment until April 1944 and so in February*

The four Estonian SS battalions lost no time in attacking the Russian bridgehead at Vopsküla, and 22-year-old Legions-Unterscharführer Harald Nugiseks was later awarded the Knight's Cross of the Iron Cross for leading three particularly stubborn attacks that finally destroyed a Russian position.

Harald Riipalu was a 2nd lieutenant (Nooremleitnant) in the Estonian Army when the 2nd World War broke out. He joined the Estonian SS Legion in 1943 as a Legions-Hauptsturmführer and commanded the 1st battalion of the 1st Estonian SS Infantry Regiment (numbered the 42nd in October 1943 and renumbered to the 45th the following month). In April 1944 he took command of the 45th SS infantry regiment as a whole and was promoted to Waffen-Obersturmbannführer on 28 July 1944.

Waffen-Unterscharführer Harald Nugiseks was the only non-officer among the four Estonians to be awarded the Knight's Cross. He was awarded this decoration on 9 April 1944 for bravery in leading the men of his section of the 20th SS Division's 46th infantry regiment in attacks against positions held by the Red Army at Vopsküla in February 1944.

Three young Estonians from the 658th Estonian Battalion receive the 2nd Class Iron Cross from their commander and Knight's Cross holder Legions-Sturmbannführer Alfons Rebane. The men at the left and center of the front row wear the uniform of the German Army (note that the boy in the center wears an Estonian Army cap badge), whereas the man at the right of the front row is in German Police uniform. Men in the background can be seen to be wearing the SS runes on the collar patch. Since Rebane is in Waffen-SS uniform, this photograph was probably taken soon after his battalion was transferred from the German Army to the Waffen-SS in April 1944 and redesignated the IInd battalion of the 20th SS Division's 47th infantry regiment (SS-Freiw.Gren.Rgt. 47). The Police uniform could indicate prior service in a Police (previously "Schutzmannschafts-) Battalion, and it can be assumed that all would later have been issued with Waffen-SS uniform.

Defensive fighting along the Narva River continued throughout March 1944. On 23 March the SS-FHA decided to create the post of Waffen-SS Commander-in-Chief for the "Ostland" (Befehlshaber der Waffen-SS Ostland) and with effect from 15 March, Walter Krüger took over a rôle he was to hold until 25 July 1944.[102]

April 1944 saw the completion of the Division's third infantry regiment (47th) as well as three of the four artillery detachments required for the divisional artillery regiment, and so can be taken as the month in which the Estonian Brigade effectively achieved divisional status. As of 24 April 1944 the Division was made up of the 45th, 46th and 47th infantry regiments (each having an HQ, two battalions of four companies each and 13th infantry gun and 14th antitank companies); SS-Divisions-Füsilier-Btl. 20 (forming); SS-Pz.Jg.Abt. 20; SS-Art.Rgt. 20 (HQ + 4 detachments); SS-Flak-Abt. 20; SS-Pi-Btl. 20 (HQ + 3 companies); SS-Nachr.Abt. 20 (HQ + 2 companies); SS-Ersatz-Regiment 20.

Command of the new 47th SS infantry regiment (SS-Freiw.Gren.Rgt. 47 (estn. Nr. 3)) was given to Legions-Obersturmbannführer Paul Vent, who handed over the Division's senior 45th infantry regiment to Harald Riipalu, who until then had led its Ist battalion.[103]

1944 was commanding I./SS 45 under regimental commander Paul Vent. (H. Rüütel, letter of 23.8.81)

[102] Klietmann, op.cit., pg. 437. On 25.7.1944 Krüger took command of the VIth (Latvian) Non-Germanic Army Corps of the SS and was succeeded as Befehlshaber der Waffen-SS Ostland by Dr. jur. Gustav Krukenberg, who went on to be Inspector of the French Waffen-SS and final commander of the "Nordland" Division (see Vol. 3 of this series, pp. 84 & 89).

[103] Eesti riik ja rahvas II Maailmasõjas, Vol. IX, pg. 33. By 1.3.1945 command of the 47th SS infantry regiment had passed to Waffen-Obersturmbannführer Juhan Vermet.

Signal, Nr. 7, 1944, pg. 8.

16 May 1944: G.O.C. Army Group "North," Generaloberst Georg Lindemann, visits the battle HQ of the 20th SS Division on the Narva front. The Waffen-SS officer at left seems amused as divisional commander SS-Oberführer Augsberger raises his right arm in the Nazi salute rather than shaking the gloved hand of the 60-year-old German Army general - who commanded Army Group "North" from 31 March 1944 until 4

Heinrich Hoffmann, 16-5-44-tw-zi-ada 260 PK Aufn. - SS Kriegsberichter Albert, HH, 64518.
Courtesy Andrew Mollo.

July 1944. Augsberger was promoted to SS-Brigadeführer und Generalmajor der Waffen-SS soon after, on 21 June 1944. The SS-Brigadeführer und Generalmajor der Waffen-SS with his arm in a sling is Fritz von Scholz, commander of the "Nordland" Division that was also engaged at Narva.

The fighting continued along the Narva River in the area of Army Group "North" and the 20th SS Division remained a part of the IIIrd (Germanic) SS Armored Corps of Army Detachment "Narva."

Himmler took particular interest in the Estonian Division while it was fighting at Narva in May 1944. At the beginning of the month he ordered a number of Estonian officers to be transferred to the Division, but in a letter to the Higher SS and Police Leader and Waffen-SS C-in-C of the "Ostland" (Jeckeln and Krüger respectively) of 14 May, the Reichsführer-SS complained that such had still not been done.[104] This letter covers various aspects and problems facing the Estonian SS Division at the time and is worthy of close attention. From it we learn that the Division had still not in fact been completed and was short of no less than 5,000 men.[105] Himmler urged that the formation be brought up to full strength by 15 June 1944 and provided two alternative methods for finding the 5,000 men. Permission could be sought from the HQ of Army Group "North" for the transfer to the Division of all officers, NCOs and men of one or even two of the Estonian Frontier Guard regiments (which had been raised by order of 4 February 1944 and had since been renamed SS Frontier Guard regiments - SS-Grenzschutz-Rgter.). Alternatively, 5,000 recruits could be raised from Estonians previously exempt from military service. In any event, Himmler insisted that Johannes Soodla, then a Legions-Oberführer and the Inspector General of the Estonian Waffen-SS, should see to the return to the Division within the end of May of the Estonians who had previously left it, for the most part to enroll in the newly-formed frontier guard regiments which held the attraction of being commanded exclusively by Estonian officers.

Himmler went on in his letter to point to what he saw as the grave danger of the Estonians looking on the Frontier Guard regiments as the nucleus of a private Estonian Army. As seen above, six of these regiments (plus a seventh training and replacement regiment) had been ordered in early February 1944 by the Higher SS and Police Leader for North Russia - at first they were called "Estonian Frontier Guard Regiments (Police)," but prior to Himmler's letter of 14 May 1944 they had been renamed "SS Frontier Guard Regiments."

---

[104]Der Reichsführer-SS, RF/M. 35/59/44g., Feld-Kommandostelle, den 14. Mai 1944 (T-175/22/2527717-9). The letter was addressed to:
1. Höheren SS- und Polizeiführer Ostland SS-Obergruppenführer Jeckeln
2. Befehlshaber der Waffen-SS Ostland SS-Gruppenführer Krüger with copies to:
3. Chef des SS-Führungshauptamtes (Hans Jüttner)
4. Chef des SS-Hauptamtes (Gottlob Berger)
5. Kommandeur der 20. Waffen-Gren.Div. SS (estn. Nr. 1) (Franz Augsberger)
6. Verbindungsoffizier des RFSS zum Führer (Hermann Fegelein)
7. Chef Kommandostab RFSS (Ernst Rode)
8. SS-Sturmbannführer Christoph (Friedrich - Waffen-SS liaison officer at General Staff, Army, Organization Section (Verb.-Offz. der Waffen-SS b. Gen.St. d. H. Org.Abt.)
9. SS-Sturmbannführer Grothmann (Werner - 1st Adjutant to the Reichsführer-SS)

[105]From a strength return prepared by divisional commander Augsberger, the 20th SS Divison was under-strength by 3,715 men. To these had to be added 892 "Hiwis" (see fn. 74 on pg. 157) in SS-Feldersatz-Bataillon 20 whom Himmler had earlier ordered to be replaced by Estonians. As a provisional measure, Himmler ordered postponement of this substitution, and it is not known if it was ever carried out.

Johannes Soodla had been instrumental in the raising of these regiments and had not only seen to it that their officers were Estonians, but also engineered the transfer to them of men from the 20th SS Division. Himmler was far from pleased by Soodla's nationalistic behavior and criticized him openly in his letter, ordering that the six Estonian SS Frontier Guard regiments were henceforth to be under his personal control. They were to be paired off and each pair was to be placed under the tactical control of a German divisional HQ and supported by artillery and signals units provided by the German Army and Luftwaffe and personnel from these regiments were to be supplied to the 20th SS Division as and when required.[106] In the end, the survivors of these regiments were transferred to Germany after the fall of Estonia and were used to reform the Estonian Division in October 1944 - January 1945.

Himmler ended his letter by setting out agreements he had reached with the Chief of Staff of Army Group "North," Generalleutnant Eberhard Kinzel:[107]

- Only the Reichsführer-SS and the SS were responsible for Estonian and Latvian affairs.
- The 20th Estonian and 15th and 19th Latvian SS divisions had to be brought back to strength and reinforced.
- A second Estonian SS division was to begin formation by 15 July 1944 and raised during the following two months to the west of Lake Peipsi. Himmler thought SS-Oberführer Gustav Lombard would be a suitable commander for the new division. Each of the 20th SS Division's regiments would have to provide a battalion upon which the new division would be formed, while all additional officers, NCOs and men would come from the SS Frontier Guard regiments (in other words, these Estonian-led regiments would have to be disbanded to provide the manpower for a second German-led SS division).
- The new 2nd Estonian SS division would be linked with the existing 20th SS Division under an Estonian SS Army Corps by 1 October 1944.

As events would have it, the proposed second Estonian Waffen-SS division was never formed (the Russians had overrun Estonia before work could even be begun) and so there never was an Estonian SS Army Corps.

In May 1944 the redesignation of what the Germans considered "non-Germanic" formations of the Waffen-SS brought about further changes in title within the 20th SS Division. The divisional title itself was changed to "20. Waffen-Grenadier-Division der SS (estn. Nr. 1)" and its infantry and artillery regiments were renamed from "Freiwilligen-" to "Waffen-" and rank titles held by Estonian members of the formation (not Germans) changed from "Legions-" to "Waffen-."[108]

---

[106]*In fact, only the 2nd, 3rd, 4th & 6th were so paired and placed under the tactical control of Divisionsstab z.b.V. 300 - see under ORDER OF BATTLE on page 199 of this book.*

[107]*Kinzel held this post from 22.1.1943 until 18.7.1944, when he became Chief of Staff of Army Group "Vistula."*

[108]*"Freiwilligen-," meaning "volunteer," had become a meaningless prefix in any case. At best, appropriate for those divisions having a large number of West European volunteers, it had never been an accurate definition of the formations raised in the East, which relied heavily on conscription.*

While the Estonian Division continued to fight on the Narva front, in June SS-Pz.Gren.Btl. "Narwa" returned to the formation and the following month was used as a cadre for the divisional infantry reconnaissance battalion that had been ordered on 18 April 1944. The battalion had served the "Wiking" Division as the IIIrd battalion of SS-Pz.Gren.Rgt. "Westland" and rejoined the 20th SS Division in time to fight for the town after which it had been named. To maintain the tradition of its former name, at least one member of the new battalion ignored regulations and wore a hand-made cuffband with the inscription "Narwa" during the battle for the city.[109]

Static fighting was interrupted on 14 July by the launching of the Russian summer offensive that was inexorably to drive the divisions of Army Detachment "Narva" westward and finally out of the Baltic States altogether.

The Russians had managed to re-establish a bridgehead at Riigi on the west bank of the Narva, and on 25 July men of the 20th SS Division trying to contain it came under heavy artillery fire. The Estonian Division was forced to withdraw and the following day managed to hold temporary positions between Udria and Repiknu. In the afternoon of 26 July 1944, the Russians advanced on the Estonians under heavy artillery cover and close air support and succeeded in gaining more ground.

On 20 July 1944 a Russian force smashed the German line and entering Estonia took the town of Irboska.

The deteriorating situation during July 1944 led to the decision to replace Juhan Tuuling as commander of the Division's 46th infantry regiment by Knight's Cross holder Alfons Rebane, who had been transferred at the head of his 658th Estonian Battalion to the formation in April 1944. After Soodla, Tuuling was the senior Estonian officer in the Waffen-SS with the rank of Waffen-Standartenführer, but in spite of his posing for SS-PK photographers heroically in the front lines with machine pistol in hand, he was considered too old to continue to lead an infantry regiment in battle at such a difficult and critical time. Tuuling was relieved of his command on 26 July 1944 and transferred to the staff of the IIIrd (Germanic) SS Armored Corps, which had controlled the Estonian Division since March 1944 and was to continue doing so for about another month.[110]

Events worsened for the Germans and their Estonian allies during August 1944. While a desperate stand was being made by the men of Army Detachment "Narva" to the north, further south following the capture of Pskov the Germans had withdrawn westward past Riga in Latvia and so left southern Estonia virtually undefended. The Germans sent no reinforcements to the area before the Russians resumed their advance on 10 August and so the towns of Petseri to the southwest and Võru (Werro) could only be defended by local

---

[109] *According to Jan Poul Petersen of Copenhagen, such a cuffband is to be seen being worn in a film held by the Imperial War Museum in London. Members of the "Narwa" battalion are known to have worn the divisional "Wiking" cuffband (see photograph on page 223), and a veteran of the battalion claims he wore a "Narwa" cuffband over the "Wiking" one (H. Rüütel, July 1981).*

[110] *Eesti riik ja rahvas II Maailmasõjas, Vol. IX, pg. 44.*

Waffen-Obersturmbannführer Harald Riipalu. Promoted as such on 28 July 1944, he was awarded the Knight's Cross on 23 August 1944 as commander of the 45th SS infantry regiment of the Estonian Division (Waffen-Gren.Rgt. der SS Nr. 45 (estn. Nr. 1)). In this photograph, probably taken soon after his award of the Knight's Cross, Riipalu wears the metal collar insignia that had been presented to the Ist battalion of the 45th regiment by the town of Tartu in February 1944. Riipalu had been the battalion's commander at the time and was instrumental in preventing the Germans from introducing their 1st pattern collar patch. Note the outsize collar patch rank pips and the German Police issue tunic converted to Waffen-SS.

Estonian Omakaitse (self-defense) and other units and so fell after bloody fighting to the Red Army.

The assault gathered momentum and by 25 August the university town of Tartu fell and all territory between lakes Peipsi and Võrts up to the Emajõgi River was in Russian hands. The Russians halted on this line and their advance was also held on other sectors of the front.

The Germans reacted and taking advantage of a respite in the Russian attack on Narva begun on 10 August, rushed all available reinforcements to face the new threat in the southeast of the country.

Juhan Tuuling in the uniform of the former Estonian Army wears the distinctive regimental badge of the 8th Independent Infantry Battalion from his left shoulder strap button. Before the outbreak of the Second World War, Tuuling had commanded a battalion in the 7th Infantry Regiment, then the 8th Independent Infantry Battalion (8 Üksik Jalaväe Pataljon) and finally the Tallinn Guard Battalion (Vahipataljon).

Bundesarchiv

Waffen-Standartenführer Juhan Tuuling, one of the two most senior Estonian officers in the Waffen-SS (he was promoted to Kolonel on 24.2.1940 with Johannes Soodla), and commander of the 46th SS infantry regiment of the Estonian Division, poses dramatically with MP 38 machine pistol on the Narva front in the summer of 1944 (probably in July). Tuuling was considered too old for front-line duty and had to hand over his command to Alfons Rebane on 26 July. He joined the staff of the IIIrd (Germanic) SS Armored Corps and died in Denmark in 1945.

By 26 August the Red Army was ranged along the entire length of the Emajõgi River that connects the huge Lake Peipsi in the east to the smaller Lake Võrts further to the west. They also held Tartu and a 20 kilometer wide bridgehead to the west of the city.

In August 1944 the main part of the 20th SS Division withdrew from the Narva sector and was sent southward to try and halt the massive Russian offensive around Tartu. Its men fought in a number of battle groups that were formed to cope with specific emergencies as they arose, not a few of which resulted from German elements pulling out without even advising their Estonian allies. These battle groups were named after their commanders, and men of the 20th SS Division found themselves fighting alongside soldiers of the German Army and other Waffen-SS elements and under the orders of various formations. It was a confused and complicated phase of the Division's history, and a complete listing of the battle groups involving Estonian Waffen-SS may never be possible, let alone a clear account of their histories. Heavy losses were sustained all round, and the 20th SS Division was virtually destroyed in the running fight that saw its survivors driven from their country forever.

The following order of battle for the Division comes from the 25 August 1944 Waffen-SS field post number guide and gives a highly optimistic and theoretical view of the formation's composition at that time:[111]

20. WAFFEN-GRENADIER-DIVISION SS (ESTN. NR. 1)

Stab	HQ
Kriegsberichter.Tr.	war correspondent section
SS-Gren.Rgt. 45, 46 & 47[112]	3 infantry regiments
SS-Panzer-Jäger-Abt. 20	antitank battalion
SS-Füsilier-Btl. 20	infantry reconnaissance battalion
SS-Art.Rgt. 20	artillery regiment
SS-Nachr.Abt. 20	signals battalion
SS-Pionier-Btl. 20	engineer battalion
SS-Flak-Abt. 20	antiaircraft detachment
SS-Nachsch.Tr. 20	supply troops
SS-San.Abt. 20	medical battalion
SS-Wi.Btl. 20	accounting battalion
Werkst.Kp. 20	workshop company
Vet.Kp. 20	veterinary company
Feldgend.Tr. 20	military police section
Feldpostamt 20	field post office

Missing from this list is the field replacement battalion, which even if incomplete would have organized at least a divisional combat school.

[111] *Geheime Kommandosache! Feldpostübersicht Teil III, Band 12 SS-Einheiten, 11. Neudruck Stand vom 25.8.1944 (enthält Berichtingungslisten Nr. 1 bis 1543, Berlin, 1944, pp. 81-83).*

[112] *Of course, such designation had been changed in May 1944 and subsequent correction by hand deleted these entries and replaced them by "W.Gr.Rgt.d.SS (estn. Nr. 1, 2 & 3)." The field postal authorities were thus several months out of date when their 25.8.1944 guide went to press. This is a good example of how field post numbers cannot always be relied upon for accurate dating.*

Subsequent corrections entered by hand to one copy of this guide deleted SS-Flak-Abt. 20, which must consequently have been destroyed after August 1944, and changed some of the unit designations.[113]

As has been mentioned already, the major part of the fighting in the closing months of the war in Estonia was carried on by ad hoc battle groups.[114] All available details of those known will be found after the composite order of battle later in this chapter.

Estonians from the former 200th (Estonian) Infantry Regiment of the Finnish Army parade at Camp Männiku near Tallinn on 22.8.1944 - the first and last time their color would be carried in Estonia.

---

[113] *SS-Nachsch.Tr. 20 and SS-Wi.Btl. 20 were deleted and replaced by Versorg.Rgt. 20 and SS-Verw.Tr.Abt. 20, respectively.*

[114] *"Kampfgruppe" in German or "Võitlusgrupp" in Estonian. Although led by Waffen-SS officers and composed principally of Waffen-SS men, the prefix "SS-" was not used (just as was the practice with the Latvians).*

The battered Estonian Division was to receive welcome, hardened reinforcements from an unusual source while fighting in the Tartu area after the city's fall to the Red Army on 25 August 1944. Estonians anxious to fight the Russians but unwilling to do so in the Estonian SS Legion and other German-controlled units had begun to make their way by boat to Finland in March 1943 and by the end of the year about 2,500 Estonians were serving in the Finnish Army. These were concentrated into the IIIrd battalion of the Finnish 47th Infantry Regiment and with more Estonians stepping forward to fight, Marshal Gustaf Mannerheim was able to order the raising of a whole Estonian volunteer regiment in the Finnish Army on 8 February 1944. This was the 200th Infantry Regiment (J.R. 200), comprising two rifle battalions (III./J.R. 47 became I./J.R. 200), antitank and mortar companies, a signals unit and an engineer platoon.[115]

The Ist battalion of this Estonian regiment began to fight in Finland but already by July 1944 steps were being taken to repatriate the Estonian soldiers and allow them to take a direct part in the defense of their homeland. Before the Estonians could be sent home to fight, the Finnish High Command had to obtain assurances from the Germans that they would not be treated as deserters, for by leaving home and joining the Finnish Army they had broken German laws and were thus subject to punishment on return. On 15 August 1944 the Wehrmacht High Command (OKW) confirmed that should the men return to Estonia they would not be punished and advised that they would be taken into the 20th SS Division.[116]

One thousand seven hundred twenty-eight of the regiment's 1,891 men accepted disbandment of their unit, and on 20 August 1944 the 200th Infantry Regiment was struck from the order of battle of the Finnish Army.[117] The men gave up their arms, but having removed the Finnish cockade from their caps, were allowed to retain their Finnish uniforms and rank insignia.[118] On 19

---

[115]For a concise history of J.R. 200 in English, see Uustalu, For Freedom Only.

[116]An initial positive answer over the amnesty had come from the OKW on 8 August, at which time mention was made that the regiment of returning volunteers would be included in the "1st Estonian SS Divison" (Uustalu, For Freedom Only, pg. 71). J.R. 200 was officially advised of the full amnesty by the Germans on 15.8.1944. Four men were, however, specifically excluded from the amnesty, one of whom was Captain Karl Talpak, who as we have seen above led the "Company of Captain Talpak" alongside the Germans in July/August 1941 but disbanded his unit rather than have it fight outside Estonia. After that he had grown more disillusioned with the Germans and through active membership of a resistance cell in Tartu was responsible for the flight of many Estonian youths to Finland. In time he too escaped to Finland and with the raising of J.R. 200 in February 1944 became its deputy training officer until 13.6.1944 when he was given command of a machine gun company. The German refusal to extend the amnesty to Talpak probably came from his association with the Tartu resistance cell - something he had in common with the other three men similarly denied amnesty.

[117]Ninety-two officers, 106 NCOs and 1,530 other ranks for a total of 1,728 agreed - 10 officers, 10 NCOs and 143 other ranks for a total of 163 disagreed. Uustalu, For Freedom Only, pg. 71.

[118]ibid. Great ill-feeling was created upon the men's return to Estonia when they were forced to exchange their Finnish uniforms for those of the Waffen-SS (pg. 74).

August, 1,752 Estonian soldiers sailed aboard the M/V "Wartheland" from Hanko in Finland and arrived the same day at Paldiski, about thirty kilometers west of Tallinn, and two other vessels later brought the total number up to 2,002. On 22 August 1944 the Estonians, still wearing their Finnish uniforms and with their regimental color flying for the first and last time in Estonia, were assembled at Camp Männiku in Tallinn to be addressed by SS-Brigadeführer und Generalmajor der Polizei Hinrich Möller, who after serving as SS and Police Leader in Tallinn was then on the staff of the SS Main District "Ostland."[119] Möller welcomed the returning soldiers, but having confirmed that their illegal service in the Finnish Army would be forgiven, went on to warn them against any further breaches of loyalty towards the Third Reich and Adolf Hitler.

For reasons of their own, the Germans decided not to send all the returning Estonians to the 20th SS Division as promised, but rather only the former Ist battalion of J.R. 200, which was redesignated as the IIIrd battalion of the Division's 46th infantry regiment, when it joined the Division at Tartu.[120]

III./SS 46 arrived by train 25 kilometers north of Tartu on 26 August. Two days later its 350 men launched a successful attack three and a half kilometers north of Pupastvere, and on 30 August, with three companies in the line and one in reserve, the battalion proceeded to attack the villages of Ovi 1 and Noela, 12 kilometers northwest of Tartu.

Aided by the Estonian 37th and 38th Police Battalions, III./SS 46 managed to drive the Russian forces back across the Emajõgi River and lost 34 killed and 136 wounded in the process.

On 2 September divisional commander Franz Augsberger decorated the commander of III./SS 46, Waffen-Hauptsturmführer Voldemar Pärlin and 43 of his men with the Iron Cross 1st and 2nd class respectively. The battalion then set off for another sector of the Tartu front, but on the march were strafed by a Russian fighter which mortally wounded Pärlin (he died of his wounds ten days later and was replaced by Waffen-Obersturmführer Karl Pärnoja) and injured his adjutant and many others. Attached to the 87th Infantry Division, the battalion was placed in reserve in the village of Pilka, about five kilometers behind the front line. While at Pilka it received 200 fresh Estonian recruits who had barely received three weeks training at an SS camp. The veterans of the tough Finnish Army set about teaching the newcomers what they knew, but within a week the Russians resumed their attack. III./SS 46 suffered severe losses while trying to withdraw from the ensuing Russian assault, and less than 200 of its 525 men managed to reach the safety of nearby woods. Refusing to accept the order of 23 September 1944 to abandon Estonia and

---

[119]Möller had been promoted to SS-Brigadeführer on 30.1.1944, when he was SS and Police Leader in Tallinn (SS- und Polizeiführer Reval). By 9.11.1944 he still held this rank, but was listed as simply being on the staff of the SS Main District Ostland (Stab SS-Oberabschnitt Ostland - Dienstaltersliste der SS der NSDAP).

[120]Uustalu, For Freedom Only, pg. 76. Of the others, 13 officers and 600 men were sent as replacements to different German regiments (the officers are believed to have gone to SS-Ausbildungs-Bataillon 20). By the beginning of September 1944, 41 officers were serving in "Nordland" and "Nederland" at the Narva front.

Voldemar Pärlin

Karl Pärnoja

Kapten Voldemar Pärlin commanded the Ist battalion of the 200th (Estonian) Infantry Regiment of the Finnish Army (I./J.R. 200), which in August 1944 became the IIIrd battalion of the 46th SS infantry regiment of the Estonian Division. Awarded the Iron Cross 1st Class by divisional commander Franz Augsberger on 2.9.1944, he was mortally wounded by a Russian aircraft that evening and died in hospital ten days later. He was succeeded by Waffen-Obersturmführer Karl Pärnoja, who led the battalion until 26.9.1944.

pull back to Riga, the highly-successful battalion dispersed on 26 September at the village of Siberi, and its hardened veterans became "Brothers of the Forest," and groups of them are reported to have continued to fight the Russians for up to 15 years.

The Russians had been able to launch their assault on 17 September following Finland's acceptance of an armistice with the Soviet Union on 4 September. This freed vast Russian forces previously tied down on the Finnish front who were then used in a massive offensive launched on two fronts in mid-September, one between the Gulf of Finland and Lake Peipsi in the north, and the other across the Emajõgi River further to the south between Lakes Peipsi and Võrts (four Russian divisions took part in the latter attack alone that had so battered the IIIrd battalion of the Division's 46th infantry regiment).

Hitler had already ordered the abandonment of Estonia in early September following Russian successes in neighboring Latvia, and the might of the two Russian offensives, gaining momentum when they joined at the northeastern corner of Lake Peipsi, drove the Germans and their many foreign volunteers southwestward and out of Estonia. The Narva front was abandoned on 18 September after seven and a half months of continuous fighting, and the German forces pulling back along the coast to the west were driven out of Tallinn by tanks of the Red Army four days later. All German forces were ordered on 23

H. Rüütel

Senior German and Estonian officers confer soon after the 20th SS Division's withdrawal from Estonia (in either September or October 1944, somewhere in Germany, possibly Danzig). Partially hidden at the extreme left is Colonel A. Sinka, commander-in-chief of the Estonian Self-Defense League (Omakaitse), which had been destroyed in the last desperate defense of Estonia and its survivors incorporated into the Waffen-SS to rebuild the 20th SS Division. Sinka wears the Estonian Army M1936 field uniform. The Waffen-Brigadeführer in profile at left is Johannes Soodla, promoted as such on 15.9.1944, and Inspector General of the Estonian Waffen-SS units 1943-1945. On his right breast pocket he wears the badge of the Estonian Higher Military Academy (see illustration), which establishment he was commanding when the Russians invaded his country in 1940. The German SS-Oberführer at right wearing the Golden Party Badge is Viktor Knapp who, having served with Dutch Waffen-SS units in 1943 and 1944 (as at 30.1.1944 he commanded the 1st Regiment of "Landstorm Nederland"), was on the staff of the IIIrd (Germanic) SS Armored Corps by 9.11.1944.

September to withdraw from Estonia and make their way to Riga in Latvia.[121] The Red Army took Haapsalu on 26 September and Kuressaare on the Island of Saaremaa fell on 7 October. The Estonian territorial self-defense organization, Omakaitse, grouped into combat battalions and then combat regiments, and other units, fought to the death in the last desperate attempt to stem the

---

[121]*Also on 23.9.1944 the post of Waffen-SS C-in-C for the Ostland (Befehlshaber der Waffen-SS Ostland) was canceled - introduced by SS-FHA on 23.3.1944 to supervise all Waffen-SS elements in the Ostland, it had been held from 15.3.1944 to 25.7.1944 by SS-Gruppenführer und Generalleutnant der Waffen-SS (promoted on 21.6.1944 to SS-Obergruppenführer und General der Waffen-SS) Walter Krüger, and from then until 23.9.1944 by SS-Oberführer (promoted on that day to SS-Brigadeführer und Generalmajor der Waffen-SS) Dr. jur. Gustav Krukenberg. (Klietmann, op.cit., pg. 437).*

tide. But there was no stopping the massive Russian assault and Estonia was totally overrun by the Red Army by the end of November 1944.

The inevitable and tragic end had come to Estonia's three years of occupation by the Germans. The 20th SS Division, having assembled at Koeru, was faced with no alternative but to abandon its homeland and make its way through Latvia and Lithuania to East Prussia, where it would be reformed to fight again in a war that could no longer save or even help its country.[122] Its losses had been terrible, and a situation report drawn up at Koeru on 20 September 1944 showed that its three infantry regiments were lacking no less than four of their nine battalions.[123]

Estonian Combatants Association in GB

SS-Brigadeführer und Generalmajor der Waffen-SS Franz Augsberger, commander of the 20th SS Division, and Waffen-Obersturmbannführer Harald Riipalu, commander of the formation's 45th SS infantry regiment, watch Estonians training in the use of an MG 42 during an inspection of the Division reforming at the Neuhammer training grounds on 1.12.1944. This is one of a series of photographs taken by SS-PK Schultz and released to the press in early December 1944 (see Eesti Sõna, Berlin, 6.12.1944 & Runnak, 18.12.1944).

---

[122]Sources are unclear over how the survivors of the Division made their way back to Germany, and where they went upon arrival. According to Duprat (Histoire des SS, pg. 365), after having participated in the withdrawal from Riga, the Division was sent to the Stalluponen sector and then placed in reserve to the southwest of Warsaw, where it had to face the Russian offensive of January 1945. In his later Les Campagnes de la Waffen-SS, Vol. 2, pg. 165), he writes that the Division was trapped in the Courland pocket and was then sent by sea to the Polish front.

Three Estonian Knight's Cross holders at Truppenübungsplatz Neuhammer during the reforming of the 20th SS Division in the winter of 1944. At left is Waffen-Obersturmbannführer Alfons Rebane, commander of the 46th infantry regiment. In the center is Waffen-Unterscharführer Harald Nugiseks, a section leader in Rebane's regiment. At right Waffen-Obersturmbannführer Harald Riipalu, commander of the Division's 45th infantry regiment. All three wear the final 2nd German pattern collar patch and Nugiseks wears the Waffen-SS pattern sleeve shield.

OCTOBER 1944 - MAY 1945: REFORMING AND THE LAST BATTLES IN GERMANY:

The strength of the 20th SS Division had been drastically reduced by the time Estonia fell back under Russian control and the formation reached Germany.[124] In addition to the losses sustained in the desperate fighting to try to keep the Red Army out, large numbers of Estonians from the Division simply refused to abandon their country and families to the mercy of the Russians and disobeyed the order to withdraw. These men joined the "Brothers of the Forest" and continued to fight the invader as guerrillas for many years after the end of the Second World War.

Heinrich Himmler decided that the Estonian Division of the Waffen-SS should be rebuilt, and its survivors and those of the six destroyed SS Frontier Guard regiments were ordered by the SS-FHA on 6 October 1944 to the German Army's training area (Truppenübungsplatz) Neuhammer near Breslau in

---

[123]The 45th, 46th & 47th SS infantry regiments were lacking their Ist, IInd & IIIrd and IInd battalions, respectively (Klietmann, op.cit., pg. 513).

[124]As late as March 1945 Allied Intelligence (MID, German OB) was uncertain as to whether the Division had been transferred to Germany. Manpower Study reported the Division to be forming at Neuhammer under the SS-FHA in October 1944 but gave no listing for November 1944.

Silesia.[125] Work on rebuilding the formation under the Army's Department of Armaments and the SS-FHA[126] was begun in November but had to be curtailed in January 1945 when the Red Army launched its new offensive by breaking out of the Baranów bridgehead and crossing the Vistula River in mid-January.[127] On 21 January Russian troops crossed the Oder River at Borkenhaim, and the unprepared 20th SS Division had to be committed to battle once more.

To face the Russian offensive in Silesia, Army Group "Center" (Heeresgruppe "Mitte") was reformed on 25 January 1945 under Generaloberst Ferdinand Schörner by redesignating Army Group "A" and was made up of the German 1st and 4th Armored Armies and the 17th Army (the 7th Army joined the Army Group in May 1945).[128] The Estonian Division was to fight the remaining months of the war as a component of this new Army Group "Center," primarily within the VIIIth Army Corps of its 17th Army, but also under the LVIth Armored Corps, and for a short period in February/March 1945 with Corps Group "Silesia" (Korpsgruppe "Schlesien") of the 1st Armored Army.[129]

Most of the Division left Neuhammer by rail on 21 January 1945 and were rushed through Breslau and Brieg to the area south of Oppeln in Upper Silesia to help check the Russian advance on the northern flank of the Silesian front.[130] The Red Army was ranged roughly parallel to the Oder River which

---

[125]SS-FHA, Amt II Org.Abt. Ia/II, Tgb.Nr. 3572/44 g.Kdos., v. 6.10.1944, Verlegung 20. Waffen-Gren.Div. der SS (estn. Nr. 1) (T-175/141/2669112). The German Red Cross, Divisionsschicksale, Band II, pg. 804, gives the Division reforming at Tr.Üb.Pl Neuhammer from October 1944 until January 1945. To be noted that Neuhammer was an establishment of the German Army, not an SS-Tr.Üb.Pl of the Waffen-SS. Training was also carried out at Hohenstein and company commanders attended a course at Neveklau (H. Uus, letter of 8.10.81).

[126]"in Aufst. HRüst. (SSFHA) in Neuhammer" (Tessin, op.cit., Vol. 4, pg. 151).

[127]Der Freiwillige, 22. Jahrgang, Heft 4, April 1976, pg. 20.

[128]Schörner had held the rank of Generaloberst since 1.4.1944 and was promoted Generalfeldmarschall on 5.4.1945. He was given command of Army Group "Center" on 17.1.1945. For details of Army Group "Center" (1945) see Tessin, op.cit., Vol. 14, pg. 157.

[129]Charts show the 20th SS Division making up Korpsgruppe "Schlesien" along with the 168th Infantry Division in the 1st Armored Army on 1 March 1945 - but at 19 February and 12 April 1945 the Estonian Division was a part of the 17th Army. An eyewitness report (see fn. 132 below) gives the Division under the LVIth Armored Corps in March 1945, which is not given by Tessin or Klietmann. But Tessin (op.cit., Vol. 5, pg. 203) does show the HQ of the LVIth Armored Corps as having been reformed in February 1945 from the substitute HQ of the VIIIth Army Corps Breslau, at the disposal of Army Group "Center" in February and March 1945 (it was in Berlin at the disposal of Army Group "Vistula" in April 1945) and it was the G.O.C. LVIth Armored Corps, General der Kavallerie Rudolf Koch-Erpach, who seconded the proposal for Rebane's award of the Oak Leaves in April 1945 (for Rebane had been responsible for the rescue of the Corps HQ from the Oppeln pocket). Manpower Study gives the Division under "Jeckeln" of the 4th Armored Army, Army Group "Center" in February 1945 and under the VIIIth Army Corps of the 17th Army, Army Group "Center" from March 1945 until the end of the war (its compilers were thus unaware of the transfer to Prague).

[130]Most of the Division left Neuhammer by train on 21.1.1945, but the 46th SS infantry regiment left on 26.1.1945, and the 47th SS infantry regiment, SS-Ausbildungs-

flows in a northwesterly direction past Oppeln, Brieg, Breslau and Steinau. Behind this line (known both as the "Oder Front" and "Oppeln Front"), with its HQ at Tillowitz, the 20th SS Division was to fight for the next seven weeks, at first around Breslau, then gradually being beaten back with severe casualties to the southeast past Brieg and Oppeln. Fighting is reported at Dambrau, Schönwitz, Karbischau (some four kilometers from the Oder and fifteen from Oppeln) and Wolfsgrund. Particular and unexpected success in a battle near Wolfsgrund was due, in part, to the paralytic state of the attacking Russian soldiers, for they had overrun the well-stocked local distillery and were in no fit state to take on the men of the Waffen-SS.[131] The Estonian Division played a significant rôle in halting the enemy advance and stabilizing the upper Silesian front, and elements are reported to have been able to complete their reforming at Lamsdorf in Upper Silesia.[132]

und Ersatz-Regiment 20, part of a Nachrichtenstaffel and part of a Kranken-Kraftwagenzug and other elements did not leave for the Oder front and remained behind at Neuhammer to be formed into Kampfgruppe "Rehfeldt" (see page 188 of this book and fn. 173 (Waffen-Untersturmfuhrer Elmar Silm in Võitleja, Nr. 3/4, 1970; Der Freiwillige, 21. Jahrgang, Heft 5, Mai 1975, pg. 17; H. Uus, letter of 9.10.1981).

131 Võitleja, Nr. 6, 1970.

132 "Die letzte Schlacht - Der Einsatz der 20. (erste estnische) Panzergrenadierdivision [sic] der Waffen-SS in Oberschlesien im Frühjahr 1945," in Der Freiwillige, 22. Jahrgang, Heft 12, Dezember 1976, pp. 14-15. This eyewitness account of the last battle was signed "SS-Hstuf. (F) Wg." and was probably written by the commander of SS-Gau-Btl. 20, SS-Hstuf. Prof. Dr. W. Willing (H. Uus, letter of 30.9.81). The fact that neither author nor publisher was able to include the correct divisional title in the heading casts some doubt on the accuracy of the article's contents. It has appeared in English under the title "The Last Battle of the 20th Waffen-Grenadier-Division der SS (Estonia Nr. 1)" - An eyewitness report of an officer of the division in Siegrunen, Vol. IV, Nr. 4 (22), November 1980, pp. 16-18.

Waffen-Obersturmbannführer Alfons Rebane wears the 2nd German pattern divisional collar patch and outsize rank pips at Tr.Üb.Pl Neuhammer in the winter of 1944/45, while the Estonian Division was being reformed after its withdrawal from Estonia. Rebane had been transferred from the German Army to the Waffen-SS in April 1944, and his 658th Estonian Battalion had become the IInd battalion of the new 47th SS infantry regiment (SS-Freiw.Gren.Rgt. 47). On 26 July 1944 Rebane replaced Waffen-Standartenführer Juhan Tuuling as commander of the 20th SS Division's 46th infantry regiment, and having been promoted to Waffen-Obersturmbannführer on 9 November 1944, was recommended for the Oak Leaves of the Knight's Cross in early April 1945 by the G.O.C., LVIth Armored Corps. This recommendation was entered into the Awards Book (OKH/PA/P5) on 12 April 1945, and the award was approved and signed by Grossadmiral Karl Dönitz on 9 May 1945. Rebane thus became the 875th recipient of this high award, together with the Belgian Léon Degrelle (commander of the 28th SS Division "Wallonien"), he was one of the only two non-German recipients (not only in the Waffen-SS but throughout the German armed forces). Promoted to Waffen-Standartenführer in March 1945, he acted as deputy commander of the 20th SS Division in the last months of the war. Rebane (whose name appropriately translates as 'fox' in English) was highly regarded for his leadership and tactical skills and was affectionately known as 'the Estonian Rommel.' He died on 8 March 1976 in Augsberg, Bavaria.

Heinz Stutterecker

Here Waffen-Obersturmbannführer Harald Riipalu had replaced his Tartu pattern collar patch by the 2nd German pattern. The photograph was probably taken at Tr.Üb.Pl. Neuhammer in the winter of 1944/1945 while the Estonian Division was reforming after its withdrawal from Estonia. Riipalu led the 45th SS infantry regiment until the end of January 1945, when heart trouble forced him to be sent on sick-leave via Prague to Denmark. After the war Riipalu settled in England but never fully recovered and died in Yorkshire on 4 April 1961 at the age of 49.

Harald Riipalu, on sick-leave and here in civilian clothes, with Estonian Waffen-SS officers and men at Odense, Denmark in early 1945.

Harald Riipalu fell ill at the end of January 1945 and was sent on sick-leave to Denmark, where he was to stay until the end of the war.[133] Command of Riipalu's 45th SS infantry regiment passed first to SS-Obersturmbannführer Fritz Störtz, who had joined the Estonian SS Legion at the head of his 1st Company, Waffen-SS Battalion for Special Employment, in January 1943, and remaining with the Estonian formation, had been promoted to SS-Sturmbannführer on 9 November 1944 and by the beginning of March 1945 was commanding the divisional field replacement battalion (SS-F.E.B. 20). But Störtz was wounded soon after assuming command, and control of the Estonian Division's senior infantry regiment passed to Waffen-Hauptsturmführer Paul Maitla, previously commander of its first battalion, who was to lead the unit until the end of the war.

During February 1945 the Division was under the VIIIth Army Corps of the 17th Army of Army Group "Center," and it was so weakened that it had to be down-graded to the status of a battle group.[134] Towards the end of the month, while remaining a part of Army Group "Center," it came under the control of Corps Group "Silesia" of the 1st Armored Army.

For most of February 1945 Estonian divisional elements that had remained behind at Neuhammer in late January fought alongside Hungarian Waffen-SS troops in a battle group. This was SS-Kampfgruppe "Rehfeldt," led by SS-Obersturmbannführer Emil Rehfeldt, who had been operations officer of the Estonian Waffen-SS formation since 1943. This battle group fought near Bober, Queis and Lausitz Neisse from 4 to 28 February 1945 and included the 47th infantry regiment, SS Training and Replacement Regiment 20, part of a signal section and part of an M.T. ambulance section.[135] It was disbanded on 28

---

[133]Riipalu fell ill at the end of January or beginning of February 1945 according to H. Rüütel (letter of 15.10.81), who believes that his being shown in the Stellenbesetzungsliste as commander of the 45th SS infantry regiment was a mistake.

[134]Tessin, op.cit., Vol. 4, pg. 151.

[135]Der Freiwillige, 21. Jahrgang, Heft 5, Mai 1975, pg. 17 prefixes the battle group "SS-." See page 158 of this book for a photograph of Rehfeldt as "Ia" of the Estonian

February, and while Rehfeldt and 60 percent of his men were sent to Odense in Denmark, the remainder marched to rejoin the Estonian Division on the Oder front.

The Division was a part of Corps Group "Silesia" on 1 March 1945, and its order of battle of that day shows how its 45th and 46th infantry regiments were both missing their third battalions, whereas the 47th had all of its three. Apart from these infantry regiments, the following elements were listed as being in existence on that 1 March 1945:[136]

SS-Füsilier-Bataillon	infantry reconnaissance battalion
Waffen-Artillerie-Regiment 20	artillery regiment (4 detachments)
Nachrichten-Abteilung 20	signals battalion
Pionier-Bataillon 20	engineer battalion
Panzerjäger-Abteilung 20	antitank battalion
Dina 20	divisional supply elements
Feldersatz-Bataillon 20	field replacement battalion

The Russians resumed their advance on 10 March 1945 in the Grottkau area. Following heavy artillery fire, the Red Army managed to break through the left sector of the 20th SS Division on 15 March, positions that had been held by the 46th infantry regiment, and an attached infantry battalion of the German Army (Grenadier-Bataillon 486).[137] The Division's 45th infantry regiment was sent in and succeeded in driving back the enemy and sealing the breach.

Placed under the newly reformed LVIth Armored Corps of General der Kavallerie Rudolf Koch-Erpach, the survivors of the Estonian Division fell back fighting through Rossdorf, Jatzdorf, Korndorf, Tillowitz and Friedland, and the divisional HQ is known to have been transferred from Falkenberg to Friedland.[138]

Russian troops that had been advancing on the town of Neisse along the left bank of the river of that name linked up at Neustadt with other Red Army elements that had been advancing from Oppeln. By so doing they managed to trap the survivors of the 20th SS Division, along with soldiers of other German formations, in what became known as the Oppeln pocket.[139]

Divisional commander Augsberger saw that the only way to save his division from capture or destruction was to attempt a breakout from the pocket

SS Brigade in August 1943 as an SS-Sturmbannführer. He was promoted to SS-Obersturmbannführer on 9.11.1943, but although listed as being with the 20th SS Division on 1.10.1944, he is not shown with the formation in the 1.3.1945 Stellenbesetzungsliste. It is possible that the involvement of Hungarians had something to do with Berthold Maack's later arrival/choice as divisional commander, for he had been put in command of the 26th (Hungarian) SS Division on 25.1.45.

[136] Stellenbesetzungsliste der Waffen-SS, v. 1.3.1945.

[137] Source is as fn. 132, which states that the battalion's number is unconfirmed. This Grenadier-Bataillon was probably a former training/replacement unit and not a part of Grenadier-Regiment 486; it may have been the former Grenadier-Ausbildungs- und Ersatz-Bataillon 486.

[138] See fn. 132 above.

[139] The name of the pocket has been given in various forms by different authors ("Oppeln-Neisse" by Klietmann, op.cit., pg. 224; "Tillowitzer-Falkenberger" by a German eyewitness - see fn. 132 above), but Estonians who were there remember it simply as the "Oppeln pocket" (H. Uus, letter of 30.9.1981).

Waffen-Hauptsturmführer Paul Maitla, in a photograph probably taken soon after his award of the Knight's Cross of the Iron Cross on 23 August 1944. Maitla, a Hauptsturmführer since 30 January 1944, had been recommended for the award by the "Nordland" Division for his leadership of the Ist battalion of the 45th SS infantry regiment of the 20th SS Division - neither he nor his regiment were a part of the "Nordland" Division (as Schneider suggests, op.cit., pg. 231). Maitla was still a Waffen-Hauptsturmführer in command of I./SS 45 on 1 March 1945, but later that month succeeded SS-Obersturmbannführer Fritz Störtz as commander of the whole 45th infantry regiment. Sources give Maitla as being promoted to Waffen-Sturmbannführer, but this is unconfirmed. He disappeared, almost certainly killed, in Czechoslovakia in May 1945 (v. Seemen, op.cit., pg. 232 & Schneider, op.cit., pg. 231).

westwards, and for this he divided his forces into three groups.[140] The left group consisted mainly of Paul Maitla's 45th infantry regiment. Alfons Rebane was to lead his 46th regiment as the central group, and Augsberger himself took charge of the right group.

The 45th and 46th infantry regiments were holding the front north of Falkenberg on 18 March 1945 when Augsberger gave the order to break out of the encirclement and try to reach Ziegenhals to the west. The divisional antitank battalion, under its German commander SS-Hauptsturmführer Bernhard Langhorst, led the breakout and managed to pave the way to Ziegenhals - it was soon followed by the workshop company, engineer and signals battalions and artillery regiment.[141] Having successfully covered the withdrawal, the 45th and 46th infantry regiments finally made good their escape and reached the rest of the formation that was assembling at Ziegenhals.[142] Last to reach

---

[140]*Der Freiwillige, 22. Jahrgang, Heft 4, April 1976, pg. 20. They were known as "Durchbruchsgruppen," literally, "break-out groups."*

[141]*The source given under fn. 132 refers to engineers who had previously been at Rossdorf.*

[142]*8th Company, IInd Battalion of Waffen-Grenadier-Regiment 45, for example, retreated under orders along with 'several thousand German soldiers' south from Tillowitz to Ziegenhals on 19.3.1945. Forced to abandon their burning vehicles after being attacked after only an hour's travel, the main part of the journey (about 75 kms taking some 15 hours) had to be on foot off the road, and the men were under fire from Russian AFVs as they advanced on Ziegenhals. (Translation of memoirs of the*

Ziegenhals were the survivors of the divisional HQ - Augsberger, who had led the Estonians in the Waffen-SS since July 1943, had been killed, together with his adjutant, SS-Obersturmführer Hinz, on the first day of the breakout near Neustadt on 19 March.[143]

Augsberger was to be replaced by SS-Oberführer Berthold Maack, who since 25 January 1945 had been titular commander of the stillborn 26th (Hungarian) SS Division, but in the time it took him to arrive, the divisional "Ia" (operations officer - 1. Generalstabsoffizier (Führung)), SS-Sturmbannführer Hans-Joachim Mützelfeldt, assumed temporary command.

The breakout had been rendered all the more difficult because only one usable road was available, but was executed without panic and with only minor disorder. Apart from divisional commander Augsberger, some 25 percent of the formation's manpower had been lost with almost all of the heavy equipment.[144]

SS-Sturmbannführer Mützelfeldt and his men were ordered by a Major Schiller from the HQ of the LVIth Armored Corps to regroup and establish a stronghold to the south of Ziegenhals, but before this could even be begun, fresh orders were received that placed the Division in Army Corps reserve.[145] During the evening of 22 March 1945, the Division withdrew from Ziegenhals and was ordered on 1 April 1945 to the northern edge of the Riesengebirge area south of Hirschberg. There it regrouped and received new heavy weapons and an Estonian battalion coming from Dresden and two Police companies as reinforcements.[146]

The withdrawal was unavoidable and had been ordered by divisional commander Augsberger on 18 March - it was the only way to prevent the total destruction or capture of the Division and so kept it in action for the remaining weeks of the war. The retreat must have been misinterpreted at Corps level in the confusion that followed, and with Augsberger dead and unable to clarify what

---

former Waffen-Obersturmführer and commander of 8./II./SS 45, provided by Henno Uus, letter of 8.10.81).

[143]See fn. 132. After the successful breakout, Rebane, with a small group of men, were ordered to go back to the pocket to rescue their Army Corps HQ. Rebane was again successful and later believed this was the action that earned him the Oak Leaves to his Knight's Cross (H. Rüütel, letter of 4.10.1981).

[144]H. Uus, letter of 30.9.1981.

[145]See fn. 132.

[146]D.R.K., Divisionsschicksale, Band II, pg. 804 gives the Division reforming in the Riesengebirge March/April 1945. According to one source (see fn. 132), it was an Estonian engineer battalion from Dresden that was added to the Division in the Riesengebirge area after the successful escape from the Oppeln pocket. This can hardly have been the Division's own SS-Pionier-Btl. 20 for this had itself successfully escaped from the encirclement, and so could have been a mistaken report for an Estonian construction (Bau-) or labor (Arbeits-) battalion. It may have been (SS-) Bau-Bataillon 20/Bau- und Pionier-Bataillon 20 that had been formed at Lamsdorf on 15.2.1945.

There was possibly some connection with SS-Kampfgruppe "Ebelt" (see page 201 below), which had its origins with the SS Engineer Training & Replacement unit at Dresden (SS-Pionier-Ausbildungs- und Ersatz-Regiment/Bataillon 1), which was responsible for the training of Waffen-SS engineers. The two police companies remain unidentified.

had taken place to his superiors, reports started to come through that the Estonian Division had disintegrated. The source of this confusion appears to have been a report prepared by the HQ of the LVIth Armored Corps, according to which the Division had been routed and ceased to exist. As soon as he became aware of this unfairly damning report, Ia Mützelfeldt made his way to Corps HQ and insisted to his surprised superiors that the 20th SS Division was still well organized and ready for combat. Meanwhile, however, Hitler had raged on 23 March 1945 when told by his senior aide, General Wilhelm Burgdorf, that the Estonian Division of the Waffen-SS had collapsed.[147]

That Hitler was soon told that the report was all a misunderstanding is evident from the subsequent awards to officers of the Division of the Knight's Cross. When this most prestigous of German decorations was awarded to a unit commander, it usually honored not only the recipient as an individual, but also the men under his command. If the Estonian Waffen-SS Division was in disgrace, then the Germans would certainly never have recommended its deputy commander, Waffen-Standartenführer Alfons Rebane, for the Oak Leaves in April 1945, so making him one of the two most highly-decorated non-Germans in the entire Wehrmacht and Waffen-SS.[148] Nor would SS-Hauptsturmführer Bernhard Langhorst, commander of the divisional antitank battalion that had led the breakout to Ziegenhals, have been awarded the Knight's Cross of the Iron Cross on 5 April 1945.[149] But these facts have been ignored by at least two post-war historians of the Waffen-SS, who have unfairly put this courageous division on record as "falling apart" and "collapsing, refusing to continue to fight once their homeland was lost."[150]

---

[147]Duprat, Histoire des SS, pg. 365; Stein, op.cit., pg. 194, fn. 70; Der Freiwillige - as fn. 132). The alleged 'collapse' of the Estonian Division was one of the many topics raised in a rambling conversation between Hitler and Burgdorf on the night of 23.3.1945. Burgdorf, Chief of Army Personnel Office and senior aide to Hitler in succession to General Schmundt who had died of the wounds he received in the 20.7.1944 "bomb plot," provided inaccurate information in that he confused the Estonians with the Latvians and mistakenly said that the 20th SS Division had been attacked frontally, whereas it was in fact surrounded along with some four other divisions. Burgdorf committed suicide in the Reich Chancellery on 1.5.1945. (H. Uus, letter of 30.9.1981).

[148]Rebane, also commander of the 20th SS Division's 46th infantry regiment, and the Belgian Lēon Degrelle (both members of the Waffen-SS) were the only two non-Germans serving with the German armed forces in the Second World War to receive the prestigious Oak Leaves to the Knight's Cross and so were the most highly decorated foreign volunteers. Seventy-six of the 882 known awards of the Oak Leaves went to men of the Waffen-SS (8 percent) - a further 7, bringing the total to 889, went to soldiers of allied nations (3 Romanians, 2 Japanese, 1 Spaniard and 1 Finn). These 7 were not numbered awards, nor for some reason was Degrelle's, but Rebane was recorded as the 875th "soldier of the German Wehrmacht" to receive it. He was proposed for the award on 3 April 1945, seconded by General der Kavallerie Koch-Erpach (G.O.C. LVIth Armored Corps) and the Reichsführer-SS, and the proposal was registered by OKH/PA/P 5 on 12 April 1945.

[149]Augsberger had received the Knight's Cross as divisional commander 11 days before his death and the breakout. Schneider (op.cit., pg. 218) is correct in giving Bernhard Langhorst's rank as SS-Hauptsturmführer - von Seemen (op.cit., pg. 217) makes the mistake of giving his Allgemeine-SS rank of SS-Sturmbannführer.

[150]Stein, op.cit., pg. 194: "The previously reliable 20th Waffen-Gren.Div. der SS (estn. Nr. 1) fell apart when it was again committed to battle in Silesia early in 1945."

In April 1945 the Estonian and German survivors of the 20th SS Division were not attached to any specific corps, but rather were listed as being available for employment ("zur Verfügung") in Silesia under the 17th Army of Army Group "Center."[151] They were engaged in bloody defensive fighting on the Schönau-Bolkenhain-Löwenberg line, around Hirschberg and then further to the north in the Goldberg area. Finally what remained of the Estonian Division was forced to retreat southwestward back past Hirschberg through Reichenberg, Oberschreiberhau and Tannwald towards Prague, where they took up what were to be their last battle positions of the war at Turnau near the town of Melnik to the north of the Czech capital.[152]

When Germany capitulated on 8 May 1945, the main concern of all the Division's survivors was to try to be taken prisoner by the Western Allies rather than by their bitter enemies the Russians. There was no unified plan, and individual unit commanders were left to their own devices, each trying to get themselves and those of their men fit to travel to the West. For the majority there was no alternative but to surrender to the Red Army on 8 May in and to the north of Prague, but some did escape, and a number are known to have reached the lines held by the U.S. 3rd Army around Pilsen.[153] But for some of the Estonians among them (many were Germans), the initial relief soon turned to bitter and disbelieving disappointment, for the decision had been taken to hand the Estonians back to the Russians as part of the shameful program of

---

Stein felt the Estonian Division had fought well in the 'futile' (hopeless, perhaps, but no Estonian would have thought it 'futile'! - ed.) defense of its homeland during the Russian advance of 1944, but "lost much of its zeal" once the Red Army had occupied Estonia (ibid, pp. 178 & 194). Duprat, Histoire des SS, pg. 365: ". . . (the Division) cracked in Silesia in March 1945, as is shown by the Führer conference of 23 March. It felt less need to fight so far from its homeland, which is quite normal." Duprat, Les Campagnes de la Waffen-SS, Vol. 2, pg. 166: ". . . exhausted and demoralized, the Division collapsed, refusing to continue to fight once its homeland was lost." On the other hand, post-war Estonian claims that the Division had a perfect record without a single case of desertion being recorded appear equally far-fetched. Two sentries who disappeared without a trace may have been captured by the Russians rather than have deserted, but the 200 survivors of the IIIrd battalion, 46th SS infantry regiment who dispersed into the woods on 26.9.1944 were clearly deserting their formation, no matter how valid their motives. The same is also true for all those who refused to abandon Estonia and joined the "Brothers of the Forest."

[151]Tessin, op.cit., Vol. 4, pg. 53. On 12.4.1945 Army Group "Center" was made up of the 1st Armored Army, 17th Army and XXIXth Army Corps. In turn, the 17th Army contained the VIIIth & XVIIth Army Corps, XXXXth Armored Corps and elements at "Fortress Breslau" (Div. Stab z.b.V. 609, Fest.Kdt. Breslau). The survivors of the 20th SS Division joined those of the 18th SS Division "Horst Wessel," Fallschirm-Panzer-Division 1 "Hermann Göring" and Div.Stab z.b.V. 603 as being part of the 17th Army, but not any of its constituent corps. (Keilig, Das Deutsche Heer 1939-1945, pg. 31/7).

[152]Melnik is given by Tessin, op.cit., Vol. 4, pg. 151.

[153]D.R.K., Divisionsschicksale, Band II, pg. 804; Tessin, op.cit., Vol. 4, pg. 151. See also Gliederung des deutschen Heeres in den Jahren 1944/45 (Schematische Übersicht) - 1.3.1945, KTB/OKW, IV., 189 ff. The Division surrendered in Prague itself according to Abschrift, Einheiten-Archiv, Estnische Einheiten (see fn. 1 on page 122 of this book). Duprat, Les Campagnes de la Waffen-SS, pg. 166. 8./II./SS 45 is said to have been at Hirschberg on 9.5.1945 (H. Uus, letter of 8.10.1981).

forced repatriation that was to be carried out so effectively by the British and Americans after Germany's defeat.[154]

Among the fortunate Estonians who managed to survive the war and escape Russian captivity and revenge were Waffen-Brigadeführer Johannes Soodla, Knight's Cross holders Waffen-Standartenführer Alfons Rebane and Waffen-Obersturmbannführer Harald Riipalu, Waffen-Obersturmbannführer Ain Mere and Waffen-Sturmbannführer August Vask. Soodla, the senior Estonian officer in the Waffen-SS who had been appointed Inspector General of the Estonian SS Legion in 1943 and retained this responsibility for all Estonian Waffen-SS troops throughout the war, escaped to Florida in the U.S.A through the French-occupied zone of Germany. He later returned to Europe and spent the rest of his life in West Germany, where he died in 1967. Rebane, who with Lēon Degrelle were the only two non-Germans in the whole German armed forces to receive the Oak Leaves to the Knight's Cross, also settled in Germany and died in Augsburg on 8 March 1976. Riipalu, who had received the Knight's Cross as commander of the 20th SS Division's 45th infantry regiment from Felix Steiner on 23 August 1944, fell gravely ill as the war drew to a close and handing over his command to Waffen-Hauptsturmführer Paul Maitla, was forced to Denmark on sick-leave. He settled in England after the war and published a book of his experiences in London in 1950.[155] He never fully recovered and died at the age of 49 at Heckmondwike, Yorkshire, on 4 April 1961, dispelling any doubt anyone may have had that this brave officer had escaped the fate of his men by feigning sickness.

While their fellow Estonians were being handed back to certain death by the Americans, back in Prague an equally tragic and shameful fate befell many sick and wounded survivors of the Estonian SS Division as they lay in their hospital beds in the Czech capital. The Czechs had suffered under the German occupation of their country, and on the day following the capitulation, 9 May

---

[154]See Victims of Yalta by Nikolai Tolstoy & other sources quoted in his Notes. The following summary is provided by H. Rüütel (letter of 23.4.1978): "Forcible repatriation of Balts took place in France, French occupied Zone of Germany, on French territory by the United States Army, in Finland and in Sweden. On 17 August 1945 the U.S. Army forced 48 Estonians to return to the Soviet Union from Camp Cherbourg (D.E.F. Nr. 23) and on the same day another 18 Estonians started their journey to unknown destinations from a U.S. Army camp near Marseille (C.C.P.W.E. Nr. 404). Also on the same day about 200 General Vlassov officers were brutally forced onto lorries by the Americans, which took them to a Soviet ship. The French authorities forced an unknown number of Balts to return including the high-ranking Estonian officer, Colonel Juhan Vermet, formerly C.O. of Estnische Grenzschutz-Regiment 2 (at 1.3.1945 a Waffen-Obersturmbannführer and C.O. of the 47th SS infantry regiment - ed.). On 25.1.1946 Sweden forcibly repatriated 150 Latvians, 10 Lithuanians, 7 Estonians and 1,250 Germans to the Soviet Union. Of the Estonians, one was 37 years of age and the remaining six were only 18 years old. In Finland a small number of Estonians were handed over to the Russians. In the British controlled POW Camp 2227 (Zedelghem, Belgium) there was only once trouble, when the Russians came for a Latvian colonel and a Latvian captain. The colonel stabbed himself with a pocket knife, was taken to hospital and survived. The Russians took the captain, and he was never heard of again. The Latvian colonel's action settled the future for us (POW Camp 2227 was also my 'home" for a time). Nobody was forced to do anything against their will any more."

 [155]See bibliography.

1945, Prague townspeople took to the streets and set about seeking revenge upon anyone they thought to be a German or associated in some way with the German occupation of their country. Groups are reported to have stormed hospitals and to have tortured and killed not only veterans of the 20th SS Division, but also the totally innocent nurses and doctors who were attending them.[156]

ORDER-OF-BATTLE (COMPOSITE) (* - unconfirmed)

Stab der Divison/Div.-Kommando[157] (ordered 24.1.1944 by reorganizing Stab 3. Estn. SS-Freiw.Brig.,[158] which had been formed from Stab Estn. SS-Legion)

SS-Kradmeldestaffel/Kradmeldezug

SS-Div-Kartenstells (mot.)/SS-Kartenstelle 20

SS-Musikzug

SS-Div.-Begleit-Kompanie

Waffen Grenadier Regiment der SS 45 (estnisches Nr. 1) (regimental sized Estn. SS-Legion began to form at SS-Tr. Üb. Pl. Debica on 1.10.1942. March 1943 I. Btl. was detached and became an SS-Gren.-Btl. (mot.) & attached to SS-Div. "Wiking" (see SS-Pz.Gren.Btl. "Narwa" below). March 1943: IV. Btl. renamed as new I. Btl. & remainder of Legion renamed as 1. Estn. SS-Freiw.Gren.Rgt. Later renamed to SS-Freiw.Gren.Rgt. 1 (Estn. Brigade). 22.10.1943: SS-Freiw.Gren.Rgt. 42.[159] 12.11.1943: SS-Freiw.Gren.Rgt. 45.[160] 22.1.1944: SS-Freiw.Gren.Rgt. 45 (estnisches Nr. 1).[161] 26.5.1944: Waffen-Gren.Rgt. der SS 45 (estn. Nr. 1).[162] 29.9.1944: I. Btl. missing.[163] Rebuilt at Tr. Üb. Pl. Neuhammer 11/1944 - 1/1945. Listed 1.3.1945 with only I. & II. Btl. Broke out of Oppeln pocket in mid-March 1945.

Waffen-Grenadier Regiment der SS 46 (estnisches Nr. 2) (raised in early 1943 as 2. Estn. SS-Freiw.Gren.Rgt. for Estn. SS-Freiw.-Brig., which ordered 5.5.1943. Later renamed to SS-Freiw.Gren.Rgt. 2 (Estn. Brigade). 22.10.1943: SS-Freiw.Gren.Rgt. 43.[159] 12.11.1943: SS-Freiw.Gren.Rgt. 46.[160] 22.1.1944: SS-Freiw.Gren.Rgt. 46 (estnisches Nr. 2).[161] 19.8.1944: former 200th (Estonian) Infantry Regiment of the Finnish Army left Finland for Estonia & its I. Btl. (I./J.R. 200) became new III./Waffen-Gren.Rgt. der SS 46 in September 1944. Attached to 87. Inf.Div. from 3.9.1944 - known as "Einheit Pärnoja" after its C.O., who disbanded the unit on 23.9.1944 rather than obey order to withdraw from Estonia. Regiment listed on

---

[156]*This horrifying story is given by the not-always-reliable Duprat in his 1968 Histoire des SS, on page 365 of which he writes that "all" the occupants of the hospitals in Prague, doctors and nurses included, were tortured and killed. In his later book on the campaigns of the Waffen-SS (Les Campagnes de la Waffen-SS, Vol. 2, 1973, pg. 166) he limits himself to say that "certain elements were taken in the Czech uprising." It is possible that unpleasant action was taken at the SS hospital in Prague (SS-Lazarett at Sanatorium Praha-Podol & Sokol Building at Podoli).*

[157]*Not to be confused with the German formation staff (Aufstellungsstab) that arrived at SS-Tr.Üb.Pl Debica on 23 November 1942 from SS-Totenkopf-Infanterie-Ersatz-Bataillon III, Brno.*

[158] *See fn. 6 on pg 122 of this book.*

[159]*See fn. 4 on page 122 of this book.*

[160]*See fn. 79 on page 159 of this book.*

[161]*See fn. 80 on page 159 of this book.*

[162]*Klietmann, op.cit., pp. 223 & 228.*

[163]*ibid, pg. 513.*

20.9.1944 as missing its II. & III. Btls. Rebuilt at Tr. Üb.Pl. Neuhammer 11/1944 - 1/1945. Listed 1.3.1945 with only I. & II. Btl. Broke out of Oppeln pocket in mid-March 1945.

Waffen-Grenadier Regiment der SS 47 (estnisches Nr. 3) (ordered 24.1.1944 as SS-Freiw.Gren.Rgt. 47, the intention was to build it from III./45 & III./46, but its I. & II. Btle. were provided by transferring Estnisches Bataillon 659 & 658 respectively from the Army. 22.1.1944: SS-Freiw.Gren.Rgt. 47 (estnisches Nr. 3).[161] Completed 24.4.1944 but without its III. Btl. 26.5.1944: Waffen-Gren.Rgt der SS 47 (estn. Nr. 3).[162] 20.9.1944: II. Btl. missing.[163] Rebuilt at Tr.Üb.Pl. Neuhammer 11/1944 - 1/1945. Listed 1.3.1945 with I., II. & III. Btle.

SS-Panzer-Grenadier-Bataillon "Narwa" (The 800 strong I./Rgt. 1 der Estn. SS-Legion was detached on 4.4.43 and renamed as an SS-Gren.Btl. (mot.) was attached to SS-Div. "Wiking" in the summer of 1943.[164] Renamed Estnisches SS-Freiwilligen-Bataillon "Narwa" & later SS-Pz.Gren.Btl. "Narwa," it served "Wiking" as III./SS-Pz.Gren.Rgt. 10 "Westland" and is reported to have reached a strength of 1,280 men.[165] Survivors of the Btl. returned to the 20. SS-Div. & in 7/1944 were used as the cadre for SS-Freiw.Div.-Füs.-Btl. 20, which ordered 18.4.1944 (see below).

estn. SS-Füsilier-Bataillon 20/SS-Freiwilligen-Divisions-Füsilier-Bataillon 20/SS-Füsilier Bataillon 20/Waffen-Füsilier-Bataillon der SS 20 (ordered 18.4.1944 & formed 7/44 on basis of survivors of SS-Pz.Gren.Btl. "Narwa" returning from SS-Div. "Wiking." Still forming 24.4.1944. 26.5.1944: Waffen-Füsilier-Bataillon der SS 20.[162] Listed on 1.3.1945. Name "Narwa" may unofficially have been retained in title after return to the 20. SS-Div.)

estn. SS-Panzerjäger-Abteilung 20/SS-Panzerjäger-Abteilung 20/SS-Waffen-Panzerjäger-Abteilung 20 (ordered 24.1.1944 as SS-Panzerjäger-Abteilung 20 with its 1. Kp. based on the 14. Pz.Jäg.Kp of SS-Freiw.Gren.Rgt. 46.[166] Completed 10.7.1944.[167] 26.5.1944: SS-Waffen-Panzerjäger-Abteilung 20.[162] Listed 1.3.1945. Broke out of the Oppeln pocket in mid-March 1945.

*SS-Fla.-Kompanie

*Sturmgeschütz-Abteilung/Kompanie

*Gren.Begleitzug

*SS-Waffen-Sturmgeschütz-Abteilung/Batterie 20 (possibly part of the Panzerjäger-Abteilung).

Waffen-Artillerie-Regiment der SS (estnisches Artillerie-Regiment Nr. 1) (ordered 24.1.1944 as SS-Freiw.Art.Rgt. 20 with SS-Art.Abt. 53 providing its I. Abt. New HQ & II. & III. (le.) Abt. raised 4.4.1944 - IV. (schw.) Abt. began forming at Benešov on 31.3.1944. 26.5.1944: Waffen-Artillerie-

---

[164]*ibid, pg. 134 - on page 225 it is stated that the battalion was detached from the Legion on 23.3.1943. See fn. 64 on pg. 151 of this book.*

[165]*The battalion retained field post number 48 314 throughout - first in 1943 as I./Estnische SS-Legion (see fn. 61 on page 149); then in the summer of 1944 as SS-Pz.Gren.Btl. "Narwa" with "Wiking" (Klietmann, op.cit., pg. 140), and by August 1944 as SS-Füs-Btl. 20 (see fn. 111 on page 177). By August 1944 a new III./SS-Pz.Gren.Rgt. 10 "Westland" had been formed and given the field post number 35 703. SS-Sturmbannführer Georg Eberhardt was commander of the battalion while serving in "Wiking." See Tessin, op.cit., Vol. 4, pg. 151 & Vol. 14, pg. 184. The strength of 1,280 is given by Jüri Remmelgas in Kolm kuuske, pg. 130.*

[166]*According to Tessin, op.cit., Vol. 4, pg. 151, the battalion was based on SS-Pz.Jäg.Abt. 53 (i.e., the former Brigade's battalion).*

[167]*Klietmann, op.cit., pg. 227.*

Regiment der SS 20 (estnisches Art.Rgt. Nr.1).[162] Listed 1.3.1945 with 4 Abt. Broke out of the Oppeln pocket in mid-March 1945).

estn. SS-Freiwilligen-Flak-Abteilung 20/SS-Flak-Abteilung 20 (ordered 24.1.1944 as SS-Freiw.Flak-Abt. 20 from SS-Flak-Abt. 53. 26.5.1944: SS-Waffen-Flak-Abt. 20.[162] Destroyed in Estonia in August/September 1944 & deleted by hand from FpÜ of 25.8.1944. Not reformed at Neuhammer because Corps Flak units were by then preferred to divisional Flak units for SS infantry & field post numbers dropped from lists in 1945.)

SS-Waffen-Nachrichten-Abteilung 20 (ordered 24.1.1944 & formed as SS-Freiw.Nachr.Abt. 20 from SS-Nachr.Kp. 20 on 13.4.1944. 26.5.1944: SS-Waffen-Nachrichten-Abteilung 20.[162] Listed 25.8.1944 & 1.3.1945. Broke out of the Oppeln pocket in mid-March 1945. An exclusively German unit throughout.)

SS-Nachrichten-Kompanie 20 (ordered 24.1.1944 & formed by renumbering SS-Nachr.Kp. 53. Used as basis for SS-Nachr.Abt. 20.)

SS-Waffen-Pionier-Bataillon 20 (ordered 24.1.1944 as SS-Freiw.Pi.Btl. 20 & formed from the 15. Pi.Kpen. of SS-Freiw.Gren.Rgt. 45 & 46. 26.5.1944: SS-Waffen-Pionier-Bataillon 20.[162] Listed 1.3.1945. Broke out of the Oppeln pocket in mid-March 1945.)

SS-Nachschubführer 20/ Kommandeur der SS-Divisions-Nachschubtruppen 20 (formed 24.1.1944 with the former Versorgungs-Einheiten 53 - became SS-Versorgungs-Regiment 20).

SS-Divisions-Nachschubtruppen 20 (listed on 25.8.1944 - later renamed SS-Versorgungs-Regiment 20, which see for sub-units. Dina 20 still listed on 1.3.1945.)

SS-Versorgungs-Truppen 20 (newly formed from the corresponding elements of the Estn. SS-Freiw.Brigade - after 25.8.1944 reformed with Nachschubtruppen into SS-Versorgungs-Regiment 20, which see for components).

SS-Versorgungs-Regiment 20 (formed after 25.8.1944 from SS-Divisions-Nachschubtruppen 20 & SS-Waffen-Versorgungs-Truppen 20)

SS-Versorgungs-Staffel (reported in 1944)

SS-Nachschub-Kompanie/Zug (listed as a Kompanie on 25.8.1944, later reduced to a Zug).

1. (& 2.)* SS-Kraftfahr-Kompanie (90t) (only one Kompanie shown at 25.8.1944)

1. & 2 SS-Fahrschwadron (60t) (both listed on 25.8.1944)

*1., 2. & 3. SS-Fahrkolonne

leichte SS-Artilleriekolonne (listed on 25.8.1944, but field post number subsequently given to SS-Kraftfahrzeug-Instandsetzungs-Zug)

SS-Kraftfahrzeug-Instandsetzungs-Zug (probably the forerunner of SS-Kraftwagenwerkstatt-Kompanie &/or SS-Werkstatt-Kompanie 20)

SS-Werkstatt-Kompanie 20[168] (formed from SS-Kraftwagenwerkstatt-Kompanie of the Estn. SS-Freiw.Brigade. Broke out of the Oppeln pocket in mid-March 1945)

---

[168]Hand entered amendments to a copy of the 25.8.1944 Waffen-SS field post number guide suggest that sometime after 25.8.1944 SS-Werkstatt-Kp. 20 became SS-Feldzeug-Kp. 20. This is unlikely by the differing natures of the two companies (workshop on the one hand, an ordnance stores on the other), and it is more likely that the field post number of the one company passed to the other, and that SS-Feldzeug-Kp 20 was formed from the Waffenwerkstattzug.

SS-Feldzeug-Kompanie 20[168]

SS-Wirtschafts-Bataillon 20 (listed as such on 25.8.1944, but should have been renamed SS-Verwaltungstruppen-Abteilung 20 from 15.8.1944)

SS-Bäckerei-Kompanie/Zug 20 (listed as a Kompanie on 25.8.1944, later reduced to a Zug)

SS-Schlächterei-Kompanie/Zug 20 (listed as a Kompanie on 25.8.1944, later reduced to a Zug)

SS-Verpflegungs-Amt (cancelled after 25.8.1944)

SS-Verwaltungstruppen-Abteilung 20 (formed by renaming SS-Wirtschafts-Bataillon 20, which see above for components)

SS-Sanitäts-Abteilung 20 (listed on 25.8.1944 but later reduced to a single SS-Sanitäts-Kompanie)

1. SS-Sanitäts-Kompanie 20 (listed on 25.8.1944)

SS-Truppenentgiftungszug 20 (deleted after 25.8.1944)

2. SS-Sanitäts-Kompanie 20 (deleted after 25.8.1944)

SS-Krankenkraftwagen-Kompanie/Zug 20 (listed as a Kompanie in 1944 & 1945, but eventually reduced to a Zug)

SS-Sanitäts-Nachschub-Kompanie (reported in summer 1944)

SS-Feldlazarett 20 (listed summer 1944 with same field post number as SS-Krankenkraftwagen-Kompanie 20)

SS-Veterinär-Kompanie 20 (ordered 24.1.1944 & formed by renumbering the SS-Veterinär-Kompanie 53 of the Estn. SS-Freiw.Brigade)

SS-Feldpostamt (mot.) 20 (listed 25.8.1944)

SS-Kriegsberichter-Zug 20/SS-Kriegsberichter-Trupp 20 (based on the SS-KB-Zug that was sent to the Legion on 23.3.1943 from the SS-KB-Abt. Listed as SS-KB-Trupp on 25.8.1944)[169]

SS-Feldgendarmerie-Trupp (mot.) 20/SS-Waffen-Feldgendarmerie-Trupp 20 (SS-FG-Trupp 20 listed on 25.8.1944)

SS-(Ausbildungs- und) Ersatz-Regiment 20 (Division's original SS-F.E.B. 20 was renamed SS-Ausbildungs- und Ersatz-Bataillon 20 & on 6.12.1944 expanded to SS-Ausbildungs- und Ersatz-Regiment 20. From 10.2 - 12.2.1945 part of Kampfgruppe "Rehfeldt." 15.2.1945 Regiment sent from Forst/Neisse to Odense in Denmark, where it stayed to end of the war. When Kampfgruppe "Rehfeldt" disbanded on 28.2.1945, Rehfeldt & 60 percent of his men joined SS-A.-u.Rgt. 20 in Denmark)[170]

*SS-Ersatz-Bataillon "Narwa" (received field post numbers in February & in March 1944 became III./Ers.Rgt. Reval - later known as Estn. Ersatz-Btl. "Narwa" - not confirmed as having served the 20. SS-Division)

SS-Waffen-Feldersatz-Bataillon 20 (ordered January 1944 as SS-F.E.B. 20 & formed 7.2.1944 by renaming SS-F.E.B. 53. Later reorganized as SS-Ersatz-Regiment 20 - see above).

*Divisions-Kampfschule

---

[169]Jüri Remmelgas, a former war correspondent now living in Stockholm, wrote that the Estonian war correspondents platoon was attached to the Estonian Division under the designation of 20. Estn. Kreigsberichter-Zug (it was administratively under the SS-Kriegsberichter-Abteilung in Berlin, which later became SS-Standarte "Kurt Eggers") Eesti riik ja rahvas II Maailmasõjas, Vol. VII, pp.

[170]Klietmann, op.cit., pg. 227. Given as SS-Ersatz-Regiment 20 on 24.4.1944. When at Odense, Denmark, in 1945 the unit was still referred to by its old name: SS-F.E.B. 20.

SS-Waffen-Feldersatz Bataillon 20 (a new SS-F.E.B. 20 was formed when the original was expanded to SS-Ersatz-Regiment 20. Listed on 1.3.45)

(SS-) Baubataillon 20/Bau- und Pionier-Bataillon 20 (this battalion for the construction of field fortifications was formed 15.2.1945 at Lamsdorf in Upper Silesia from men of SS Construction Inspectorates (SS-Bauinspektionen) Krakau & Breslau. Led by SS-Hstuf. (F.) Prof. Dr. W. Willing, it was made up of 80-100 German Waffen-SS men from the two Inspectorates and 250 Volkssturm members from the Falkenberg district of Upper Silesia. It could have been the "Estonian Pionierbataillon" reported to have joined the 20. SS-Division in March 1945 in the Riesengebirge area)[171]

*SS-Alarm Regiment 20

NON-DIVISIONAL ELEMENTS ABSORBED BY OR ATTACHED TO THE 20th SS DIVISION, OR WHICH PROVIDED THE FORMATION WITH MEN:

A: GERMAN ARMY:

1) ABSORBED:

Estnische Kompanie 657 (formed late 1941 as Ostkompanie (estn.) 657 - absorbed by Brigade in July 1942)

Estnische Bataillon 658 (formed 1.1.1943 by renaming Ostbataillon (estn.) 658. 100 men were transferred to the Division in February 1944 & the whole battalion became II./SS-Freiw.Gren.Rgt. 47 on 24.4.1944)[172]

Estnische Bataillon 659 (formed 1.1.1943 by renaming Ostbataillon (estn.) 659. 250 men were transferred to the Division in February 1944 & the whole battalion became I./SS-Freiw.Gren.Rgt. 47 on 24.4.1944)[172]

Estnische Bataillon 660 (formed 1.1.1943 by renaming Ostbataillon (estn.) 660 & absorbed by SS-Freiw.Gren.Rgt. 46 in July 1943)

Note: The 657th Estonian Company and 658th, 659th, and 660th Estonian Battalions were all ordered to be transferred from the German Army to the Waffen-SS in July 1943, but in fact their actual transfer was staggered (OKH, Gen.St.d.H., Org.Abt. II/17893 geh., v. 21.7.1943 - P. H. Buss).

Divisionsstab z.b.V. 300 (formed 1.5.1944 from the HQ of the 13. Luftwaffen-Feld-Division under Army Group "North." While fighting on Lake Ilmen, it controlled the 2nd, 4th, 5th & 6th Estonian Frontier Guard Regiments (see under B: Police below), which were later all absorbed by the Division).

2) ATTACHED (POSSIBLY BETWEEN 22.1.1945 & 20.3.1945):

Heeres-Sturmartillerie-Batterie 236 (presumably one of the 4 batteries of Heeres-Sturm-Art.Brigade 236)

Grenadier-Regiment 417 (destroyed at Baranōw in 1945, its survivors went to Silesia)

Heeres-Pionier-Brigade 655 (Radf.) (formed November 1944 with its Ist battalion from Pionier-Btl. 655 & its IInd battalion from Pionier-Btl. 676. Under 4.Pz.Armee at Görlitz)

---

[171] *Tessin's reliance on field post data (op.cit., Vol. 4, pg. 152) makes him late in dating the forming of SS-Bau-Btl. 20 as April 1945. See fn. 146 on page 191 of this book.*

[172] *See fn. 89 on page 163 of this book.*

Panzerjäger-Kompanie 1348 (the only German Army element bearing this number was Sturmgeschütz-Abteilung 1348, which became Panzerjäger-Abteilung 348)

Kampfgruppe "Fritsch"

Kampfgruppe "Hamann"

B: GERMAN POLICE:

Estnische Schutzmannschafts-Bataillon 29 (disbanded 1943 & some of its men volunteered for the Estonian SS Legion)

Estnische Schutzmannschafts-Bataillon 33

Estnische Schutzmannschafts-Bataillon 36

Estnische Schutzmannschafts-Bataillon 37

Estnische Polizei-Bataillon 38

Estnische Schutzmannschafts-Bataillon 39 (disbanded October 1943 & its men went to the Brigade)

Estnische Polizei-Bataillon 287(disbanded and its men went to the Division on 29.10.1944)

2 Polizei-Kompanien (added to the Division as reinforcements while in the Riesengebirge area in March/April 1945 - numbers & other details not known)

Polizei-Kampfgruppe "Breul" (attached to the Division, possibly between 22.1.1945 & 20.3.1945)

The following frontier guard regiments were raised by the Higher SS & Police Leader for North Russia (HSSPF Russland-Nord) and after the fall of Estonia to the Russians their survivors were used in the reforming of the 20th SS Division at Tr.Üb.Pl. Neuhammer in late 1944/early 1945:[173]

SS-Grenzschutz-Regiment 1 (formed 7.2.44 as Estnische Grenzschutz-Regiment 1 (1. Piirikaitse Rügement) with 3 infantry battalions and a (13th) infantry gun company. Redesignated by 14.5.1944 and destroyed 17.9.44).

SS-Grenzschutz-Regiment 2 (raised in February 1944 as Estnische Grenzschutz-Regiment 2 (2. Piirikaitse Rügement) with 3 infantry battalions & a (13th) infantry gun company. Paired with Estnische Grenzschutz-Rgt. 4, it became part of Kampfgruppe "Nord" under Divisionsstab z.b.V. 300. Redesignated by 14.5.1944, its commander Juhan Vermet had become a Waffen-Obersturmbannführer by 1.3.1945 when he was commanding Waffen-Gren.Rgt. der SS 47 (estn. Nr. 3))

Estnische Grenzschutz-Regiment 3 (3. Piirikaitse Rügement) (raised early February 1944 with its I., II., & III. Btle. formed at Pärnu, Tartu, and Viljandi, respectively. Sent to Tallinn, the regiment was renamed Estnische Regiment "Reval" (Reval is German for Tallinn), but this designation was valid for only three days & its battalions were sent to fill gaps in Division "Feldherrnhalle" (I.Btl.) & 170. Infanterie-Division (II. & III. Btle.))

SS-Grenzschutz-Regiment 3 (3 new battalions & a (13th) infantry gun company were formed when the original Estnische Grenzschutz-Rgt. 3 was broken up. Paired with Estnische Grenzschutz-Rgt. 6, it became part of Kampfgruppe "Süd" under Divisionsstab z.b.V. 300. Final designation in use by 14.5.1944).

SS-Grenzschutz-Regiment 4 (formed February 1944 - field post numbers only introduced in April 1944 - in Tartu & Tartumaa with 3 battalions. Paired

[173]*See Tessin, Die Stäbe und Truppeneinheiten der Ordnungspolizei, in Zur Geschichte der Ordnungspolizei 1936-1945, Teil II, pp. 60-61.*

with Estnische Grenzschutz-Rgt. 2, it became part of Kampfgruppe "Nord" under Divisionsstab z.b.V. 300. Redesignated by 14.5.1944 and destroyed in Puhatu swamps).

SS-Grenzschutz-Regiment 5 (raised 26.2.1944 - but field post numbers not issued until April 1944 - in Põltsamaa, Paide & Türi, this also consisted of 3 infantry battalions & a (13th) infantry gun company, but was the largest of the frontier guard regiments by having 3,500 men.)

SS-Grenzschutz-Regiment 6 (field post numbers introduced in April 1944) in Pärnu & Kilingi-Nomme as Estnische Grenzschutz-Regiment 6 with 3 battalions & a (13th) infantry gun company. Paired with Estnische Grenzschutz-Rgt. 3, it became part of Kampfgruppe "Süd" under Divisionsstab z.b.V. 300. Final title in use by 14.5.1944.

1. Ersatz- und Ausbildungs-Regiment (Viljandi Tagavara Rügement or I Tagavara ja Väljarõppe Rügement - 3 battalions. It absorbed the 37th, 38th & 287th Estonian Police battalions)

Estnische Regiment "Reval" (see Estnisches Grenzschutz-Regiment 3)

C: FINNISH ARMY:

Jalkaväkirykmentti 200[174] (an infantry regiment of Estonians serving in the Finnish Army which was formed in early 1944. In August 1944 it was disbanded and its 2,002 volunteers were shipped to Estonia. Beginning September 1944, 41 of its officers were serving with the "Nordland" and "Nederland" formations of the Waffen-SS on the Narva front. Its Ist battalion (I./J.R. 200) was sent to the Tartu front and became III./SS-Freiw.Gren.Rgt. 46, which was also known as "Pärlini pataljon" after its commander, Waffen-Hauptsturmführer Voldemar Pärlin (died of wounds 12.9.1944). Refusing to abandon Estonia to the Russians, it was disbanded by its new commander, Waffen-Obersturmführer Karl Pärnoja on 23.9.1944. Remaining companies mutinied while holding defensive positions near Tallinn. II. & III. Btl. did not go to the 20. SS-Div. upon arrival in Estonia in August 1944; they were first sent to training camps and their men were absorbed by the 20. SS-Div. later)

KAMPFGRUPPEN & EINHEITEN:[175]

The following can only be considered a partial listing of the ad hoc units raised by and with elements of the 20th SS Division:

Kampfgruppe "(Léon) Degrelle"

While fighting at Narva the whole "Wallonien" Brigade was reduced to only 300 men fit for combat, and these were grouped into a battle group led by the Belgian Rexist leader and commander of the "Wallonien" SS Brigade, SS-Obersturmbannführer Lēon Degrelle. It fought on the Tartu front and is believed to have included elements of the 20th SS Division. Only 32 men survived and all were subsequently awarded the Iron Cross and sent home. Degrelle himself was awarded the Knight's Cross on 27 August 1944 as commander of the SS-Sturmbrigade "Wallonien."

SS-Kampfgruppe "Ebelt"

There is evidence to suggest that SS-Kampfgruppe "Ebelt" was attached for a time to SS-F.E.B. 20 of the 20th SS Division in early 1945 while in the Neisse

---

[174]Finnish for "infantry regiment 200," abbreviated "J.R. 200." In Estonian it was called Jalaväerügement 200, so retaining the same abbreviation.

[175]See fn. 114 on page 178 of this book.

area.[176] SS-Kampfgruppe "Ebelt" was formed in late February/early March 1945 by the 1st SS Engineer Training and Replacement Battalion in Dresden (SS-Pionier-Ausbildungs- und Ersatz-Bataillon 1) from about 1,000 men drawn from the Volkssturm and Organization Todt. Led by SS-Hauptsturmführer Heinz Ebelt and divided into four companies, it served as a second defensive line behind the Neisse River in the Niesky area, and having fought near Seifersdorf, found itself cut off behind the Russian lines following the Red Army's thrust between Bautzen and Görlitz. Ebelt and his men continued to fight behind the lines until relieved by the LVIIth Armored Corps on 22 April 1945. The survivors gathered in the Löbau area and while a group made its way on foot to join the engineer battalion of the "Frundsberg" Division (SS-Pi.Btl 10), the remainder traveled to Kampnitz in Bohemia, where on arrival on 7 May 1945 they met up with the remaining elements of the 1st SS Engineer Training and Replacement Battalion. The following day these men made their way westwards to surrender to the Western Allies.

Kampfgruppe "Hints"

Led by Waffen-Hauptsturmführer Eduard Hints, commander of the 4th company, Ist battalion of the 20th SS Division's 45th infantry regiment.[177]

Einheit "Lessing"

The German SS-Hautpsturmführer Lessing was adjutant to Rebane in the 20th SS Division's 46th infantry regiment, and this element may have been a part of Kampfgruppe "Rebane" (see below). Lessing is said to have been replaced as he was considered unreliable.

"Pärlini pataljon"

This was the name given to III./Waffen-Gren.Rgt. der SS 46 (formerly I./J.R. 200) after its first commander, Waffen-Hauptsturmführer Voldemar Pärlin, who died ten days after being mortally wounded on 2 September 1944. See also Einheit "Pärnoja."

Einheit "Pärnoja"

Another name for what was more usually known as "Pärnoji pataljon," III./Waffen-Gren.Rgt. der SS 46 (formerly I./J.R. 200), after its second and

---

[176]*Kampfgruppe "Ebelt" (without the "SS-" prefix) was added by hand to both a copy of the 25.8.1944 edition of the Waffen-SS field post number guide (see fn. 111 on page 177) and Deutsches Rotes Kreuz, Suchdienst München Abt. NZW Einheiten-Rahmen 20. Waffen.Gren.Div. SS (estn. Nr. 1). vorher 3. estn. SS Freiw.Brigade under SS-F.E.B. 20 (VBL Band WC - Seiten 644-645). Surprisingly neither entry gave a field post number. That the battle group should have been attached to SS-F.E.B. 20 is confirmed by Deutsches Rotes Kreuz, Feldpostnummern Aufstellung 23.2.1956 for this gives 38 087 as its field post number - the same number as the battalion itself. Details of the battle group's history are provided by Wolfgang Vopersal (letter of 28.7.81), who claims that SS-Kampfgruppe "Ebelt" was never a part of the 20th SS Division, and Der Freiwillige, Heft 7, Juli 1971, pg. 20 - Heft 10, Oktober 1973, pg. 19 - Heft 12, Dezember 1977, pg. 20.*

[177]*Hints is given in the Stellenbesetzungsliste der Waffen-SS of 1.3.1945 as having held the rank of SS-Hauptsturmführer since 24.2.1938, which suggests he was a German. In fact, Eduard Hints is an Estonian (in 1978 he was living in Canada), confirmed by the date of his promotion to Kapten (equivalent to Hauptsturmführer) in the pre-war Estonian Army, for all promotions were traditionally dated 24 February, the anniversary of the independence of the Republic of Estonia in 1918. As of 1.3.1945 Hints was still a Waffen-Hauptsturmführer and commanding the IIIrd battalion of Waffen-Grenadier-Regiment der SS 47. There was possible confusion with Augsberger's German adjutant, SS-Obersturmführer Hinz, K.I.A. near Neustadt on 19.3.1945.*

last commander who succeeded Pärlin, Waffen-Obersturmführer Karl Pärnoja.

Kampfgruppe "Rebane"

Led by Waffen-Sturmbannführer Alfons Rebane, it included the IInd battalion of the Estonian Division's 47th infantry regiment (what had been until April 1944 Rebane's 658th Estonian Battalion) under Waffen-Hauptsturmführer Jahn Sepa, IInd and IIIrd battalions of the 5th Frontier Guard Regiment (5. Grenzschutz-Regiment) under Waffen-Hauptsturmführer Jakustant and Tania and an unidentified German battalion. In July 1944 the battle group was referred to as "Regiment (Rügement) Rebane" and was sent to the Tartu front in August - by which time Rebane had replaced Juhan Tuuling as commander of the Division's 46th SS infantry regiment.

(SS-) Kampfgruppe "Rehfeldt"

Formed at Neuhammer as an "alarm unit" (Alarmeinheit) in January 1945 from elements of the 20th SS Division (Waffen-Gren.Rgt. 47, SS-Ausbildungs- und Ersatz-Regiment 20, parts of a Nachrichtenstaffel and a Kranken-Kraftwagenzug, etc) and Hungarian Waffen-SS personnel. Commanded by SS-Obersturmbannführer Emil Rehfeldt,[178] it was not sent with the main body of the 20th SS Division to the Oder front, but engaged in defensive fighting between 4/5 and 28 February 1945 in the Bober, Queis and Lausitz/Neisse area. Disbanded on 28 February 1945 at Rotenburg/Neisse, Rehfeldt and 60 percent of his men were sent on 1 March 1945 by rail to join SS-Ausbildungs- und Ersatz-Regiment 20 in Odense in Denmark. Rehfeldt is reported to have led (another?) SS-Kampfgruppe "Rehfeldt" in Berlin from 1 April 1945. The remaining 40 percent of the disbanded (original) battle group was marched to join the 20th SS Division on the Oder front. If Rehfeldt, in fact, commanded two different battle groups, then it is possible that the first, that had been raised at Neuhammer in January 1945, was called Kampfgruppe "Rehfeldt," whereas the second that fought in Berlin was called SS-Kampfgruppe "Rehfeldt." Up to 12 February 1945, Kampfgruppe "Rehfeldt" was a part of Festungsabschnitt Niederschlesien, and after that date of Korpsgruppe "Friedrich."

Kampfgruppe "Riipalu"

Led by Waffen-Obersturmbannführer Harald Riipalu, who on 23 August 1944 was awarded the Knight's Cross as commander of the 20th SS Division's 45th infantry regiment (until April 1944 he had commanded the same regiment's first battalion). The battle group fought in northern Estonia around Narva and was made up of the first battalion of the 45th SS infantry regiment, the former SS-Panzer-Grenadier-Bataillon "Narwa" that had returned to the Estonian Division after serving with "Wiking" and other elements.[179]

---

[178]SS-Sturmbannführer Rehfeldt was "Ia" of the Estonian SS Brigade in August 1943 and promoted to SS-Obersturmbannführer on 9.11.1943. He was still serving with the 20th SS Division on 1.10.1944 but was not listed with the formation at 1.3.1945. Listed as SS-Kampfgruppe "Rehfeldt" in Der Freiwillige, Heft 5, Mai 1975, pg. 17.

[179]Known in Estonian as "Riipalu võitlusgrupp," it is shown on pg. 34 of Eesti riik ja rahvas II Maailmasõjas, Vol. IX, as containing "I./45, Pat. "Narva," 227. Merij. Pat., 111. Julg. Rüg. & Eesti Diviisi Runnakkahurid" (111. Julg. Rüg. translates as the 111th Security Regiment, but no trace of a 111. Sicherungs-Regiment has been found in the German armed forces that could have been there at the time - "Eesti Diviisi Runnakkahurid" means "Estonian Division assault guns," presumably a reference to the self-propelled sub-unit of the divisional antitank unit - 2./SS-Panzerjäger-Abt. 20 - P. H. Buss).

Kampfgruppe "Vent"

This battle group fought on the Tartu front and was led by Waffen-Obersturmbannführer Paul Vent, who had commanded the Division's 47th infantry regiment since April 1944. It consisted of Ist, IInd and IIIrd battalions, led by Waffen-Sturmbannführer Friedrich Krug, Waffen-Hauptsturmführer Paul Maitla and Waffen-Hauptsturmführer H. Rannik, respectively.[180]

BRIGADE & DIVISIONAL STRENGTHS:*

DATE	OFFICERS	NCOs	MEN	TOTAL
31.12.1943	178	864	4,037	5,099
30. 6.1944	431	1,637	11,355	13,423
15. 9.1944	439	1,978	12,965	15,382

On 31.3.1943 there were 37 Estonian officers, 175 NCOs and 757 men. On 15.9.1944 the Division included 566 "Hiwis" (Hilfswillige).

*Actual strengths (including men in hospitals, on detachment or on leave)/Iststärke

Brigade and Divisional Commanders

1 July 1943[181] - 19 March 1945[182] . SS-Standartenführer (promotion date as yet unknown to SS-Oberführer and to SS-Brigadeführer und Generalmajor der Waffen-SS on 21 June 1944) Franz Augsberger[183]

March 1945[184] - 8 May 1945[185] . . . SS-Oberführer (promoted SS-Brigadeführer und Generalmajor der Waffen-SS on 20 April 1945) Berthold Maack[186]

---

[180]Friedrich Krug was an Estonian cavalry officer who had won the Estonian Freedom Cross (VR II/3). After the Second World War he chose to fight on and was killed as a "Brother of the Forest" (metsavend).

[181]SS-Standartenführer Augsberger was already supervising the raising of the Estonian SS Legion at SS-Tr.Üb.Pl.Debica in August 1943 when Soodla was appointed commander of the Legion's 1st regiment, and since the Germans would not allow an Estonian to lead the Legion as a whole, Augsberger must already have been chosen to lead the Estonian Waffen-SS (Klietmann, op.cit., pg. 228, dates Augsberger's command as early as 1.7.1943). Augsberger was appointed commander of the 20th SS Division when it was ordered by the SS-FHA on 24.1.1944 (see fn. 6 on page 122 of this book).

[182]Augsberger was killed on 19.3.1945 near Neustadt in Silesia on the first day of the breakout from the Oppeln pocket.

[183]See page 154 for further biographical details.

[184]It is not known exactly when Maack assumed effective command of the Division. From Augsberger's death on 19.3.1945 until Maack's arrival, Ia, SS-Sturmbannführer Hans-Joachim Mützelfeldt led the formation.

[185]Date the Division surrendered to the Russians in and to the north of Prague.

[186]Berthold Maack served as an officer in the First World War, following which he served in a Freikorps in Berlin, then joined the Jungstahlhelm and then the SS. By July 1935 he was commanding an SS foot regiment (39. SS-Standarte) and the following

NOTES

1) Legions-Standartenführer (later Legions-Oberführer and from 1 September 1944 Waffen-Brigadeführer und Generalmajor der Waffen-SS) Johannes Soodla never commanded the Estonian Legion nor its successor formations.[187] That he has been wrongly identified as the Estonian Waffen-SS commander stems from the fact that in August 1943 as a Legions-Standartenführer he was given command for a short time of the Legion's first regiment - since the Legion only had one regiment at the time, the conclusion has been wrongly drawn that he must, therefore, have commanded the Legion. This was neither true nor possible, for the Germans would never have permitted an Estonian to command the Legion, and Franz Augsberger had already been at Debica SS training area for a month when Soodla was given regimental command. Soodla became Inspector General of the Estonian Waffen-SS and, although the senior Estonian officer in the Waffen-SS, was never the Estonian Waffen-SS formation's commander.
2) Waffen-Standartenführer Alfons Rebane, the most highly decorated Estonian in the Waffen-SS, was deputy divisional commander in early April 1945 when his recommendation for the award of the Oak Leaves was submitted.[188]

---

year was leader of an SS District (at first SS-Abschnitt XXVI, by 1938 SS-Abschnitt XXV). He thus held high rank in the Allgemeine-SS (an SS-Brigadeführer since 13.9.1936) when war broke out, but once transferred to the Waffen-SS had to revert to a lower rank - he joined SS-Regiment "Germania" in January 1940 and thus served in "Wiking" during the Western Campaign as an SS-Hauptsturmführer. Promoted to SS-Sturmbannführer, he commanded SS-Pz.Jäg.Abt. 5 of "Wiking," then assumed command of the whole Regiment "Germania" (following which he also led SS-Regiment "Westland"). The next three years saw Maack serving with the "Nord" Mountain Division. At first he raised a Geb.-Jäger-Bataillon and was then in action as commander of II./Geb.-Jäger-Regiment 11. In February 1943 he took command of this regiment which he led until the end of August 1944 (during which time he was promoted to SS-Standartenführer and then SS-Oberführer der Reserve). Maack held an officers' course (Divisions-Führer-Lehrgang) at Hirschberg in Silesia before being appointed commander of the 26. Waffen-Gren.Division der SS (ung. Nr. 2) on 25.1.1945. This second Hungarian division of the Waffen-SS, in fact, never reached more than battle group status, and so Maack was available to replace Franz Augsberger as commander of the 20th SS Division when the latter was killed on 19.3.1945. (Stellenbesetzungsliste der Waffen-SS of 1.3.1945 inexplicably gives "Luidpold Maack" as commander of the 20th SS Division at that date - apart from the error in his first name, it is possible that Maack had been considered as Augsberger's replacement before the latter's death). Maack led the 20th SS Division until the capitulation on 8 May 1945, during the last days of the war he was also Chief of General Staff of the VIIIth Army Corps (to which the Division was attached at the end). He died on 26.9.81 (Der Freiwillige, 27. Jahrgang, Heft 12, Dezember 1981, pg. 19).

[187]See fn. 72 on pg. 156 and pg. 194 of this book.

[188]See pg. 165 for biographical details.

SS-Brigadeführer
Franz Augsberger

Jost Schneider

Berthold Maack, here in the uniform of an SS-Standartenführer. He was given command of the 20th SS Division after Franz Augsberger's death on 19 March 1945 as an SS-Oberführer. He was promoted to SS-Brigadeführer und Generalmajor der Waffen-SS on 20 April 1945.

Source: Der Freiwillige, 24. Jahrgang, Heft 4, April 1978, pg. 25.

Divisional and Unit Insignia

COLLAR PATCHES[189]

1) PLAIN BLACK

The SS-FHA order of 29 September 1942 raising the Estonian SS Legion provided that its members were to wear plain black collar patches on both sides of the collar.[190] A month later, the SS-FHA sent a memorandum to Heinrich Himmler proposing no less than four different designs for a special right hand collar patch for the new Legion (see pp. 208/9), but also pointing out that the SS runes could also be worn. The plain black collar patch is reported as having been worn exclusively by the Legion while forming at SS-Tr.Üb.Pl. Debica in late 1942 and early 1943.[191] It is also said to have been worn by the Brigade in the autumn of 1943.[192]

2) SS RUNES

The SS-FHA suggested to Himmler on 29 October 1942 that the men of the Estonian SS Legion could be considered as eligible for the SS runes, but in fact this was forbidden until the Estonians were in action on the Nevel front in the winter of 1943/44 when orders were received to remove the unofficial but popular hand-made collar insignia (see 3 below) and replace them with the SS runes. This order was most unpopular, for the Estonians cherished their national insignia with its message of freedom and had no desire to wear the victory runes of the SS. Since no SS runes collar patches were available and the Division was far from sources of supply, the Estonians were delighted to be unable to comply with what they saw as a stupid order and continued to wear the hand-made collar insignia.

One whole battalion of the Estonian SS Legion did, however, wear the SS runes from an early date. In March 1943 the Legion's Ist battalion was detached and sent to serve as SS-Pz.Gren.Btl. "Narwa" in the "Wiking" Division, and it was issued with SS runes collar patches before departure. These men continued to wear the runes until the survivors rejoined the 20th SS Division in June 1944.

---

[189]See Ted Koppel's detailed evaluation and analysis of contemporary photographs and post-war illustrations (The Estonian Collar Badge in German Service 1943-1945, in The Military Journal, Vol. 1, No. 1, Jan.-Feb. 1977, pp. 16-17). His figure "C" is the Tartu pattern, whereas D, E, F & G are attempts of varying quality to depict the impossible: the countless variations of hand-made versions (also confused by others' poor art work on basis of photographs of the Tartu and 2nd German patterns). Figures J, K & L are meaningless representations of the 1st German pattern (sword & letter E), distorted as they are taken from different photographs where the same collar patch is seen from different angles.

[190]See fn. 1 on page 122 of this book. Presumably this only applied to new recruits and so NCOs and officers were permitted to show their rank on the left collar patch.

[191]H. Rüütel, letter of 10.2.76.

[192]See fn. 189.

Tony Hedges

Unidentified Waffen-Untersturmführer wears a plain black collar patch with type "A" sleeve shield (introduced for Estonians serving with the German Army). Place and date unknown.

A young Estonian private soldier.

On 29 October 1942 SS-Gruppenführer und Generalleutnant der Waffen-SS Hans Jüttner, Chief of Staff of the SS Main Operational Office (SS-FHA - Jüttner assumed full command on 30 January 1943), wrote to Himmler about the insignia to be worn by the Estonian SS Legion, which had been formed a month before.* Attached to the letter were designs for four proposed collar patches for the Legion, which Jüttner described as follows:

1) The "jar-Rune," sign of togetherness and the beginning of a new life. One of the oldest Nordic symbols of belief and life.
2) The "ing-Rune" as a symbol of the companionship of the combined course of battle.
3) The "Wendhorn" (literally: turning horn) as a sign of both liberty and dependence, sign of fruitful replenishment.**

4) The shield - as a sign of duty and obligation. Symbol of fighting men.

Note:
The exact design of the shield is not confirmed - it could have had a different shape to that illustrated, and the colored bars may have been diagonal.

Himmler obviously was not impressed, and none of these badges were ever worn on collar patches by men of the Waffen-SS.

---

*SS-FHA, Kdo. W.-SS, Abt. Ia, v. 29.10.1942, Kragenspiegel und Ärmelabzeichen der Estnischen SS-Legion (T-175/22/2527812-3).
**Reported - apparently incorrectly - by H.I.A.G. as the vehicle symbol for 6. SS-Geb.Div. "Nord" (see Vol. 2, pg 155 and Vol. 3 pg. 173).

(1)

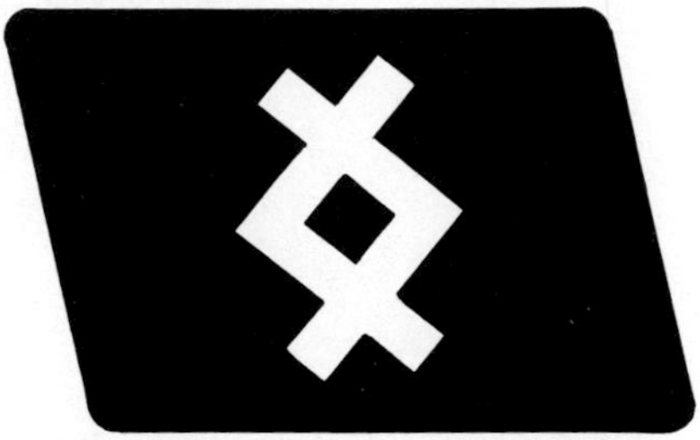

(2)

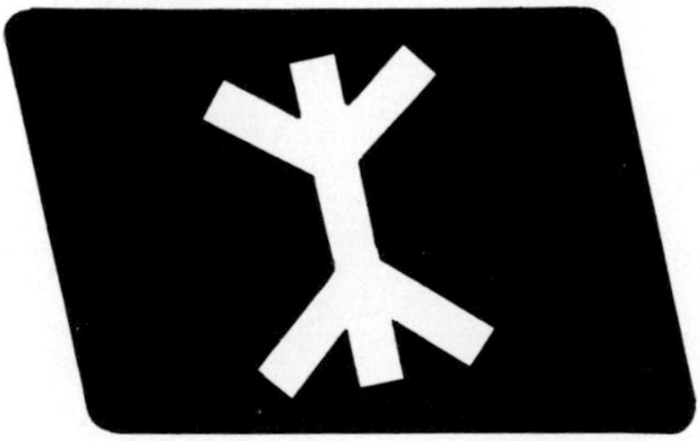

(3)

(4)

3) MAILED ARM, SWORD & "E" - HAND-MADE VERSIONS

The Estonians wanted to be able to return to their homeland after completion of their training with a collar patch of national significance. Since the Germans had failed to introduce such a collar patch, as training of the Legion's 1st Regiment drew to its close, the Estonians decided to take matters into their own hands. The central motif of the Estonian Independence (or Freedom) Cross, instituted to commemorate service in the 1918-1920 War of Independence and made up of a mailed arm holding a sword and a rounded letter "E" for "Eesti" (Estonia), was proposed and immediately accepted as being eminently suitable.[193]

---

[193]Legions-Standartenführer Johannes Soodla and Legions-Obersturmführer Kilk are reported as having been behind the idea of having a special Estonian collar patch (Harald Riipalu, Kui võideldi kodupinna eest, pg. 111).

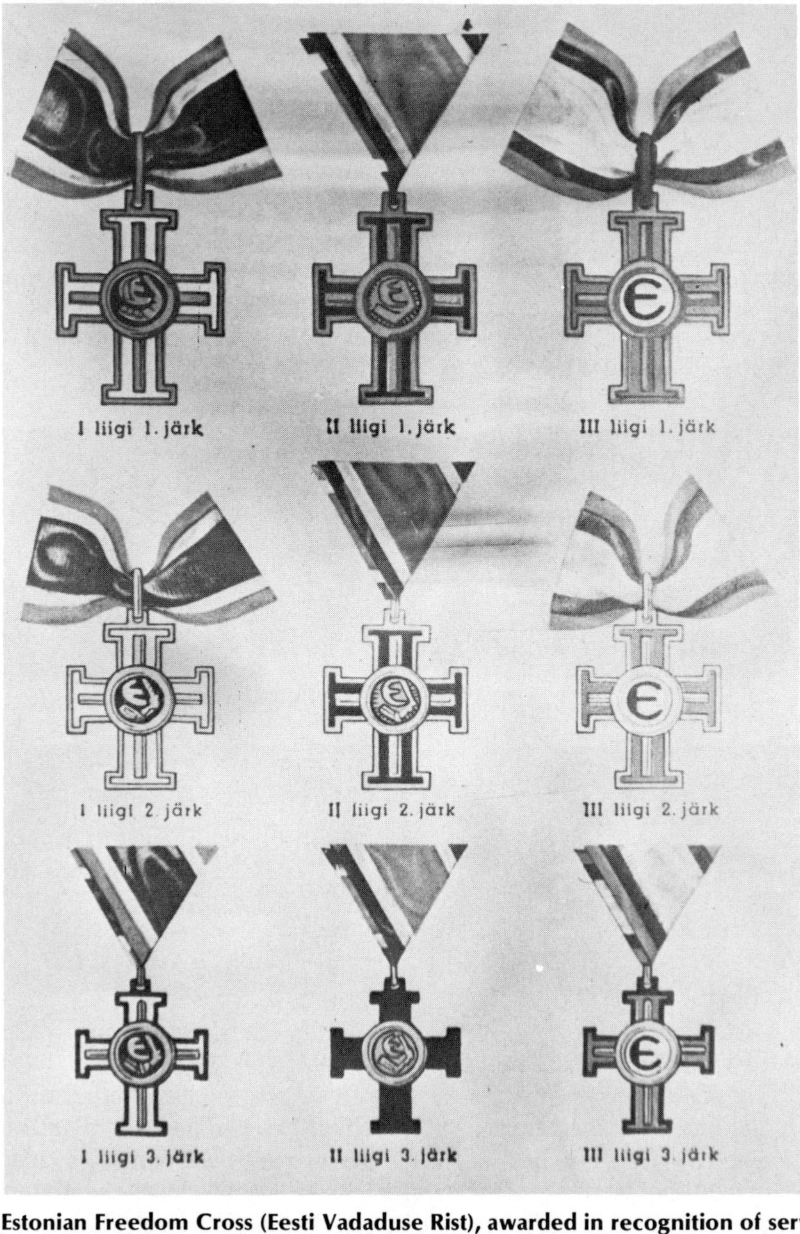

The Estonian Freedom Cross (Eesti Vadaduse Rist), awarded in recognition of services rendered during the Estonian War of Independence, 1918-1920, and from which the design for the collar patch and vehicle sign of the Estonian Waffen-SS was taken. This Cross was awarded in three divisions - I: Governmental Decorations; II: for bravery; III: for civil merit - and within each division in three grades (1, 2, and 3). One hundred-thirty Britons received the cross, including none other than King George V and Winston Churchill, who were presented with the 1st grade of the Ist division (VR I/1). The 28 recipients of the VR II/2 were known as the 28 national heroes of the War of Liberation and included Johannes Soodla, Inspector General of the Estonian Waffen-SS 1943-1945. (See Taavi R. Triumph, Eesti Teenetemärgid in Eesti Filatelist 1977, 20-21, pp. 80-84.)

Without official approval, the collar patches had to be made clandestinely and once the design had been drawn up the badges were made by hand. These first Estonian collar patches were made from aluminum taken from empty flare casings, and the quality of manufacture depended upon the skill of the individual, thus varying considerably. Positioning of the badges (by pins or stitched with cotton) on the plain black patches also varied from man to man.

Many estonians were thus wearing hand-made collar patches of varying design when they were committed to the front as the Estonian SS Volunteer Brigade in October 1943. More badges were made by hand at the front by those men who did not yet have them, and instances of needlessly firing flares just to lay hands on the aluminum are reported.

4) MAILED ARM, SWORD & "E" - THE TARTU PATTERN

Leaders of the university town of Tartu had learned of the collar patch problems from Waffen-Obersturmbannführer Paul Vent, commander of the 45th infantry regiment, and grateful for the successful containment of the Russian advance, decided to donate professionally-made insignia to the men of the Estonian SS Division. The Surgical Instruments Factory in Tartu was thus commissioned to produce high quality badges. These were finely stamped from light metal (aluminum?) and, finished by hand, were given a silvered finish. When the Ist battalion of Vent's 45th infantry regiment, under Harald Riipalu, passed through Tartu after fighting at Mehikoorma and Meerapalu in February 1944, a

The Mayor of Tartu, Paul Keerdoja, shakes hands with Harald Riipalu, commander of the Ist battalion of the 45th SS infantry regiment. Riipalu's battalion had succeeded in halting the Russian advance, and in recognition of this, the Mayor of Tartu presented his men with specially made collar patches in February 1944.

ceremony was arranged, and the mayor of Tartu presented the battalion with the new collar insignia. Although these badges were identical, their positioning on the collar patch was not always consistent because it was left to the individual to sew them onto the collar patch with needle and thread.

Regimental commander Vent obtained the dies and arranged for more badges to be made for distribution to the whole of his regiment. Divisional HQ turned a blind eye to this breach of the Germans' ban, and in time the Tartu badges were distributed throughout the Division.

Bundesarchiv

A Waffen-Sturmmann wears the Tartu pattern collar patch (another case of failure to observe the 1 November 1943 order that the SS runes shield should not be worn on the steel helmet for the duration of the war).

5) SWORD & "E" - THE 1st GERMAN PATTERN

In the summer of 1944, not long before the fall of Estonia to the Red Army, and by coincidence or design about the same time that the Estonian SS Division was redesignated from "Freiwilligen-" to "Waffen-," the Germans took action over the collar patch question. They knew that the Estonians preferred their national insignia to the SS runes but insisted that such national badge should be of official German design and manufacture. Obviously without consulting the Estonians, the SS-FHA had approved a new design that omitted the mailed arm and so consisted merely of a large capital letter "E" superimposed upon a slanting sword. This over-stylized design was machine woven in grey thread onto the usual black collar patch, and one morning in mid-June 1944 a consignment reached the HQ of the 45th infantry regiment with orders that all the unofficial hand-made insignia were to be removed at once from the collar and replaced by the new patches - confirmation that this had been done was to be given the following day.

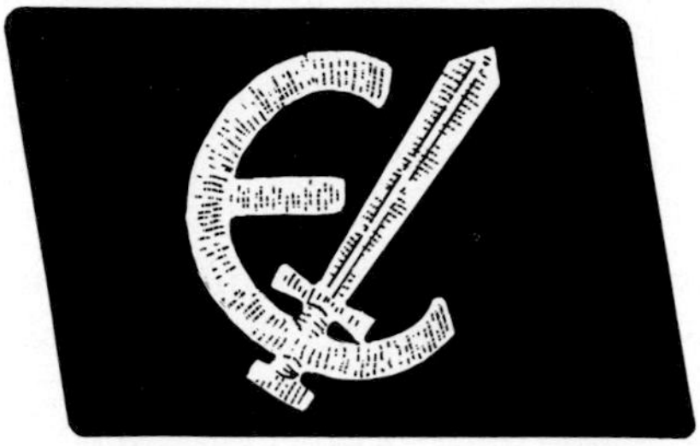

Unidentified Waffen-Rottenführer.

An unidentified Waffen-Hauptsturmführer and company commander in an observation post with a private soldier in Estonia, 1944. He wears the unpopular 1st German pattern collar patch and the final Waffen-SS pattern sleeve shield on his upper left sleeve (the top stripe of the shield appears surprisingly light in this photograph - possibly a photographic defect). He clearly disobeys the 1 November 1943 order that banned the wearing of the SS runes shield on the steel helmet for the duration of the war (<u>Verordnungsblatt der Waffen-SS</u>, 4. Jahrgang, Berlin, 1.11.1943, Nr. 21, Z 402).

Regimental commander Harald Riipalu (he had succeeded Paul Vent in April 1944) and his staff were astonished and horrified, for not only were they being told to give up their prized Estonian-made insignia that had been presented to them by the town of Tartu, but also the SS-FHA had rendered the design ugly and meaningless by removing the mailed arm and superimposing the "E" and sword.[194] Riipalu dispatched within the hour a letter to his divisional HQ in which he argued for the rejection of the SS-FHA pattern and retention of the Tartu insignia, at the very least for the men of his 45th infantry regiment who had been presented with the badges by the Mayor of Tartu.

Riipalu was not the only Estonian unit commander to complain about the new collar patches, and divisional commander Augsberger decided to pass on his letter to Himmler himself. Pleasure and relief must have been accompanied by no small degree of surprise when just a few days later the following telegram was received from the Reichsführer-SS:

> "Confirming the symbol of the 20. Est. Waffen-Gren.Div.: the mailed arm, hand holding the sword, letter "E" in curvature...
>
> Himmler!"[195]

In spite of the Estonians' violent and immediate reaction, and the Germans' prompt acceptance of their demands, photographs show that the unpopular German-made "sword & E" collar patch was worn by officers, NCOs and men of the Estonian SS Division. This may have been in the period following introduction of the patches and their subsequent replacement by the 2nd German pattern (see 6 below). It is probable that at least Riipalu and his 45th infantry regiment refused to remove their Tartu pattern patches until the 2nd German pattern patches were received.

6) MAILED ARM, SWORD & "E" - THE 2nd GERMAN PATTERN

Himmler's acceptance of Riipalu's plea marked a resounding success for the Estonians. The SS-FHA then designed a new, second official collar patch which was acceptable to the Estonians. They were, of course, sorry to have to remove the more meaningful and traditional Tartu-made badges, and some took advantage of the confused closing stages of the war to retain them. But the final pattern patch was in-

[194]Riipalu describes the design as "the letter E followed by an upright squiggle, probably intended to represent a sword." He and his staff suggested the combination looked like the letters "EI," which in Estonian means "no," and how this could have been interpreted to have meant "no more Estonia." To be fair, whereas the German badge may not have appealed to the Estonians and lacked heraldic meaning, its component "E" and sword are quite clear and easily distinguishable. It is possible that the Germans took the design from the cap badge of "ERNA" (see fn. 25 on page 132 of this book).

[195]Riipalu, op.cit., pg. 114.

H. Rüütel Collection

Waffen-Hauptsturmführer Aleksander Veelma, who left the 20th SS Division to take command of the Ist battalion of the 1st Frontier Guard Regiment (raised on 7.2.1944 as Estnische Grenzschutz-Regiment 1, renamed SS-Grenzschutz-Regiment 1).

troduced and issued to the Division while it was reforming at Tr.Üb.Pl. Neuhammer between October 1944 and January 1945.[196]

7) MAILED ARM, SWORD & "E" - VARIATION:

This machine-woven example appears original but differs from the 2nd German pattern and is so far unidentified.[197]

Note:

The "double-armed swastika" has often been incorrectly attributed to the Estonian SS Division. Introduced in the

[196]*The 2nd German pattern in the photograph is an original piece issued at Neuhammer in October 1944 to an Estonian who, at the time of publication, is living in Surrey, England.*

[197]*Illustration courtesy of the Jim van Fleet Collection.*

second half of 1944 for former members of the German Army and Luftwaffe who were transferred to concentration camp staffs and guard units (Totenkopf-Sturmbanne), it had nothing to do with the 20th SS Division.[198]

SLEEVE SHIELDS

The order of 29 September 1942[199] raising the Estonian SS Legion makes no mention of a sleeve shield, but when Hans Jüttner, Chief-of-Staff of the SS-FHA wrote to Himmler on 29 October 1942,[200] he enclosed an illustration of the Estonian coat of arms upon which a sleeve badge for the Legion could have been based should Himmler have decided to allow the Estonians to wear the SS runes on the collar. The SS runes were at first forbidden, and the Legion was supposed to have worn the equally anonymous plain black collar patch, but no effort seems to have been made on the part of the Waffen-SS to design, let alone introduce, a national sleeve shield (in practice, the Estonians' nationality was shown by the unofficial collar patches - see above). Even when the SS runes were later authorized for the collar, no attempt appears to have been made over issue of a Waffen-SS sleeve shield - no runes patches were, in fact, available, and so nationality continued to be shown on the collar. In June 1944 the unpopular 1st German pattern collar patch was introduced, and when the commander of the 45th infantry regiment wrote to divisional HQ urging that at least his regiment be allowed to retain the collar insignia that had been specially presented to them by the town of Tartu, he further asked that his men be allowed to wear a national sleeve badge. Himmler's telegram later that month confirmed that such a sleeve shield could be worn and this may have prompted the introduction (believed to have been in June 1944) of the one and only official Waffen-SS sleeve shield for Estonians in the Waffen-SS (type "C" below).

The following is a study of all the sleeve shields that could have been worn by men of the 20th SS Division - only types "A," "B" and "C" enjoyed wide distribution and wear, and of the many variations, only the Finnish-made type "G" is proven to have been worn by photographic evidence. Since Estonians made their own sleeve shields for a time, the number of possible variations is enormous, but all will have included either or both the three lions and national tricolor.

Although no trace has been found of the design submitted to Himmler by the SS-FHA on 29 October 1942, the Estonian coat of arms consists of three blue

---

[198]It is possible, of course, that Estonians transferred from the German Army to concentration camp duties could subsequently have been posted to the 20th SS Division and thus continued to wear the "double-armed swastika" collar patches. To date no evidence exists to prove that any Estonians wore this collar patch. (See fn. 173 on page 111 of this book for the SS orders introducing the "double-armed swastika" collar patch).

[199]See fn. 1 on page 122 of this book.

[200]SS-FHA, Kdo. W.-SS, Abt. Ia, v. 29.10.1942, Kragenspiegel und Ärmelabzeichen der Estnischen SS-Legion.

lions superimposed upon a golden shield.[201] A number of sleeve shields were designed and manufactured on the basis of the Estonian coat of arms and national flag. The following three types are known to have been worn widely by Estonians in the Waffen-SS:

"A" - the national colors divided diagonally (in the flag the subdivision is horizontal), without the lions. This pattern was officially laid down in

"A"

Waffen-Sturmbannführer Alfons Rebane, who won the Knight's Cross on 23 February 1944 as a Major and commander of the 658th Estonian Battalion of the German Army, wears pattern "A" sleeve shield that was introduced for Estonians serving in the German Army. To be noted that he also wears the unpopular 1st German pattern collar patch and that the sleeve eagle appears to be metal (and therefore intended for wear on the service cap). This original example is slightly deformed, in that the top of the shield should be pointed, not blunted.

---

[201] *The colors of Estonia are taken from the national flag which consists of three horizontal stripes of equal width of medium blue, black and white. The flag dates back to 29.9.1881 when it was adopted by the Estonian Students' Association (Vironia), at its foundation ceremony in Tartu. When the Russians recognized Estonian independence on 2.2.1920 the flag was recognized by the constitution and adopted on 4.7.1920. The blue is said to stand for mutual confidence and fidelity, the black for the nourishing soil and supposed ancestors of the Estonians (the Melanchlaeni or black-cloaked people mentioned in Book Four of Herodotus' Histories), and the white for the snow that covers the country, hope for the future and moral cleanliness. The coat of arms (blue lions on gold) was originally that of the city of Tallinn, which had been granted by the King of Denmark in 1248. (K. Dzirkails & H. Rüütel, letter of 30.9.81).*

German Army Orders on 17 July 1944 for Estonians serving in the German Army and as Luftwaffe auxiliaries.[202] It was worn by the Estonian Battalions and Company that were absorbed by the 20th SS Division in 1944.[203] This type is known to have been worn on the left upper sleeve just below the SS sleeve eagle.

"B" - a variation of the above but with three golden lions superimposed and bordered in gold was introduced for the Estonian Police (formerly "Schuma") battalions. This type, designed with no apparent regard for heraldic accuracy, is known to have been worn on either the upper left or right sleeve by Estonians in the Waffen-SS, and as the accompanying photograph shows, it was worn contemporaneously by Estonians in the German Army.[204] It is known to have been worn by members of the "Narwa" battalion that served with the "Wiking" SS Division from March 1943 until June 1944.

"B"

Type "B" sleeve shield, worn at left by an Estonian private in the Waffen-SS and at right by an Estonian NCO serving with the German Army. It is possible that the latter had been transferred to the Waffen-SS but had not yet been issued with a new uniform. Type "B" was originally intended for Estonians serving with the Police (formerly "Schuma") battalions. In the photograph on the opposite page, it is seen being worn under the SS sleeve eagle on the left upper arm.

---

[202] *Z. 289 (actually an error for 292) of Heeres-Verordnungsblatt (H.V.Bl.), 26. Jahrgang, 38. Ausgabe, Teil B, Blatt 15, v. 17.7.1944. This also laid down the cap cockade for Estonians and both shield and cockade are illustrated in the 1945 edition of Der Soldatenfreund (see fn. 205 below on page 219).*

[203] *See fn. 89 on page 163 of this book.*

[204] *Perhaps the soldier at right of the photograph has just been transferred to the 20th SS Division and so has not yet been issued with Waffen-SS uniform?*

Estonian Combatants Association in GB

An Estonian Untersturmführer wearing the type "B" sleeve shield salutes Rear Admiral Pitka.

"C" - in 1944 (possibly June) a final pattern Waffen-SS sleeve shield was introduced for wear on the upper left sleeve. This consisted of the Estonian national colors divided, as on the national flag, horizontally and mounted on a black cloth backing.[205]

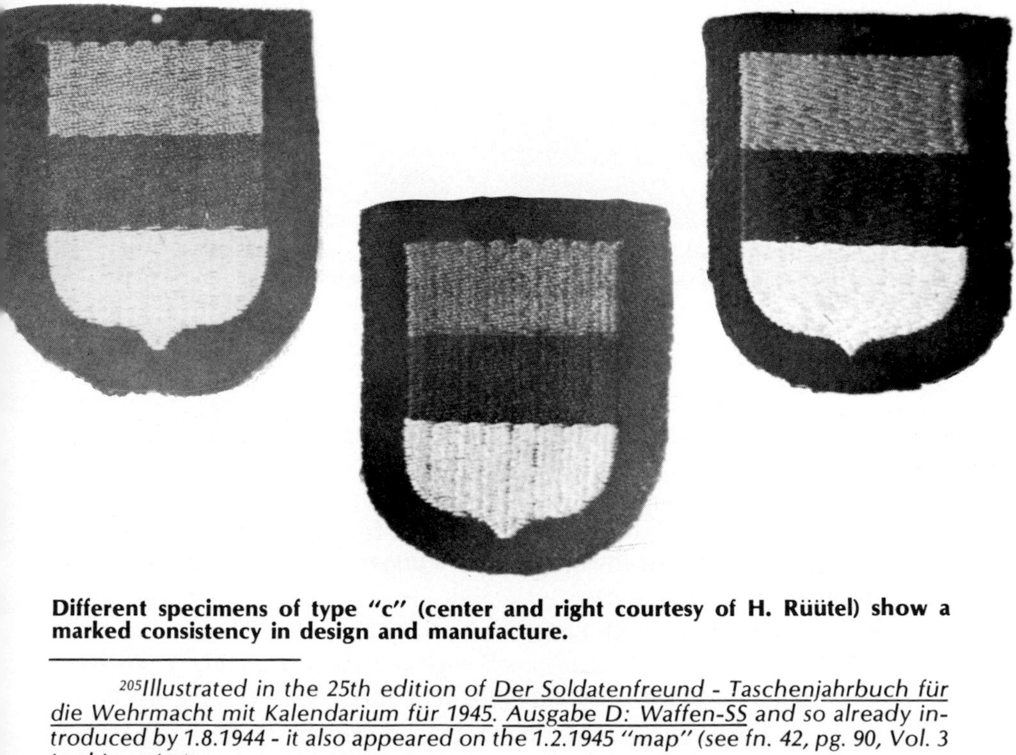

Different specimens of type "c" (center and right courtesy of H. Rüütel) show a marked consistency in design and manufacture.

---

[205] *Illustrated in the 25th edition of Der Soldatenfreund - Taschenjahrbuch für die Wehrmacht mit Kalendarium für 1945. Ausgabe D: Waffen-SS and so already introduced by 1.8.1944 - it also appeared on the 1.2.1945 "map" (see fn. 42, pg. 90, Vol. 3 in this series).*

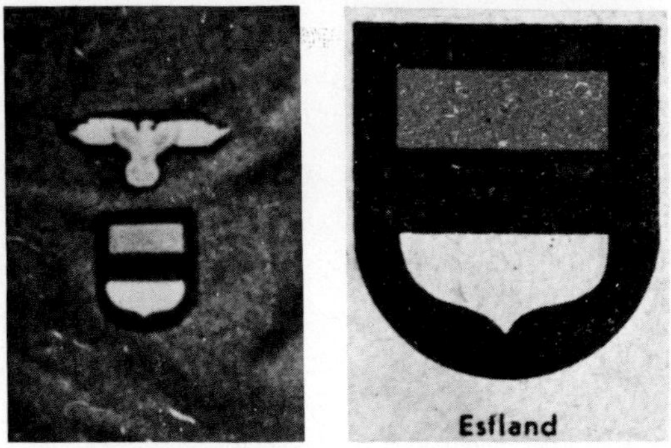

Left: The German-made final pattern being worn on the left upper sleeve by an officer (H. Rüütel).
Right: Color plate from the 1945 edition of the Waffen-SS pocket diary (see footnote 205 on page 219 of this book.

The Estonian Rear Admiral Johan Pitka visits the Estonian Waffen-SS and talks with divisional commander Franz Augsberger, who clearly wears the Waffen-SS pattern of sleeve shield.

Apart from the above three basic types, the following variations have been encountered:

"D" - the heraldically correct three blue lions on a yellow shield below the word "ESTLAND" (German for Estonia) in blue block capital letters. Produced by the Bevo company of Wuppertal, this type does not appear to have been worn.

"E" - as "D" but printed with black lions on a yellow shield below the word "ESTLAND" in light blue block capital letters. Possibly a post-war reproduction, there is no evidence that this type was ever worn.

"F" - three gold lions on a simple shield divided diagonally into the national colors. This is reported as having been worn by members of the 20th SS

"D"

"E"

"F"

Division, but may possibly have been a confused report of type "B" above.[206]

"G" - a simple shield in national colors divided horizontally, smaller than type "A" and on a black cloth base. This was manufactured in Finland for members of the (Estonian) 200th Infantry Regiment of the Finnish Army and was worn by the men of this regiment who joined the 20th SS Division in August 1944 (primarily the IIIrd battalion of the 46th SS infantry regiment).[207]

"H" - a simple shield in national colors divided horizontally, similar to type "C" but without the black underlay and not believed to be the same as "G." Reported as having been worn by members of Ost-Btl. 658 (which was absorbed by the 20th SS Division in April 1944 as the IInd battalion of the 47th SS infantry regiment).[208]

---

[206] *H. Rüütel.*
[207] *See photographs in Uustalu's For Freedom Only.*
[208] *P. H. Buss.*

Men of the former 200th (Estonian) Infantry Regiment of the Finnish Army, who had returned to Estonia in August 1944 to join the 20th SS Division. They wear Finnish-made badges on their left upper sleeve (type "G").

"I" - as "H" but with the same shield shape as "C."

"J" - a horizontally divided shield in national colors with a metal mailed arm, sword and "E" badge attached.[209]

"J"

"K" - a square patch divided horizontally into the national colors. This unusual type is reported as having been worn by a member of the 20th SS Division who wore the SS runes on the collar.[210]

---

[209]Eesti saatusaastad 1945-1960, Vol. 1, EMP, Stockholm, 1963 & H. Rüütel. Note that the badge is too large to have been worn on the collar patch.

[210]M. Lukich, letter of 12.6.72. This could have been an improvised Estonian badge or a confused report of the rectangular sleeve badge divided horizontally into the Dutch national colors (red/white/blue) worn by Dutch volunteers (see Buss/Mollo, Hitler's Germanic Legions, pg. 121). To be noted that Estonians and Dutch fought alongside one another in Waffen-SS uniform at Narva.

CUFFBANDS

No cuffband was authorized or worn by the Division.[211]

Some members of the Estonian SS Legion's original Ist battalion, detached in March 1943 and which served the "Wiking" SS Division as SS-Pz.Gren.Btl. "Narwa" until its return to the Estonian Division in July 1944, are known to have worn:

a) the "Wiking" divisional cuffband,
b) an unofficial hand-made cuffband with the word "Narwa"[212]
c) the "Wiking" and "Narwa" cuffbands together.

An unofficial cuffband with the inscription "Estland" was also worn.

Estonian Combatants Association in GB

Five Unterscharführer of SS-Pz.Gren.Btl "Narwa" of the "Wiking" Division. The 1st German pattern and SS runes collar patches are being worn on either side of the accordionist and the "Wiking" divisional cuffband is clearly seen being worn below the type "B" Estonian sleeve badge.

---

[211] *Cuffbands were specifically forbidden for the Estonian SS Volunteer Brigade by the SS-FHA on 22.10.1943 (see fn. 4 on page 122 of this book).*

[212] *See fn. 109 on page 174 of this book.*

Juhan Raagi, "Spiess" or Waffen-Stabsscharführer (Waffen-Oberscharführer in his capacity of Company Sergeant-Major) wears an unofficial cuffband "Estland" below the German "Schuma" type "B" sleeve shield and the double sleeve rings.
Source: Võitleja, No. 11, November 1967, pg. 6.

UNIFORM NOTES:

1. The SS-FHA memo to Himmler of 29 October 1942 pointed out that if the decision were taken for the Estonian SS Legion not to wear the SS runes on the collar patch, then all its full members of the SS would have to wear the special SS runes badge on the left breast.[213]
2. Harald Riipalu, Knight's Cross holder and last commander of the Division's senior 45th SS infantry regiment, carried on the tradition of the former Estonian Army by wearing two small silver buttons on the cuffs of his tunic.[214] ➡

Estonian Combatants Association in GB

SS driver in camouflage uniform with SS runes on the collar patch stands beside the staff car of SS-Sturmbannführer Georg Ahlemann, commander of SS-Ersatz-Regiment 20, Narva front, 11 April 1944. The rectangular regimental car flag on the left mudguard carries the Estonian mailed arm, sword, and "E" symbol and was probably divided horizontally black/white/black. The same car is seen in the two photographs on page 226, together with Ahlemann himself in shirt-sleeve order. Ahlemann, a Sturmbannführer since 9.11.1943, still held this rank on 1.10.1944 when he was commanding SS-Grenadier-Ersatz-Bataillon 20.

---

[213]For illustration, see Vol. 2, pg. 126.

[214]Riipalu appears to have been the only Estonian officer to have added the small buttons to the sleeve of his German tunic as was the custom in the former Estonian Army. (H. Rüütel, letter of 10.5.81). Photographs show that he favored a German Police tunic, which in peace time would have had two buttons on each cuff in any case.

Estonian Combatants Assoc. in G.B.

Estonian Combatants Assoc. in G.B.

SS-Sturmbannführer Georg Ahlemann, commander of SS-Ersatz-Regiment 20.

REGIMENTAL COLORS & FLAGS

1. The Division's senior 45th SS infantry regiment carried as its color the flag of the 1st Regiment of the Estonian SS Legion. The obverse was black with the mailed arm, sword and letter "E" between clusters of oak leaves as central design, above which were the letters "E.L." ("Eesti Leegioni," or Estonian Legion) and below "1. GREN. RÜGEMENT" (1st grenadier regiment). The reverse was divided horizontally into the national colors (black/blue/white) with the coat of arms in the center (three blue lions on a golden shield over sprigs of oak leaves) - the flag had a silver fringe and two silver tassels.[215]

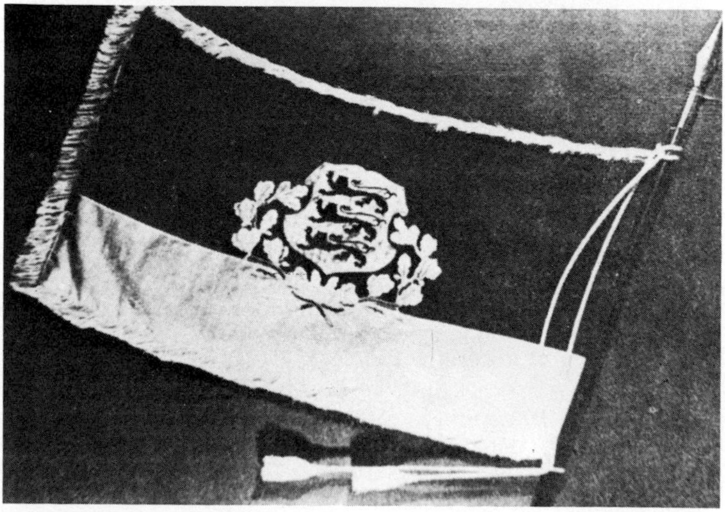

[215] *Harald Riipalu was on sick-leave in Denmark when the war ended, and he gave the flag to his female secretary. Thanks to Major (USAAF, Retd.) Henno Uus, this flag is now held by the Estonian Archives in Lakewood, New Jersey, USA.*

2. Command and staff flags are believed to have included a small white mailed arm, sword and letter "E" symbol in the top right-hand corner. A recorded example of this was the car flag of SS-Sturmbannführer Georg Ahlemann, commander of SS-Ersatz-Regiment 20.[216] In the photograph on page 225, taken on 11 April 1944 on the Narva front, his staff car (registration SS-302667) carries a regimental flag divided horizontally into black/white/black bars.[217]

3. The former (Estonian) 200th Infantry Regiment of the Finnish Army (J.R. 200), the majority of whose members were taken into the 20th SS Division in 1944, had a color that consisted of the Estonian flag (horizontal bars) with the motto "EESTI AUKS, TULEVIKU PANDIKS!" ("for the honor of Estonia, as a pledge for the future!") over the date "1944" and under the Estonian coat of arms on the obverse. The color was

Obverse of the color of the former (Estonian) 200th Infantry Regiment of the Finnish Army (J.R. 200). The motto translates as "for the honor of Estonia, as a pledge for the future!" Most of the men of this regiment joined the 20th SS Division in 1944. Note the Finnish lion on the top of the flag pole.

---

[216]*As of 1.10.1944 Ahlemann, an SS-Sturmbannführer since 9.11.1943, was commander of SS-Grenadier-Ersatz-Bataillon 20 (Dienstaltersliste der SS der NSDAP).*

[217]*The fact that Ahlemann had a flag (oblong) and not a pennant (triangular) confirms that he was commanding a regiment rather than a battalion at the time. The flag of a regimental HQ was divided horizontally into three segments (see Vol. 1, pg. 147) and the colors in this case, definitely not the Estonian national colors, may have been black/white/black. The original print from which this photograph is copied is in the collection of H. Rüütel and is marked on the reverse "P.K.H. 3350 PK Dr. Pauli/Transocean-Europress (G) 11396, 11.4.1944."*

sewn by hand in Estonia by the mother of one of the regiment's volunteers and sent to Finland, arrived just in time to be brought back home by the returning regiment. It was flown only once in Estonia on 22 August 1944, the day the regiment paraded at Camp Männiku in Tallinn and was addressed by SS-Brigadeführer und Generalmajor der Polizei Hinrich Möller. It is possible that the color was taken over by the 20th SS Division.[218]

DIVISIONAL VEHICLE SYMBOL

1. The mailed arm, sword and letter "E" symbol worn on the collar patch. First painted onto the Brigade's vehicles and equipment in the autumn of 1943, when the first unofficial hand-made collar patches were worn prior to completion of training and return to Estonia.[219]

2. Sword and letter "E." The unpopular German design, withdrawn as a collar patch soon after its introduction in June 1944.[220]

---

[218]*Uustalu, For Freedom Only.*

[219]*Koppel (see fn. 189 on page 207 above). Confirmed as the "original" design in Der Freiwillige, 15. Jahrgang, Heft 7, Juli 1969, pg. 21.*

[220]*The one and only source that can be found for this design is the illustration given in Der Freiwillige, 15. Jahrgang, Heft 7, Juli 1969, pg. 21. Many other authors have copied it, yet no photographic or other evidence has yet been found to support the theory that this design was ever painted or stencilled onto vehicles of the 20th SS Division. No symbol had been identified for this Division by Allied Intelligence as late as 1.3.1945 (German Divisional Emblems, Military Research Section, London, MIRS(D) - EMB, January 1945 & 2nd supplement, MIRS (D-1) - EMB/3/45, 1 March 1945).*

Appendix

CORRECTIONS AND ADDITIONS

Volume 1

PAGE

10 Steel Helmets: Estonian Waffen-SS men are reported to have painted the Estonian arm shield (presumably type "A" - see page 217 of this book) on the side of their steel helmets while fighting at Narva in 1944 (J. P. Petersen).

80 SS Chevrons: The "old campaigners" chevron (at first called "Armwinkel für Altegediente," by 1943 "Ehrenwinkel für alte Kämpfer") was reserved in the case of Austrians for those who had volunteered for the SS before 12 February 1938 (not 12.2.1933 as given by Mollo in Uniforms of the SS, Vol. 1, pg. 54 - nor 12.2.1935 as given in this series - see Organisationsbuch der NSDAP, 6. Auflage 1940 & 7. Auflage 1943).

81 SS Chevrons: The "former members" chevron was at first called "Armwinkel für ehem. Polizei- und Wehrmachts-Angehörige," but by 1943 it was referred to as an "Ehrenwinkel" (Organisationsbuch der NSDAP).

98/99 Trade and Specialty Badges: These designs for Waffen-SS motor transport drivers' badges were drawn up in 1942, but never introduced (doubtless because of the Motor Vehicle Driver's Badge of Merit, introduced on 23.8.1942). That at left (a) was to have been for motorcycle drivers (SS-Kraftfahrabzeichen für Kradfahrer der Waffen-SS), that at right (b) for motor car and truck drivers and tractor operators (SS-Kraftfahrabzeichen für Pkw.-, Lkw-Fahrer und Führer von Zugmaschinen der Waffen-SS) (See Der Versuch der Einführung eines SS-Kraftfahrabzeichens und das

(a)

(b)

Kraftfahrbewährungsabzeichen (1942-1945) by Wolfgang Vopersal, in Der Freiwillige, 22. Jahrgang, Heft 11, November 1976, pp. 14-17).

107 There were two types of "paired SS runes" collar patches:

(a) where the left patch bore a mirror image of the SS runes on the right (as worn below by whom Beadle/Hartmann (op.cit., pg. 30) identify as a doctor of the "Prinz Eugen" Division at Mostar in 1943.)
(b) where the "SS runes" appeared on both left and right collar patches (as worn inexplicably by SS-Oberführer Herbert-Otto Gille in October 1942 as C.O. of SS-Art.Rgt. 5 of the "Wiking" Division).

129/132 Officer Candidates: See the 2-part article Der Führer-Nachwuchs der Waffen-SS - Aufbau und Abzeichen by Jochen Nietsch in Der Freiwillige, 20. Jahrgang, Heft 4, April 1974, pp. 17-19 & Heft 5, Mai 1974, pp. 17-20.

146 Car flag of the Inspector General of the Latvian SS Legion (Kommandostandarte des Generalinspekteurs der lettischen SS-Freiwilligen-Legion). Shown in a photograph dated 20.8.1944 (see page 86 of this book) of the car of Waffen-Gruppenführer und Generalleutnant der

Waffen-SS Rudolfs Bangerskis. It is logical to assume (but so far unproven) that similar flags existed for the Inspector Generals of the other national SS legions (such as for Johannes Soodla, Inspector General of the Estonian SS Legion, which could also have incorporated the national colors).

Volume 2

PAGE

8 Introduction: Line 4: The SS-VT was at Hitler's (or Himmler's) disposal, not command.

20 The SS Race and Resettlement Main Office: Created as SS Race and Resettlement Office on 31.12.1931, it achieved Main Office (Hauptamt) status on 30.1.1935.

CHIEFS:

31.12.1931 - February 1938: SS-Obergruppenführer Walter Darré (replaced)

February 1938 - 9.7.1940: SS-Obergruppenführer und General der Polizei Günther Pancke (became HSSPF Dänemark)

9.7.1940 - 20.4.1943: SS-Gruppenführer Otto Hofmann (became HSSPF Südwest in Stuttgart)

20.4.1943 - 8.5.1945: SS-Obergruppenführer und General der Waffen-SS Richard Hildebrand.

(Research by C. Peyton Williams, letter of 12.9.1977).

27 SS Corps: Thousands of men served in the corps troops, yet these elements have generally been ignored in postwar books on the Waffen-SS. Volume 2 in this series remains the most detailed source of information available on the subject, and the additional information given below should be studied in conjunction with what has already been given in the appendices to Volumes 3 and 4. Many of the new entries given come from the 25.8.1944 field post office guide (FpÜ) of the Waffen-SS.

SS-Obersturmbannführer Rudolf ("Rudi") Lehmann, some time after receiving the Knight's Cross of the Iron Cross (23.2.1944) as "Ia" of 1. SS-Pz.Div. "LSSAH."

Our thanks go to Rudolf Lehmann, former SS-Standartenführer and Chief of Staff of the Ist SS Armored Corps from 1.10.1944 to 9.3.1945 for his comments on Waffen-SS corps troops in general and those of the Ist SS Armored Corps "Leibstandarte" in particular. His observations are given below and in several cases differ from what has been found in original documents. This can be explained partly because there were undoubtedly differences between what was laid down and believed to be the case by the SS-FHA in Berlin and what was, in fact, done by the units in the field. One should also consider just what can reasonably be expected to be remembered about such matters after the passage of more than 35 years.

According to Herr Lehmann, a Waffen-SS Corps usually had an SS-Feldgendarmerie-Zug (mot.), rarely a Trupp. Apart from the fact that there was practically very little difference (if any at all) between a FG-Zug and a FG-Trupp, and German divisions had a FG-Zug each at one time and a FG-Trupp at other times, when the SS-Gen.Kdo. (Pz.) was formed, it was supposed to have had a FG-Trupp (b) (mot.).

Herr Lehmann is joined by other sources in saying that a Corps had (at least!) a light (20-ton) lorry column (le. Lkw.Kol. (20t)).

Sources do not support Herr Lehmann in saying that no Corps had a Fliegerstaffel, and that, at best, they had a few spotter aircraft provided by the Luftwaffe. An Org.Abt. chart for the II. SS-Pz.-Korps dated 3.6.1943 gives a Fliegerstaffel (this is repeated on 1.10.1943, 14.12.1943 and 25.2.1944) and on 10.6.1943 a Fliegergruppe of two aircraft is given. In practice, a few spotter aircraft were attached to Waffen-SS Corps HQs and these were referred to as either a Fliegerstaffel or a Fliegergruppe. They were removed from Corps HQs (and also from Panzer divisions) in late 1943 or early 1944.

28 SS Corps: Other ad hoc formations, virtually large battle groups, were Korpsgruppe "von dem Bach," Korpsgruppe "Rauter" and Korpskommando "Eicke." The last of these, containing the 14,000 survivors of the 290th Infantry Division, SS-Division "Totenkopf" and the 105th Artillery Command, was commanded by Theodor Eicke from 5.5.1942 to mid-June 1942. (Sydnor, <u>Soldiers of Destruction</u>, pg. 233 & fn. 27.)

The Serbian Volunteer SS Corps (Serbisches Freiwilligen SS-Korps), transferred by the O.K.W. from the German Army to the Waffen-SS in November 1944, will be dealt with in a future volume in this series - it was an armed body, not an Army Corps, and had nothing in common with the tactical higher formations described in Volume 2.

29 <u>Ist SS Armored Corps</u>: This Corps appears named simply "Leibstandarte" in most German documents, but the form "LSSAH" is not unknown.

Corps troops (less the Nachr.-Abt. in Unna) were first assembled at Berlin-Lichterfelde and then sent to Meran. They remained at Meran until the beginning of 1944 and so were not on the Russian front during the summer of 1943.

29/30 <u>Corps troops</u>: Our sources do not agree with Herr Lehmann when he says the following did not exist:

<u>Fliegerstaffel</u>: Although this may, in fact, have consisted of "a

Fieseler Storch provided by the Luftwaffe, with, at most, a sergeant as pilot," early organizational charts of I. SS-Pz.-Korps show a Fliegerstaffel (or Fliegergruppe) which was removed from the Corps HQ in late 1943 or early 1944.

SS-Flak-Abt. 101/SS-Fla.-Kompanie: Returns sent to the Generalinspekteur der Panzertruppen indicate that the I. SS-Pz.-Korps had a Fla.-Kp. (mot.) and "1. Fla.-Kp." for the I. SS-Pz.-Korps "Leibstandarte" is confirmed with field post number 58 399.

SS-Werfer-Brigade I. SS-Korps: This was either an error for Werfer-Abteilung or, as Herr Lehmann suggests, planned but never built (in fact, it was stated in Volume 2 that the staff was only formed in April 1945).

SS-Vielfachwerferbatterie (mot.) 522: This was under the Corps' command on 1.3.1945. It is possible that one of the integral Batterien of SS-Werfer-Abt. 101 was equipped for a time with Vielfachwerfer and an additional 8cm. Batterie is shown in one chart.

SS-Wehrgeologen-Btl. 101: It is possible that the Corps had no military geologists.

SS-Korps-Sich-Kp. 101: A Sich.-Kp. (mot.) was indicated in a return by the Corps to the Generalinspekteur der Panzertruppen and the Company appeared in the 25.8.1944 FpÜ with FPNr. 59 515.

SS-Feld-Ers.-Brig. Gen.-Kdo. I. SS-Pz.-Korps/101: There is evidence that this unit existed - and not just on paper as Herr Lehmann suggests:

- as an addition it appears typed to the 25.8.1944 FpÜ as Felders.-Brigade Gen.-Kdo. I. SS-Panzer-Korps Leibstandarte, with Brigade Stab and Pz.-Aufkl.-Kp. (FPNr. 46 158 A & B respectively), SS-Felders.-Einheit 12, Waffen-Ausb.-Gruppe Panzer (1st, 2nd and 3rd companies with FPNr. 47 125 A,B & C) and SS-Felders.-Einheit 12, Waffen-Ausb.Gruppe Artillerie (4 batteries, Unterführer Lehr Batterie, Pz.-Pi.-Kp., Pz.-Nahkampf-Kp. & Divisions-Kampfschule with FPNr. 65 172 A-H).
- on 1.3.1945 the Brigade was commanded by SS-Obersturmbannführer Wilhelm Weidenhaupt. It could have become detached from the Corps and the use of the number "12" may indicate an association with the 12. SS-Pz.-Div. "Hitlerjugend."

The following comments are also prompted by Herr Lehmann:

s. SS-Beob.-Bttr. (mot.) 101/501: Although this worked with the schw. Art.-Abt., it is shown separately in the charts.

SS-Korps-San.-Abt. 101: Although SS-Feldlazarett 501 and the SS-Kr.Kw.-Zug belonged to the San.-Abt., this was later broken up to save manpower.

SS-FG-Kp. (Trupp) (mot.) 101: Herr Lehmann insists the Feldgendarmerie element was a Zug and not a Kompanie, but a FG-Kompanie was laid down in the Aufstellung order and Org.Tgb. Nr. II/4028/43 of 8.6.1943 and the 25.8.1944 FpÜ lists "Feldgend.-Kp. 101" with field post number 57 772. A FG-Trupp (b) (mot.) appeared in the returns sent by the Corps to the Generalinspekteur der Panzertruppen.

30/31 The only Corps symbol Herr Lehmann can recall on vehicles had the "skeleton key and hook" (Dietrich und Haken), without the oakleaves and swords.

31 COMMANDERS:

27.7.1943 - 25.8.1944.	SS-Obergruppenführer und Panzergeneral der Waffen-SS Josef ("Sepp") Dietrich
28.8.1944 - 20.11.1944	SS-Obergruppenführer und General der Waffen-SS Georg Keppler (as mentioned in fn. 11)
20.11.1944 - 8.5.1945.	SS-Gruppenführer und Generalleutnant der Waffen-SS Hermann Priess

CHIEF OF STAFF:

1.10.1944 - 9.3.1944.	SS-Obersturmbannführer Rudolf ("Rudi") Lehmann

31 IInd SS Armored Corps: Referring to the Corps as "1. SS-Panzer-Armee" in the late summer of 1943 in Italy and Yugoslavia was a deception ploy to confuse the enemy - the "LAH" Division was referred to as a Corps and its two infantry regiments as divisions (Rudolf Lehmann).

32/33 Corps Troops: The IInd SS Armored Corps, in fact the first Waffen-SS higher formation, was examined in Volume 2 and additional data has been given in the appendices to Volumes 3 & 4. Faced with more information on corps troops contained in the 25.8.1944 FpÜ and a detailed listing in Tieke's Im Feuersturm letzter Kriegsjahre (pp. 605/606), it has been decided to provide the following revised and enlarged composite listing. Elements underlined are those the original SS-Generalkommando (Panzer) was supposed to have had when formed:

Gen.Kdo./Korpsstab
- Fliegerstaffel
- SS-Korpskartenstelle (mot.) 102
- SS-Fla.-Kp. 102
- gemischte Flak-Kompanie 102
- SS-Kriegsberichter-Kp.
- SS-Korps-Sicherungs-Kompanie/SS-Sich.-Kp. 102

schw. SS-Pz.Abt. 102/502
- Stab
- Stabs-Kp.
- 1. - 3. Kompanie
- Versorgungs-Kp.
- SS-Pz.-Werkstatt-Kp. 102

SS-Arko 102

schw. SS-Art.Abt. 102/502
- Stab
- Stabs-Kp.

1. - 4. Batterie
schw. SS-Beobachtungs-Batterie 502
1. u. 2. SS-Gr.W.Kp. 102
SS-Werfer-Abt. 102/502
Stab
Stabs-Kp.
1. - 4. Batterie

Korps-Nachrichten-Abteilung 51/400 (Heer)/SS-Korps-Nachr.-Abt. 102
1. - 4. Kp.
Kol.
SS-Führungs-Nachr.-Rgt. 502
schw. SS-Pz.Aufkl.-Abt. 502
SS-Wehrgeologen-Kp. (mot.)
SS-Nachsch.Tr. 102/502
Korps-Nachsch.-Führer:
Stab
Stab-Kp.
1. SS-Kraftfahr.Kp. 102
2. SS-Kraftfahr-Kp. 102
SS-Kfz.-Inst.-Kp. 102
Instandsetzungsstaffel des II. SS-Pz.-Korps
Werkstatt-Zug
Kw.-Werkst.-Kp. 102/Werkstatt-Kp.
WK-Zug
1. kleine Kraftwagen-Kolonne
2. kleine Kraftwagen-Kolonne
3. grosse Kw.-Kol. f. Betr.St./3. grosse Betriebsstoff-Kolonne
1. Kraftwagen-Kompanie 102
2. Kraftwagen-Kompanie 102
3. Kraftwagen-Kompanie
Kolonne RSO
Korps-San.-Abt. (mot.)/Korps-San.-Abt. SS-Gen.Kdo./SS-Sanitäts-Abteilung 102/502
Stab
1. Sanitäts-Kp.
2. Sanitäts-Kp.
1. Kr.Kw.Zug 502
2. Kr.Kw.Zug
1. Kr.Trsp.Kp./Krankentransport-Kompanie
Bakt.Zug
le. San.Kol./Kolonne
Feldlazarett (D.R.K.)/"D.R.K."/SS-Gen.Kdo.
1. Laz. (mot.)/SS-Gen.-Kdo./1. SS-Lazarett (mot.)
2. Laz. (mot.)/SS-Gen.-Kdo./2. SS-Lazarett (mot.)
Feldlazarett 502
Kr.-Sammel-Kp.
le.Kr.Kw.Kol.
le. San.Kol.
Feldgenesenden-Kp. 102

Feldpostamt/SS-F.P.A. 102
FG-Trupp (b)(mot.)/SS-FG-Trupp (mot.) 102/SS-FG-Kp. 502
Rekr. Depot II. SS-Pz.-Korps
SS-Feld-Ers.-Brig. II/SS-Feldersatz-Brigade 102 (HQ for SS-F.E.B. 9 & 10)
SS-Kartswehr-Btl. (mot.) (formed 15.11.1942)

33 CHIEFS OF STAFF:

1943	SS-Standartenführer (promoted to SS Oberführer on 20.4.1943) Werner Ostendorff
1943 - late 1944[1]	SS-Standartenführer Rüdiger Pipkorn
late 1944[2] - 1945	SS-Obersturmbannführer Baldur Keller

N.B. Major i.G. Schiller was never Chef d. Gen.St. d. II. SS-Pz.Korps. He was operations officer (Ia) of the "Das Reich" Division from April 1945 to the end of the war under Rudolf Lehmann.

34/35 IIIrd (GERMANIC) SS ARMORED CORPS:
Corps Troops: The 25.8.1944 FpÜ also lists:
- SS-Führungs-Nachr.-Rgt. 503 (possibly not attached to the Corps)
- Werfer-Battr.
- Werkst.Zug 103 (possibly a complete company at one time)
- Bekl.Instands.-Kp. 103

and gives the following composition of the medical unit:
- SS-Sanitäts-Abteilung 103
  - Stab
  - Kr.-Trsp.-Kp.
  - Genes.-Kp.
  - Kol.
  - 1. Korps Lazarett (possibly Feldlazarett)
  - 2. Korps Lazarett (possibly Feldlazarett)
  - Kr.-Kw.Zug 503

The Kr.-Kw.-Zug (later a Kol.) was subsequently deleted.

35 COMMANDERS: Joachim Ziegler does not appear to have commanded the III. SS-Pz.-Korps in 1945; he stayed with the "Nordland" Division until the end. It was Felix Steiner who took over again after Unrein in March 1945 after commanding Pz.A.O.K. 11 for a short time in 1945 (Lennart Westberg, letter of 20.3.1981).

CHIEFS OF STAFF: The last Chief of Staff of the III. SS-Pz.-Korps is missing: von Bockelberg was replaced by SS-Standartenführer von Bock und Polach in March/April 1945 (Lennart Westberg, letter of 20.3.1981).

---

[1] *He held this post on 19.8.1944.*
[2] *He was with the V. SS-Geb.-Korps as late as 1.10.1944.*

36 IVth SS ARMORED CORPS: 1st SS Division "LAH" was never a part of this Corps (Rudolf Lehmann).

36/37 Corps Troops: The 25.8.1944 FpÜ also lists:
- Flak-Kp. (surely a Flak-Batterie or a Fla.-Kp.?)
- SS-Nachschub.-Tr. 104 (originally consisting of Stab, 1. & 2. Kraftf.-Kp. & Kfz.-Instands.-Kp.104 - later the whole entry was deleted and replaced by 1. & 2. Kraftf.-Kp. 104 - which seems inadequate).

38/39 Vth SS VOLUNTEER MOUNTAIN ARMY CORPS:
Corps Troops: The following additional entries are found in the 25.8.1944 FpÜ:
- Kraftf.-Schule 105 (also reported as Krfr.-Schule Gen.-Kdo. V. SS-Geb.-Korps)
- Pi.-Führer 105
- SS-Nachsch.-Tr. 105
  1. & 2. Kraftf.-Kp. 105 (120t)
  3. gr.-Kw.-Kol. f. Betr.-St. (later deleted)
  4. Kl.-Kw.-Kol. f. Betr.-St. (later deleted)
  5. & 6. Wasserkol. (later deleted)
  Nachsch.-Kp. 105
  Kw.-Werkst.-Kp. 105 (later deleted)
- SS-San.-Abt. 105 (previously Korps-San.-Abt. 5)
  Stab
  verst. Kr.-Trsp.-Kp.
  Kol. (later deleted)
  1. & 2. Zug San.-Kp. 505 (later deleted)
  1. & 2. Kr.-Kw.Zug 505
- SS-Veterinär Dienste
  Pferdelaz. 105
  Pferdepark 105
  Vet.-Park 105
- SS-Kampfgruppe "Becker" (V. SS-Korps) (added to list - 1945)
- SS-Werfer-Abt. 505 (added to list)

According to Tessin (op.cit., Vol. 2, pg. 285), SS-Sturmgesch.-Abt. "Skanderbeg" served as a Corps element in April 1945.

40 VIth (LATVIAN) SS VOLUNTEER ARMY CORPS:
Corps Troops: Hans Stöber's Die lettischen Divisionen im VI. SS-Armeekorps (pp. 226 & 240) confirms all corps troops listed so far, with the following modifications:
- Stabskompanie 506
- SS-Korpskartenstelle (mot) 506
- SS-Korps-Nachr.-Abt. VI. SS-Korps/SS-Nachr.-Abt. 106/506
- SS-Pi.-Kp. VI. SS-Korps
- SS-Kraftf.Kp. 506/1
- SS-Kraftf. Kp. 506/2
- SS-F.P.A. (mot.) 106/506
- SS-FG-Trupp (mot.)/SS-FG-Kp. (mot.) 106/506 (expanded from Trupp to Kompanie on 1.11.1943)
- SS-Korps-Begl.-Kp. (mot.)/SS-Sich.-Kp. 506 (German personnel)
- SS-Lehr-Btl. VI. SS-Korps/SS-Lehr-Btl. 506

The 25.8.1944 FpÜ also gives:
- Flak-Battr.

- Werkst.Kp. 106 (added to list after publication)
- San.Kp. 106 (added to list after publication)

Waffen-Grenadier Regiment der SS 106 (lettisches Nr. 7) was formed from the remnants of the 2. & 5. Grenzschutz-Rgt. and was commanded by Waffen-Obersturmbannführer Jānis Jansons. It took part in the 3rd Battle of Courland, suffered 60% casualties and Jansons died of his wounds and was replaced by Waffen-Standartenführer Eduards Stipnieks. On 3.1.1945 the Regiment took part in the counter-offensive of the VI. SS-Armeekorps north of Dobele.

41 VIth (LATVIAN) SS VOLUNTEER ARMY CORPS:

CHIEFS OF STAFF: SS-Standartenführer Nikolaus Heilmann was the first Chief of Staff of the VIth SS Army Corps. He held this post until 17.2.1944 when he took command of the 15th SS Division and was succeeded by Oberstleutnant (later Oberst) i.G. Helmut Ziervogel.

41 VIIth SS ARMORED CORPS:

Corps Troops: Although other elements were certainly planned, the only corps troops listed in the 25.8.1944 FpÜ were: Stab, Kartenstelle & SS-Nachr.-Abt. 107 (HQ + 3 companies). SS-Feldlaz. 507 & SS-Kr.-Kw.-Zug 507 were Führungstruppen.

42 IXth (CROAT) NON-GERMANIC MOUNTAIN CORPS OF THE SS:

Corps Troops: The following additional/amended entries are found in the 25.8.1944 FpÜ:
- Kraftf.-Kp. 109 (90t)
- Kfz.-Instands.Zug 109
- 1. Kr.-Kw.-Zug 509
- FG-Tr. 509/109 (in fact FG-Tr. b)
- F.P.A. 509/109 (in fact F.P.A. (mot.))

N.B. No explanation can be given for the curious fact that the last two elements were numbered "509" in the 25.8.1944 printing, but were subsequently renumbered "109."

43 Xth SS ARMY CORPS:

Corps Troops: The following were subsequently added to the 25.8.1944 FpÜ:
- SS-Nachr.-Abt. X. SS-A.K.
- Kraftf.-Kp. X. SS-A.K.
- Fahrschwdr. X. SS-A.K.
- Nachsch.-Kp. X. SS-A.K.

Arko. X. SS-Korps is also reported.

44 XIth SS ARMY CORPS:

Corps Troops: The following additions/amended entries come from typed additions to the 25.8.1944 FpÜ:
- Kfz.-Instands.-Zug 111 (possibly a company at some time)
- SS-Pz.-Jagd-Kp. 550
- Feldlaz. 511
- Kr.-Kw.-Zug 511

45 XIIth SS ARMY CORPS:

Corps Troops: The following were given in the 7.8.1944 formation order:

SS-Korps-Karten-Stelle (mot.) 112
SS-Feldgendarmerie-Trupp 112
SS-Korps-Nachrichten-Abteilung 112
  Stab
  Ffk.-Kp. (mot.)
  Korps-Fernsprech-Betriebs-Kp. (mot.)
  Korps-Funk-Kp. (mot.)
  Staffel (mot.)
SS-Kraftfahr-Kp. 112 (90t)
SS-Kraftfahrzeug-Instandsetzungs-Kp. (mot.) 112
SS-Feldpostamt (mot.) 112
The 25.8.1944 FpÜ also lists:
- Kfz.-Instands.-Zug 112
- SS-Feldlazarett 512
  Kr.-Kw.-Zug 512

45/46 XIIIth SS ARMY CORPS:

The Corps history (Spiwoks/Stöber: Endkampf zwischen Mosel und Inn, pp. 365/367 provides the following list of controlled elements:

WAFFEN-SS:
  6. SS-Geb.-Div. "Nord" (22.2.45 - 28.2.45)
  17. SS-Pz.-Gren.-Div. "G.v.B." (10.9.44 - 30.3.45)
  38. SS-Gren.-Div. "Nibelungen" (26.4.45 - 6.5.45)
  SS-Kampfgruppe "Dirnagel" (April/May 1945)

HEER:
- 11. & 21. Panzer-Division
- 3. Panzergrenadier-Division
- XIII. & 116. ("FHH") Panzer-Brigade
- Panzer-Kampfgruppe Hobe
- 47., 48., 347., & 462. Infanterie-Division
- 9., 16., 19., 36., 79., 212., 352. (z.b.V.), 353., & 559. Volksgrenadier-Division
- 2. Gebrigs-Division
- 172. Division

LUFTWAFFE: Flak-Division 9

46 Corps Troops: The corps elements laid down in the 7.8.1944 formation order were the same as shown above for the XIIth SS Army Corps, but numbered 113.

Additions to the 25.8.1944 FpÜ include:
- Kfz.-Instands.-Zug 113
- Verpfl.-Amt 526 (the entry is not clear, but the field post number is certainly 00 449 - it could have been transferred from the Army)
- SS-Res.-Fahr-Abt. XIII beim Gen.-Kdo. XIII. SS-A.K. (a most unusual identification)

SS-Arko 113 is also reported.

46 XIIIth SS ARMY CORPS:

COMMANDERS: According to Spiwoks/Stöber (op.cit., pg. 363) Max Simon assumed command on 16.11.1944

CHIEFS OF STAFF: von Einem's first name was Kurt.

49 XVIIth SS ARMY CORPS:

Although neither Klietmann nor Tessin mentions such a Corps, it was included in our original listing because (a) it is logical that something was at least planned (there was an XVIIIth SS Corps), and (b) an HQ is reported in 1944.

It now appears that the XVIIth Corps of the Waffen-SS was to have been Hungarian: XVIIth (HUNGARIAN) NON-GERMANIC ARMY CORPS OF THE SS (XVII. Waffen-Armee-Korps der SS (ungarisches). The Corps HQ is confirmed as having been formed in late 1944, but the RF-SS only ordered the two Hungarian Waffen-SS divisions (the 25th & 26th) to be grouped into such a Corps in January 1945. In fact, this Corps existed only on paper. (Andreas von Weissenbach, "Die ungarischen Verbände der SS im 2. Weltkrieg" in Der Freiwillige, 21. Jahrgang, Heft 7, Juli 1975, pg. 18).

Corps Troops should have been numbered 117 or 517, but so far only XVII. Arko./XVII. SS-Korps has been found. SS-Sturmbannführer Talbot von Pistor is said to have been appointed corps supply officer (Korps-Nachsch.-Führer) in early April 1945 (Landwehr, Siegrunen Newsletter, 2nd issue/April 1982, pg. 1).

COMMANDERS: 1945: Waffen-General der SS Franz Vitéz Feketehalmy-Czeydner
1945: Waffen-General der SS Eugen Vitéz Ruszkay-Ranzenberger

49 XVIIIth SS ARMY CORPS:

Corps Troops: Additions to the 25.8.1944 FpÜ include:
- FG-Tr./XVIII. SS-A.K.
- Kfz.-Instands.-Kp.
- Kraftfahr-Kp.
- SS-Nachr.-Abt. (formerly Korps-Nachr.-Abt. 499 (Heer))

Corps elements were probably all transferred from the Army.

60/71 1. SS-Panzer Division "Leibstandarte SS Adolf Hitler": Readers wishing to have a more detailed history of the "LSSAH" should consult Weingartner's Hitler's Guard and Lehmann's series Die Leibstandarte (Volume 1, covering the period from 1933 to June 1941, appeared in 1977 and Volume 2, July 1941 to January 1943, in 1980). The following comments come from Herr Lehmann via Jost Schneider. Anticipating a revised and enlarged coverage in a future volume in this series, we limit ourselves to corrections and not additions.

62 History:

"LAH" was not part of the occupying forces of the Rhineland.

"LAH" was sent from Poland to Prague in January 1940.

62 footnote 1: Sources stating the SS-Stabswache Berlin was formed before 17.3.1933 are wrong.

64 "LAH" did not take part in the victory parade in Paris (in fact, only von Briesen's 69th Infantry Division paraded).

"LAH" transferred to Romania from Metz, not from Berlin. It stayed there as Lehrtruppe for two weeks and was then moved to Bulgaria.

67 Boves: Stein quoted The New York Post of 29.6.1964 as the source for the report that in June 1964 West German officials disclosed that

Joachim Peiper of 1. SS-Pz.-Div. "LSSAH" was being investigated for his rôle in the destruction of the town of Boves in northern Italy and the mass execution of its inhabitants in September 1943 during an anti-Fascist partisan operation (op. cit., pp. 253 & 275/276). "LAH" was in northern Italy from 4.8.1943 to 12.12.1943, but Rudolf Lehmann claims that no such action was taken by "LAH" or any other unit and refers to proceedings for withdrawal of the charge made to the senior prosecutor of the Stuttgart Superior Court. Weingartner failed to research the incident (he quotes only Stein and Bender/Taylor) but casts considerable doubt on the allegation: "He (Peiper) may have been involved in a similar massacre (to the burning of two Russian villages and the killing of all their inhabitants) during Leibstandarte's Italian interlude in the summer and fall of 1943" and "Both the Russian and the Italian incidents associated with Peiper's name are vague and largely unsupported by documentation" (op.cit., pg. 126 & fn. 37 on pg. 176).

67 footnote 2: Not only did SS-Pz.-Rgt. 1 never have a IIIrd Panzer-Abteilung, but its IInd Abt. did not exist at all times either.

68 "LAH" was not encircled in the Korosten area, but later (beginning of March) between Proskurov and Tarnopol in a "private pocket," from where it broke out to the so-called "Hube pocket."

69 SS-Kampfgruppe "Peiper" was the spearhead of the Ist SS Armored Corps, not of the whole offensive.

71 Order-of-Battle: The numerals "1" and "2" should appear before the name "LSSAH."

72 Divisional Commanders: Dietrich officially assumed command of the nascent Ist SS Armored Corps "Leibstandarte" when it was activated on 27.7.1943 and so on the same day SS-Brigadeführer und Generalmajor der Waffen-SS Theodor (Teddy) Wisch became the second commander of the "LSSAH" Division (Weingartner, op.cit., pg. 83). Wisch was badly wounded in the escape from the Falaise-Argentan pocket and was replaced by SS-Oberführer Wilhelm Mohnke. Mohnke, who had been an officer with the Leibstandarte since 1933, gave up his command in early February 1945 to participate in the final defense of Berlin, and SS-Brigadeführer und Generalmajor der Waffen-SS Otto Kumm gave up command of the 7th SS Division "Prinz Eugen" to become Leibstandarte's last commander.

93 Photo: The officer in profile is SS-Obersturmbannführer Werner Dörffler-Schuband, C.O. of II./SS-Regiment "Germania."

100/104 History: For a detailed history of the "Totenkopt" Division, see Sydnor's Soldiers of Destruction. The SS Death's Head Division, 1933-1945.

106/107 Divisional Commanders: Eicke was badly wounded in the right leg when his staff car was blown up by a mine in Russia on 7.7.1941. When invalided from the front, he gave temporary command to SS-Standartenführer Matthias Kleinheisterkamp, but Himmler chose SS-Brigadeführer Georg Keppler to lead "Totenkopf" for the two months until Eicke's return on 21.9.1941. While the Division was being destroyed in the Demyansk Pocket, Eicke was ordered to Germany on leave in the second week of June 1942, and his place was taken until the formation was eventually withdrawn to Germany in October by SS-Oberführer Max Simon. Eicke re-assumed command of the formation, reforming in France as a Panzergrenadierdivision, in October 1942. Eicke was killed when his Fieseler Storch was shot down by Russian troops between the villages of Michailovka and Artelnoye on 26.2.1943, and he was buried with full military honors on 1.3.1943 in the village of Otdochnina (see photo and caption). Eicke was succeeded by Max Simon (by then an SS-Brigadeführer und Generalmajor der Waffen-SS), who led the Division until 16.10.1943 when he assumed command of the 16th SS Division "RFSS" and "Totenkopf" was led from 16.10.1943 until 13.7.1944 by SS-Brigadeführer und Generalmajor der Waffen-SS Hermann Priess. Priess was given command of "LSSAH" on 13.7.1944, and SS-Oberführer Helmuth Becker became the last commander of the "Totenkopf" Division. On 9.5.1945 Becker surrendered his Division to the U.S. Third Army, but the Americans handed him and his men over to the Russians.

Theodor Eicke's grave at Otdochnina, where he was buried on 1.3.1943. Himmler was preoccupied with the thought of Eicke's remains lying on soil retaken by the Russians and with the Germans in retreat in September 1943 had Eicke's body removed to the Hegewald cemetery at Shitomir. But Eicke's body was still buried at Hegewald when the Red Army drove the Germans out in the spring of 1944 (Sydnor, op.cit., pg. 273, fn. 26).

145 The mobile "sun cross" on a command flag of an element of the "Wiking" Division (photo possibly taken in February 1944 - "Gille" presumably refers to Herbert-Otto Gille, who commanded "Wiking" from May to August 1944, before becoming G.O.C. IVth SS Armored Corps). No record remains of the use the dog made of the post!

145 Company HQ pennant of one of the three infantry regiments of the "Wiking" Division (note the mobile "sun cross" within shield on the central black horizontal bar - the numerals "1./III" are confusing in that they suggest the 1st company of a IIIrd battalion, but the 1. Kompanie would have been of the I., not III., Bataillon).
(Source: Der Freiwillige, 23. Jahrgang, Heft 12, Dezember 1944.)

152

Jost Schneider

SS-Standartenführer Franz Schreiber, last commander of the 6.SS-Gebirgs-Division "Nord."

155 Divisional Vehicle Symbols: Sign no. 2, the "Wendehorn" ("turning horn" or "horn of the Wends"), was proposed for the collar patch of the Estonian SS Legion by the SS-FHA on 29.10.1942 (but not adopted - see pages 208/209 of this book).

170 Note on page 143 of Volume 1: 56 509 was, in fact, the field post number of the war correspondents' company of the 1st SS Armored Divison "LSSAH."

Volume 3

PAGE

29 Photo caption: This, in fact, shows Fegelein and members of his staff south of Kharkov in 1943. Gustav Lombard is to Fegelein's left with cigar in hand (Gustav Lombard, letter of 14.1.1976).

53 Order-of-Battle: For the history of the SS Divisional Battle School "Hohenstaufen" (SS-Divisionskampfschule "Hohenstaufen") - formed 5.6.1943 & disbanded in early March 1944 - see Wolfgang Vopersal in Der Freiwillige, 21. Jahrgang, Heft 11, November 1975, pp. 18-23.

55 footnote 16: read "have" for "habe."

72 read "badly" for "bad" in penultimate line of text.

84 line 28: Hitler relieved SS-Brigadeführer und Generalmajor der Waffen-SS Joachim Ziegler of his command of "Nordland" at noon on 25.4.1944 according to Krukenberg/Militärarchiv (Lennart Westberg, letter of 20.3.1981).

88 Sweden: There never was, in fact, a full company of Swedes in SS-Pz.-A.A. 11, but within its 3rd company there was a platoon of Swedish SS men (mortar crews). The commander of the 3rd company from the summer of 1944 was a Swede, SS-Obersturmführer Hans-Gösta Pehrsson. He was awarded the Ehrenblattspange on 25.12.1944, survived the fighting in Berlin, and died in Stockholm in 1974 (Lennart Westberg, letter of 20.3.1981).

109 line 5: read "mostly" for "most."

Volume 4

PAGE

6/57 14. Waffen-Grenadier-Division der SS (ukrainische Nr. 1): For another detailed account of this Divison's history in English, see Siegrunen No. 19 (April 1980) pp. 5-10; No. 20 (June 1980) pp. 8-14; No. 22 (November 1980) pp. 11-16; No. 24 (March 1981) pp. 12-15; No. 27 (September 1981) pp. 10-12.

18 footnote 32: The correct Ukrainian spelling of Rivno (the Russian spelling) is Rivne (Rŏwne in Polish, Rowno in German, and Rovno in English). Stupnytskyi (said to have been a Colonel, not a General) was named Leonid, not Anatol (P. C. T. Verheye).

21 footnote 38: According to P. C. T. Verheye (letter of 30.6.1976) no unit of the U.P.A. ever fought "for" the Germans, and there is no German or Ukrainian record indicating any such cooperation.

28 The English translation of the oath should more correctly end: ". . . and as a brave soldier I will always be ready to lay down my life for this oath."

35 line 25: read "seemingly" for "seamingly."

40 line 17: read "Nazis' " for "Nazi's."

44 Post-war commemorative badge of the 1st Division of the U.N.A. (from an illustration in the 1953 Ukrainian Book Club of Winnipeg history of the Ukrainian armed forces).

48 footnote 109: Walter Schimana was of German nationality but born in Troppau in Czechoslovakia. As SS-Brigadeführer und Generalmajor der Polizei he was "mit der Aufstellung und Führung beauftragt SS-Freiw.-Div. Galizien 15.7.1943 - 3.9.1943" (from his service record, via P. A. Nix).

52 footnote 120: Possibly genuine examples of the Galician sleeve shield with a black border have been found (Jim van Fleet).

55/56 There was also a round version of the Ukrainian Trident cap badge.

60 Evolution & Titles & footnote 6: The inclusion of the word "Waffen-" in the title was indicated by V.O. SS 1495 of 16.5.1944.

63 last paragraph: Latvians still cannot agree over the circumstances leading up to and the reasons behind the coup d'ētat of Prime Minister Kārlis Ulmanis on the night of 15 May 1934, and readers wishing to pursue the matter further are referred to the bibliography. Explanations for Ulmanis' action (a bloodless coup that led to what was considered a mild dictatorship that lasted until the Russians invaded Latvia on 17 June 1940) range from Ulmanis' personal ambition to his desire to save his country from chaos. The reasons we gave for the coup were taken from Encyclopaedia Britannica: "pro-Nazi" tendencies of the Baltic Germans and the threat of an overthrow of government by the right-wing "Thundercross" organization." Artūrs Silgailis contests this view, saying the left-wing Social Democrats' "SSS" (Stradnieku Sports un Sargs - Workers' Sport & Guard) presented as much if not more of a threat than the Right. He says the "Thundercross" cannot be held responsible for what took place, and that Hitler had not been in power long enough for any real German threat to have developed - the "pro-Nazi" activities of the younger generation of Baltic Germans coming later, after the coup. Mussolini and Hitler may, however, have provided examples for Ulmanis (P. H. Buss).

Silgailis suggests that the real cause was the inadequacy of the Latvian constitution, which in turn had led to a possible overthrow of government. This constitution had been drawn up in the turbulent years following the First World War, and its very wording prevented the establishment of a stable and workable government. Its highly liberal parliamentary election rules favored the formation of small political parties and groups, every elected parliament having representatives from at least 15 different parties (27 following the 1931 election!) and sure enough, no government managed to last for very long. Faced with possible civil war and a very definite public dissatisfaction, Silgailis maintains that something drastic had to be done. The coup was greeted favorably at the time by the majority of the Latvian people but was losing some ground of support for Ulmanis in the latter 1930s. Nevertheless, Ulmanis was trusted by the majority of Latvians to the very moment of his forced abdication on 21 July 1940.

67 The proclamation raising the Estonian SS Legion was made on 28.8.1942, the first anniversary of the liberation of Estonia's capital, Tallinn (Reval), from the Russians. 1.10.1942 was the date the men were to assemble at SS-Tr.Üb.Pl. Debica by order of the SS-FHA dated 29.9.1942. See fn. 1 on pg. 122 of this book.

Round version of the Ukrainian Trident cap badge.

68 Line 22 & footnote 22: Although the 16th, 19th, 21st, and 24th police battalions were absorbed by the Latvian Legion, strictly speaking only the 19th and 21st were actually serving under the 2. (mot.) SS-Infanterie-Brigade at the time of the conversion (the 16th was resting in Latvia after a year at the front with the Wehrmacht in the Dno area, and the 24th was attached to the Army's 380th Infantry Regiment near Petershof on the Leningrad Front). It is possible that the 16th and 24th were still considered as belonging to the 2. (mot.) SS-Inf.-Brig., or that the authorities in Berlin were unaware of the detachments.

70 Oath: The English translation should more correctly end: ". . . and as a brave soldier I will always be ready to lay down my life for this oath." General Bangerskis and Legions-Standartenführer Silgailis were the first Latvians to take the oath; they signed it on 20 March 1943.

70/71 Silgailis' date of birth was incorrectly shown as 13 November 1892 on the enlistment order of 19 March 1943 (reproduced on page 96 of Volume 4) - he was, in fact, born exactly three years later on 13 November 1895 and so was 48 years old when appointed Chief of Staff of the Division.

72 footnote 42: Only the 28th Latvian Police Battalion was, in fact, absorbed by the 15th SS Division. Latvian Police Battalions 17 and 27 were disbanded at about the time the Latvian Legion was formed and their men absorbed by other police battalions. The 269th Latvian Police Battalion became a frontier guard unit (Silgailis & Buss).

73 footnote 47: Only alternative a) is correct, according to Silgailis.

73 footnotes 48 & 49: Delete (Silgailis).

76 footnote 65: The correct number of the antiaircraft unit was "SS-Flak-Abteilung 506" - the number "106" being used only at the beginning of the merger of the units of the 15th and 19th divisions (Silgailis).

78 Photo caption: Col. C. M. Dodkins, not Shape Pictorial Section.

81 Last paragraph: It was not just 'lack of barracks and supplies' that prompted some desertions, but mainly the sustained defeats of the German Army, the loss of a great part of the Baltic area, and mostly the lack of hope of avoiding the occupation of Latvia by the Bolsheviks (Silgailis).

82 Hinrich Lohse, in fact, had no involvement with the 15th SS Division.

83 footnote 83: SS-Art.-Rgt. 15 had survived the Russian summer offensive of 1944 almost intact and with the exception of its Ist detachment was taken over by the 19th SS Division and served with it to the end of the war. I./SS-Art.-Rgt. 15 was disbanded in November 1944 and its manpower taken to Germany as cadres for a newly-raised artillery regiment for the 15th SS Division.

84 footnote 87: "The figures given by Daugavas Vanagi must be correct. The figure of 20,000 included: remnants of the 15th Division, men of disbanded police battalions and other units as well as new recruits. At that turbulent time it was, in fact, impossible to account exactly the number of men transferred from Latvia to Germany on any given day" (Silgailis).

86 Line 16: read "Lübgust" for "Lüngust" (Silgailis).

87 The 19th Division did not lose "much of its ardor" once Latvia was

retaken by the Red Army (see divisional coverage in this volume).

87 Last paragraph & footnote 97: In fact, SS-Kampfgruppe "Janums" was made up of "lettisches Füsilier-Battalion 15" and the first battalions of the 32nd and 33rd regiments. During the move to Berlin, Füsilier-Btl. 15 was separated from the battle group and took part in the defense of Berlin, where the survivors were taken prisoner by the Red Army. For details of the surrender of all elements of the 15th SS Division, see pp 24/28 of this volume.

89 32nd Regiment & footnote 99: Silgailis confirms the unit's title as "SS-Freiwilligen- und Ausbildungs-Regiment" and adds: "In reality, it was an early designation of the 32nd Regiment. The name was assigned for the regiment not by higher command but was chosen only as a temporary name by SS-Brigadeführer Hansen to indicate the primary task of this unit - to train the first batches of recruits as training cadres for the whole Division. Therefore, the word "Ersatz-" was left out on purpose. As soon as the assigned task was completed, the unit was referred to by its proper name "SS-Freiwilligen-Rgt. 1 (lettische Legion)."

90 footnote 105: After the 34th Regiment received its Latvian number "5," this number was never altered back to "3." "I assume reference to the 34th Regiment as 'Latvian No. 3' must have arisen from a printing error in the SS-FHA order" (Silgailis).

90 footnote 107: Since Grobina is situated quite close to Liepāja, elements of the "SS-Waffen-Panzerjäger-Abt. 15" were dispersed among both locations at that time. The unit's H.Q. was at Liepāja. (Silgailis)

91 footnote 113: Delete (Silgailis).

92 SS-Pionier-Bataillon 15 was reorganized and sent to Pomerania by SS-Pionier-Ausbildungs- und Ersatz-Regiment 1, Dresden.

92 SS-Versorgungs-Regiment 15 could also have been known as SS-Nachschub-Regiment 15, depending on date.

92 SS-Feldgendarmerie-Trupp 15 shared the same field post number as the military police element of the 19th SS Division (SS-FG-Trupp 19 - F.P.Nr. 34 062), possibly because one sprang from the other. (P. H. Buss)

92 SS-Feldersatz-Bataillon 15 was reformed near Berent in West Prussia in August/September 1944. It consisted of a number of companies and an Alarm Einheit and numbering eight officers and 375 other ranks was then under command of a German Major Jahnke. Combat elements of the battalion were organized into a battle group under the Latvian Waffen-Hauptsturmführer Ansis Eglītis. Eglitis was killed in action and the battle group suffered heavy losses in the fighting near Marienburg. Sent to defend Danzig, the battle group arrived on 7.3.1945 and the following day was disarmed and on 13.3.1945 disbanded and its men scattered among the German forces defending Danzig and Gotenhafen. Those of SS-F.E.B. 15 who had not been organized into the battle group were sent to Gotenhafen under the Latvian Waffen-Hauptsturmführer Jansons. He succeeded in transferring the medical battalion (2 companies with 68 officers and 604 other ranks) over Swinemünde to Korser in Denmark, where it was on 9.5.1945. (Indulis Kažociņš).

93 footnote 115: Delete (Silgailis).
93 footnote 116: Himmler made the decision at a meeting with the operations officer (Ia) of the 15th SS Division, SS-Obersturmbannführer Erich Wulff at his H.Q. Fuchsbau. Unfortunately, the copy of Himmler's letter addressed to the Chef des SS-FHA, Jüttner, did not bear any date. The copy was received by the General Inspector of the Latvian Legion in early December 1944. In accordance with this letter, the SS-FHA (by its order Amt II, Org.Abt. Ia/II, Tgb.Nr. II/-20908/44 geh.) changed the subordination of these units, ordered by its previous order of 29.11.1944 (Tgb.Nr. II/19982/44 geh.).
94 Actual strengths at 17 April 1944 were: 417 officers + 1,542 NCOs + 13,777 men - a total of 15,736.
95 footnote 118: SS-Waffen-Art.-Rgt. 15 was listed separately because its II. & III. Abteilungen were attached to the 19th Division at the time (Silgailis).
95 footnote 120: See page 29 of this volume.
96 CHIEFS OF STAFF: SS-Sturmbannführer Erich (not Horst) Wulff was Ia of the 15th SS Division until his death at Flederborn on 3.2.1945 and was recommended for the Knight's Cross of the Iron Cross (BA/DÖ 9.5.1945 - Stöber, Die lettischen Divisionen, pg. 338). SS-Sturmbannführer Kopp took over as Ia and held this post until the end of the war.
96 footnote 122: Nikolaus Heilmann was commander of the 28th SS Divison "Wallonien" from 12.12.1944 to his death on 30.1.1945 (from his service record, via P. A. Nix).
97 Photo: Latvian experts suspect this photograph of being retouched because of the lack of the cap eagle and the generally strange shape of the peak.
98 Sleeve shields: See page 40 of this volume.
102 Cuffbands: See page 48 of this volume.
103 Colors: See page 50 of this volume.
103 Divisional Vehicle Symbol: Assigned but never used, see page 51 of this volume.
115 Marzabotto: Thorough and objective research of what actually took place at Marzabotto still needs to be done and would warrant a complete volume. The source for the 2,700 Italian civilians massacred by "RFSS" in reprisal for the activities of a partisan brigade in the Apennines is Reitlinger (The SS - Alibi of a Nation, pg. 245, nf. 3) which Stein merely copied (op.cit., pg. 276). According to a more recent coverage by Renato Giorgi (see bibliography), the following numbers of civilians (not partisans) were killed in the borough ("Comune") of Marzabotto (made up of 13 mountain villages) during the period between 29 August and 3 September and on 1 October 1944: 184 (Coprara); 195 (Casaglia); 104 (Cadotto); 111 (Sperticano); 95 (Villa Ignano); 560 (S. Martino) = 1,249 plus 421 who were left unburied in the mountains.
129 Photo caption: SS-Hauptsturmführer Josef Kiermaier was an SD officer on the staff of the RF-SS (Stab RF SS, Reichssicherheitsdienst), which explains why he wore a plain black right hand collar patch.
153 Photo caption: The tall SS-Sturmbannführer in the center of this photograph cannot have been the Division's Ic (intelligence officer)

SS-Hauptsturmführer von le Coq (not SS-Sturmbannführer La Cocq in any case).

157 photo: The combination of officer's and NCO's insignia is, of course, due to this young man's having been an SS-Standartenoberjunker.

Bibliography

Aitken, Leslie, Massacre on the Road to Dunkirk - Wormhout 1940, William Kimber, London, 1977.

Artzt, Heinz, Mörder in Uniform. Organisationen, die zu vollstreckern Nationalsozialistischer Verbrechen wurden, Kindler Verlag, München, 1979

Bangerskis, Rudolfs, Mana Mūža Atmiņas, 4 vols., edited by Pāvils Klāns, Imanta, Copenhagen, 1960

Barkov, L., Mörvarid ei Pääse Karistusest, Kirjastus "Eesti Raamat," Tallinn, 1966

Bayer, Hanns, Die Kavallerie der Waffen-SS, Selbstverlag der Truppenkameradschaft der Kavallerie-Divisionen 8. "Florian Geyer," 22. "Maria Theresia," 37. "Lützow" und deren Ersatzeinheiten, Gaiberg/Heidelberg, 1980

Befehl des Gewissens. Charkow Winter 1943, Munin-Verlag, Onasbrück, 1976

Best, Walter, "Dreimal gegen den Bolschewismus Estnische Freiwillige vor ihrem Einsatz," in Deutsche Zeitung im Ostland, 14.5.1942 (3)

Best, Walter, "In einer Front. Besuch bei einem lettischen Bataillon," in Deutsche Zeitung im Ostland, 26.4.1942 (3)

Bļodneiks, Adolfs, "The Latvian Legion and Its Fate," in The Undefeated Nation, pp. 260-264

Buchbender, O., Das Tönende Erz, Slewold Verlag, Stuttgart, 1978

Bunge, Fritz, Musik in der Waffen-SS. Ein Blick zurück auf die Entwicklung Deutscher Militärmusik, Munin-Verlag, Osnabrück, 1975

Buss, Philip Henry, The Non-Germans in the German Armed Forced 1939-1945, (a thesis submitted for the degree of Master of Arts in the University of Kent at Canterbury, England), September 1974

Buss, Philip Henry and Mollo, Andrew, Hitler's Germanic Legions - An Illustrated History of the Western European Legions with the SS, 1941-1943, Macdonald and Jane's, London, 1978

Butler, Rupert, The Black Angels. The Story of the Waffen-SS, Hamlyn Paperbacks, Feltham, 1978

Chabanier, Colonel Jean, "The Battle of Kurzeme from October 1944 Until May 1945" in Historique de l'Armeé, French Defense Ministry, August 1963

Daugavas Vanagi, Latviesu Frontes Laikraksts (at first published by the Latvian Volunteer Organization Committee - a voluntary civilian body created in late 1941 - and the first issues appeared in March 1942. From August 1943 publication was taken over by the Inspector-General of the Latvian Legion. October 1944 publication was transferred to Berlin. Printed in 13,500 to 14,000 copies, the last issues were printed in Halle, Germany, in January 1945)

Daugavas Vanagu Menesraksts (monthly, begun in 1953)

Davis, Brian Leigh, German Ground Forces Poland and France 1939-1940, Almark, London, 1976

Davis, Brian Leigh, German Uniforms of the Third Reich 1933-1945, Blandford Press, Poole, 1980
Deutsche Zeitung im Ostland, Tageszeitung, Rīga, 1941-1944
Dietrich, Der (educational leaflet of the "LSSAH" Division)
Dunsdorfs, Edgars, The Life of Kārlis Ulmanis (An Outline), Daugava, 1978
Eerme, Karl, Päevata Päevad ja ööta ööd I-II, Kirjastus Kultuur, s.l., New York, 1962-1963
Eesti riik ja rahvas II Maailmasõjas, 10 Vols. (VII+VIII:1959; IX: 1960; X: 1962), EMP, Stockholm
Eesti Sõna (Estonian Voice), Editor: August Oinas, Verlag Eesti Ajaleht, Berlin, 1941-1945
"Einer für alle und alle für einen. Die feierliche Vereidigung der ersten lettischen SS-Freiwilligen-Legionäre," in Deutsche Zeitung im Ostland, 29.3.1943 (3)
"Estland kämpft für Europa," in SS-Leitheft, Heft 8, 1944, pp. 11-14
"Estlands Söhne unter den Fahnen des neuen Europas," in Die Wehrmacht, Heft 1, 1944, pp. 20-21
Estonia - Basic Facts on Geography, History, Economy, Estonian Information Centre, Stockholm, 1943
Estonia - Story of a Nation, Konstantin Pats Fund, New York, 1974
Ezergailis, Prof., in Nationalities Papers, Spring 1977 (review of coverage of the 15th SS Division in Volume 4 of this series)
Feldpostübersicht Teil III Band 12 SS Einheiten 11. Neudruck Stand vom 25.8.44 (enthält Berichtigungslisten Nr. 1 bis 1543), Reichsdruckerei, Berlin, 1944
Gilbert, Felix (translator + editor) Hitler Directs His War, Oxford University Press, 1950 (in paperback from Charter Books, New York)
Giorgi, Renato, Marzabotto Parla, La Resistenza in Emilia-Romagna 1, Edizioni La Squilla, 6th ed., 1976
Greil, Lothar, Oberst der Waffen-SS Joachim Peiper und der Malmedy-Prozess, Schild-Verlag, München-Lochhausen, 4. Auflage, 1977
Guten Glaubens Waren, Die - Band III: Bildband. 4 SS-Polizei-Panzer-Grenadierdivision (SS-Polizei-Division) 1939-1945, Munin-Verlag, Onasbrück, 1977
Hampden, Jackson, J., Estonia, London, 1941
Hastings, Max, Das Reich - Resistance and the March of the 2nd SS Panzer Division through France, June 1944, Michael Joseph, London, 1981
Haupt, Werner, Heeresgruppe Nord 1941-1945, Verlag Hans-Henning Podzun, Bad Nauheim, 1966
Haupt, Werner, Kurland - Die letzte Front - Schicksal für zwei Armeen, 2. Auflage, Podzun-Verlag, Bad Nauheim, 1960
von Hehn, Jürgen "Lettland zwischen Demokratie und Diktatur," in Jahrbücher für Geschichte Osteuropas, Beiheft 3
Historie pour tous - Numéro Spécial: Naissance de la Waffen SS, Hors série No. 9, Novembre-Decembre 1978
Historie pour tous - Numéro Spécial: Les Waffen SS, Troupes Maudites, Hors série No. 10, Janvier-Février 1979
Historie pour tous - Numéro Spécial: Les Crimes de la Waffen SS: Le Blason Souillé, Hors Série No. 11, Mars-Avril 1979
Holzmann, Walther-Karl, Manual of the Waffen-SS. Badges, Uniforms, Equipment, Bellona Publications, Watford, 1976
Istorija Ukrainskogo Vijska (History of the Ukrainian Armed Forces) 2nd revised edition, Ukrainian Book Club of Winnipeg, Canada, 1953
Janums, Vilis, Mana Pulka Kauju Gaitas, published by the author, 1953
Jürissaar, V., Kahe Rinde Vahel. Kolonel Rebasega koos Idavöitlustes, Orto, Göteborg, 1951
Junda (The Reveille), Latvian soldiers' monthly, Inspector-General of the Latvian Legion, Rīga, 1943-1944
Kadak, Paul, Mitme Taeva All, Kirjastus Välis - Eesti, Stockholm, 1974
Kannapin, Norbert, Die Deutsche Feldpost Organisation und Lokalisation 1939-1945, Biblio Verlag, Osnabrück, 1979
Kauener Zeitung, Kauen
Kažociņš, Indulis, in Daugavas Vanagu Mēnešraksts (review of Volume 4 of this series), 1979, Nr. 4, pg. 53
Ķīlītis, Major Jūlijs, Es Karā Aiziedams, published by the author, 1956
Klapdor, Ewald, Mit dem Panzerregiment 5 Wiking im Osten, Siek, 1981

Klesment, Johannes, The Estonian Soldiers in the Second World War (mimeographed, 35 pp.), The Estonian National Council, Stockholm, 1948

Kompanie-Kameradschaft: Die 3. Kompanie - SS-Panzer-Regiment 12 12. SS-Panzerdivision "Hitlerjugend," 1978

Koppel, Ted, "The Estonian Collar Badge in German Service 1943-1945," in Military Journal, Vol. 1, No. 1, Vermont, January-February 1977

Kubbo, Alf, Tulises Katlas, Kirjastus Kultuur, s.l., New York, 1966

Kuby, The Russians and Berlin, Heinemann, London, 1968

Kumm, Otto, Vorwärts Prinz Eugen! Geschichte der 7. SS-Freiwilligen-Division "Prinz Eugen," Munin-Verlag, Osnabrück, 1978

Lācis, Augusts, Ozolovīru pulki. Aizsargu Organizēšanās, Iekārta, Darbība, Cīņas un Pametumi, Vaidava, 1974

Laikmets (The Epoch), weekly magazine for the Latvian civilian population, but popular among soldiers, Riga, 1944

Landwehr, Richard, Siegrunen - The Waffen-SS in Historical Perspective, bimonthly newsletter published privately, Glendale (Volume I, Number 1 published September 1976 - latest issue received at time of going to press: Volume V, No. 3 (27), September 1981

Landwehr, Richard, Siegrunen Bulletin, published privately, Glendale (Volume 1, Number 1 published August 1979 - latest issue received at time of going to press: Issue Number 8, summer 1981)

Latvia Country and People, Chief Editor: J. Rutkis, Latvian National Foundation, Stockholm, 1967

Latviešu karavīrs otra pasaules kaŗa laikā. I: No. 1939. Gada Septembŗa Līdz 1941. Gada Jūnijam, Daugavas Vanagi, 1970

Latviešu kaŗavīrs otra pasaules kaŗa laikā. II: Pirmās Latviešu aizsardzības vienības otrā pasaules kaŗā, Daugavas Vanagi, 1972

Latviešu kaŗavīrs otra pasaules kaŗa laikā. III: Latviešu Leģions, Daugavas Vanagi, 1974

Latviešu kaŗavīrs otra pasaules kaŗa laikā. IV: Cīņas Latvijas Robežu Tuvumā, Daugavas Vanagi, 1976

Latviešu kaŗavīrs otra pasaules kaŗa laikā. V: Kaujas Vidzemē, Zemgalē un Kurzemē, Daugavas Vanagi, 1977

Latviešu kaŗavīrs otra pasaules kaŗa laikā. VI: Latviešu kaŗavīru cīņas Vācijas telpā. Otra pasaules kaŗa beigu cēliens, Daugavas Vanagi, 1978

Latviešu kaŗavīrs otra pasaules kaŗa laikā. VII: Latviešu aviācija. Latviešu kaŗavīru papildus un palīgvienības. Kaŗavīru aprūpe. Latviešu leģiona generalinspekcija. Otrā pasaules kaŗa noslēgums, Daugavas Vanagi, 1979

Latvijas armija 20 gados, Latvian Army HQ, 1940, Raven Printing, 1974

Latvju Enciklopēdija, Sweden, 1952-1953, Trīs zvaigznes

Lehmann, Rudolf (nach Vorarbeit durch Karl-Heinz Schulz) Die Leibstandarte - Band I (Von der Aufstellung 1933 bis zum Juni 1941), Munin Verlag, Osnabrück, 1977

Lehmann, Rudolf, Die Leibstandarte. Band II (Juli 1941 bis Januar 1943), Munin Verlag, Osnabrück, 1980

Lesiņs, Vilis, Butkuss, Apgāds Zelta, Ābele, 1954

Lettonie Réclame la Liberté, La, Rapport DV No. 10, Le Bureau Central d'Information, Daugavas Vanagi, London, 1968

Limberg, Fred, Isamaa Eest, Boreas Publishing House, Cardiff, 1980

Littlejohn, David, M.A., A.L.A., Foreign Legions of the Third Reich - Volume 1: Norway, Denmark, France, Bender, California, 1979

Luts, Alfred, Heitluste Keerises II, Kirjastus Välis - Eesti & EMP, Stockholm, Sweden

Mabire, Jean, La Division Wiking dans l'enfer blanc: 1941-1943, Fayard, 1980

Mabire, Jean, Les Jeunes Fauves du Führer - La Division SS Hitlerjugend dans la Bataille de Normandie, Fayard, 1976

Mabire, Jean, La Panzerdivision Wiking - La Lutte Finale: 1943-1945, Fayard, 1981

Mamers, Oskar, Häda Vôidetuile

Mengel, Hamilkar, Suurim Armastus I-IV, Kirjastus Kultuur, s.l., New York, 1960-1963

Meņgelis, Ainis, Capt. USAR, in Zintis - American Latvian Quarterly for Art, Literature and Science, Volume III, Nr. 11/12, 1964. (Review of an article by Jean Chabanier "The Battle of Kurzeme. . ." in Historique de la'Armée, August 1963)

Mesturini, Franco & Fossati, Ivo: 1933-1945 le Cartoline della Forze Armate Tedesche - Post Cards of the German Armed Forces, Edizioni Pubblibaby S.r.l., Trezzano S/N

(Milano, Italy), 1st ed. November 1981
Minsker Zeitung, Minsk
Mollo, Andrew, The Armed Forces of World War II - Uniforms, Insignia and Organisation, Orbis Publishing, London, 1981
Mollo, Andrew, Army Uniforms of World War 2, Blandford Colour Series, Blandford Press, London, 1973
Mollo, Andrew, A Pictorial History of the SS 1923-1945, Macdonald and Jane's, London, 1976
Mollo, Andrew, Uniforms of the SS - Volume 7: Waffen-SS Badges and Unit Distinctions 1939-1945, Historical Research Unit, London, 1976
Nākotne (Future), monthly, Inspector-General of the Latvian Legion, Rīga, begun in May 1944
Nietsch, Jochen, "Uniformen und Abzeichen der 15. Waffen-Grenadier-Division der SS (lettische Nr. 1)," in Der Freiwillige (part 1: Heft 4, April 1978, pp. 14-16; part 2: Heft 6, June 1978, pp. 15-17 & 22)
Oras, A., Baltic Eclipse, London, 1948
Ostland, Rīga
Piekalkiewicz, Janusz, "Pferd und Reiter im Zweiten Weltkrieg" (pp. 243-244: SS-Kavallerie)
Pusta, K.R., The Soviet Union and the Baltic States, New York, 1942
Quarrie, Bruce, 2nd SS Panzer Division 'Das Reich,' Vanguard Series 7, Osprey Publishing, London, 1979
Quarrie, Bruce, Waffen SS in Russia. A Selection of German Wartime Photographs from the Bundesarchiv, Koblenz, World War 2 Photo Album Number 3, Patrick Stephens, Cambridge, 1978
Raid, Robert "Vergessene und Verfemte (Estnische Freiwillige)," in Europa in Flammen, Band I (pp. 335-338)
Raud, V., Estonia: A Reference Book, New York, 1953
Reichsführer-SS, Der - SS-Hauptamt/IV/1: Der Soldatenfreund - Taschenjahrbuch für die Wehrmacht mit Kalendarium für 1942 - Ausgabe D: Waffen-SS, 22. Jahrgang, Adolf Sponholtz Verlag, Hannover, 1941
Reichsführer-SS, Der - SS-Hauptamt: Der Soldatenfreund - Taschenjahrbuch für die Wehrmacht mit Kalendarium für 1943 - Ausgabe D: Waffen-SS, 23. Jahrgang, Adolf Sponholtz Verlag, Hannover, 1942
Reichsführer-SS, Der - SS-Hamptamt: Der Soldatenfreund - Taschenjahrbuch für die Wehrmacht mit Kalendarium für 1944 - Ausgabe D: Waffen-SS, 24. Jahrgang, Adolf Sponholtz Verlag, Hannover, 1943
Reichsführer-SS, Der - SS-Hauptamt: Der Soldatenfreund - Taschenjahrbuch für die Wehrmacht mit Kalendarium für 1945 - Ausgabe D: Waffen-SS, 25. Jahrgang, Adolf Sponholtz Verlag, Hannover, 1944
Reider, Frédéric, Histoire de la SS par l'Image - l'Ordre SS, Éditions de la Pensée Moderne, Paris, 1975
Reider, Frédéric, Histoire de la SS par l'Image - La Waffen SS, Éditions de la Pensée Moderne, Paris, 1975
Remmelgas, Jüri, Igavesti, Kirjastus EMP, Stockholm, 1959
Remmelgas, Jüri, Kolm Kuuske, Kirjastus EMP, Stockholm, 1955
Remmelgas, Jüri, Tuline Värav, Kirjastus EMP, Stockholm, 1955
Revaler Zeitung, Tallin (Reval)
Riipalu, Harald, Kui Voideldi Kodupinna Eest. Mälestuskilde Soja-Aastast 1944, Eesti Hääl, London, 1951 (1st ed.), 1962 (2nd ed.)
Rünnak (Attack), Chief Editor: Elmar Tõnismäe, (20) Hildesheim, Haus Germanien, published by SS-Hauptamt, Germanische Leitstelle (number of issues unknown: issue 3 was dated 18.12.1944)
Rüstzeug für den Politischen Soldaten, Das. Schwert und Pflug. Schulungsbrief der SS-T-Div.
Sawka, Jaroslaw in The Ukrainian Quarterly (review of Volume 4 of this series)
Schill, Paul, Die Geschichte der lettischen Waffen-SS, Selbstverlag Paul Schill, 7505 Ettlingen mit Unterstützung durch die "Kameradschaft der ehem. Angehörigen der SS-Nachr.Abt. 19," 1. Auflage, 1977
Schneid, Sadi, SS-Beutedeutscher. Weg und Wandlung eines Elsässers, Askania Verlagsgesellschaft, Lindhorst, 1979
Schneider, Jost W., Verleihung Genehmigt! Eine Bild- und Dokumentargeschichte der Ritterkreuzträger der Waffen-SS und Polizei 1940-1945 - Their Honor Was Loyalty! An Il-

lustrated and Documentary History of the Knight's Cross Holders of the Waffen-SS and Police 1940-1945, edited and translated by Dr. Winder McConnell, R. James Bender Publishing, California 1977
Speer, Albert, The Slave State. Heinrich Himmler's Masterplan for SS Supremacy, Weidenfeld and Nicolson, London, 1981
Spekke, Arnolds Mag. Phil., History of Latvia - an Outline, M. Goppers, Stockholm, 1951
Spiwoks, Erich & Stöber, Hans, Endkampf zwischen Mosel und Inn. XIII. SS-Armeekorps, Munin Verlag, Osnabrück, 1976
SS Dienstaltersliste der Waffen-SS - SS-Obergruppenführer bis SS-Hauptsturmführer - stand vom 1. Juli 1944 (The copy held by the Militärarchiv was SS-Ogruf. von Herff's personal copy, up-dated by hand to 31.8.1944, 8.11.1944, 29.12.1944 & 31.1.1945)
SS-Führungshauptamt, Kommandoamt der Waffen-SS, Abt. Feldpostwesen, Geheime Kommandosache: Feldpostübersicht der Waffen-SS. I. Teil. Vorliegende Ausgabe enthält Blatt I und 1 - 30, SS-FHA, Berlin, 1943
SS-Personalhauptamt: Dienstaltersliste der Schutzstaffel der NSDAP (SS-Obergruppenführer - SS-Standartenführer) - Stand vom 30. Januar 1942, Berlin, 1942
SS-Personalhauptamt: Dienstaltersliste der Schutzstaffel der NSDAP (SS-Obersturmbannführer und SS-Sturmbannführer) - Stand vom 1. Oktober 1943, Berlin, 1943
SS-Personalhauptamt, Dienstaltersliste der Schutzstaffel der NSDAP (SS-Obersturmbannführer und SS-Sturmbannführer) - Stand vom 1. Oktober 1944, Berlin, 1944
Stern, Robert C., SS Armor. A Pictorial History of the Armored Formations of the Waffen-SS, Squadron/Signal Publications, 1978
Steurich, Alfred, Gebirgsjäger im Bild. 6. SS-Gebirgsdivision Nord 1940-1945, Munin-Verlag, Osnabrück, 1976
Stöber, Hans, Die Lettischen Divisionen im VI. SS-Armeekorps, Munin-Verlag, Osnabrück, 1981
Stöber, Hans, Die Sturmflut und das Ende. Die Geschichte der 17. Panzergrenadierdivision 'Götz von Berlichingen' - Band I: Die Invasion, Munin-Verlag, Osnabrück, 1976
Strassner, Peter, Vorwärts - Voran, Voran! Das Panzerbuch der Waffen-SS, Druffel-Verlag, Leoni am Starnberger See, 1978
Strawson, John, The Battle for the Ardennes, B.T. Batsford, London, 1972
Sydnor, Jr., Charles Wright, "The History of the SS Totenkopt-Division and the Postwar Mythology of the Waffen-SS," in Central European History, Volume VI, Number 4, December 1973
Sydnor, Jr., Charles Wright, Soldiers of Destruction. The SS Death's Head Division, 1933-1945, Princeton University Press, 1977
Tieke, Wilhelm, Im Feuersturm letzter Kriegsjahr. II. SS-Panzerkorps mit 9. und 10. SS-Division 'Hohenstaufen' und 'Frundsberg,' Munin-Verlag, Osnabrück, 1975
Tieke, Wilhelm, Ein Ruheloser Marsch war unser Leben. Kriegs-Freiwillig 1940-1945, Munin-Verlag, Osnabrück, 1977
Tolstoy, Nikolai, Victims of Yalta, Hodder and Stoughton, London, 1977
Uustalu, Evald, For Freedom Only - The Story of Estonian Volunteers in the Finnish Wars of 1940-1944, Northern Publications, Toronto, 1977
Uustalu, Evald, The History of Estonian People, Boreas Publishing, London, 1952
Vanadziņš, Ints, Veiss, Apgāds Zelta, Ābele, 1955
Varemetest Tõuseb Kättemaks - newspaper of the Estonian Division (From Ruins Comes Revenge)
Verweht sind die Spuren. Bilddokumentation 5. SS-Panzerregiment 'Wiking,' Munin-Verlag, Osnabrück, 1979
Võitleja (Estonian ex-servicemens' monthly - "The Fighter"), published in Heidelberg from 1952-1979 and from 1980 in Toronto, Canada
"Waffen-SS - SS-Verfügungstruppe und Waffen-SS 1939-1945," Soldat und Waffe der II. Weltkrieg, Heft 12, Jahr Verlag KG
Warma, Aleksander, Diplomaadi Kroonika, Eesti Kirjanike Kooperatiiv, Lundi, Sweden, 1971
Weidinger, Otto, Division das Reich. Der Weg der 2. SS-Panzer-Division "Das Reich." Die Geschichte der Stammdivision der Waffen-SS. Band IV: 1943, Munin-Verlag, Osnabrück, 1979
Weidinger, Otto, Division Das Reich im Bild, Munin-Verlag, Osnabrück, 1981

Weingartner, James J., Hitler's Guard. The Story of the Leibstandarte SS Adolf Hitler 1933-1945, Southern Illinois University Press, 1974
Wilnaer Zeitung, Wilna
Zintis - American Latvian Quarterly for Art, Literature and Science, 1961 - 1964 (?)